REGULATION
The Politics of Policy

Other Books
by Michael D. Reagan

THE MANAGED ECONOMY

SCIENCE AND THE FEDERAL PATRON

THE NEW FEDERALISM

POLITICS, ECONOMICS AND THE GENERAL WELFARE (editor)

THE ADMINISTRATION OF PUBLIC POLICY (editor)

REGULATION

The Politics of Policy

Michael D. Reagan
University of California
Riverside

Little, Brown and Company
Boston   Toronto

Library of Congress Cataloging-in-Publication Data

Reagan, Michael D.
  Regulation: the politics of policy.

  Bibliography: p.
  Includes index.
  1. Trade regulation—United States. 2. Trade
regulation—Social aspects—United States. I. Title.
HD3616.U47R134 1987   338.973   86-20846
ISBN 0-316-73630-9

Library of Congress Catalog Card Number 86-20846

ISBN 0-316-73630-9

9 8 7 6 5 4 3 2 1

MV

Published simultaneously in Canada by Little, Brown & Company (Canada)
Limited

Printed in the United States of America

ACKNOWLEDGMENTS

From Michael Reagan, *The Managed Economy* (NY: Oxford University Press, 1963).
Reprinted by permission of the publisher.

From Marver H. Bernstein, *Regulating Business by Independent Commission.*
Copyright 1955, © renewed 1983 by Princeton University Press. Reprinted with
permission of Princeton University Press.

Excerpted from Clair Wilcox, *Public Policies Toward Business*, Revised ed., © 1960
by Richard D. Irwin, Inc., Homewood, IL 60430. Reprinted by permission of the
publisher.

PREFACE

It is time for a new synthesis of the field of government regulation from a political-institutional perspective, and this book is written to help fill that need.

During the 1940s, 1950s, and most of the 1960s, political, legal, and institutional approaches to regulation dominated the field. Traditional economic regulation and the alphabet soup of New Deal regulatory commissions were addressed as matters of controlling abuses of private economic power, and institutional arrangements were evaluated from the perspective of political accountability in a democratic polity. There was less attention to and criticism of economic efficiency dimensions, and almost no concept of what we now call social regulation: programs designed to achieve positive social benefits in such areas as protection of health, safety, and individual rights.

The picture then changed. Questions of economic efficiency and inefficiency, for particular industries and for the economy as a whole, became dominant in the 1970s and continue to be so today. Economists, rather than political scientists and legal scholars, supply the analytic framework for the current conventional wisdom. The earlier imbalance that ignored significant economic questions, has been more than redressed. Now equity, accountability, and institutional considerations are slighted.

This book is designed as one of a growing number of contributions to a counterswing of the pendulum, one that tries to bring political-institutional aspects and broader social values—more than efficiency alone—back into the picture, while also retaining the essential economic perspective.

Regulation is political. It is an activity of government, and it involves values, interests, conflicts, and the making of choices by persons concerned with constituencies and elections. It can, therefore, never be a simple application of microeconomic principles. There is, in short, a political rationality to be considered in evaluating regulatory policy, and this book shows how that relates to and improves the vision obtained by looking only through the lens of economic rationality.

While there are recent books of case studies, and ones covering special aspects of regulation, the overall historical, organizational, and contextual dimensions seem in need of a unified exposition. It is hoped that the reader will find that synthesis in the pages that follow.

Writing a book, although essentially a solitary activity, also depends on a supportive context. Support was provided most essentially by my wife, Celeste. The Academic Senate of the University of California, Riverside, supplied intramural research funds; bibliographic searching was done by an able graduate student, Arlene Strasilla; and a congenial office setting was provided by a fine departmental staff, with special thanks due for excellent typing and cheerful adherence to my deadlines on the part of Roseanna Barron-Lopez. I also want to thank my editor at Little, Brown, John Covell, for his strong support of my writing effort, and Cynthia Chapin, who guided the manuscript through the production process. Very helpful comments and suggestions were made by three scholars who read the manuscript for the publisher: Professors R. Shep Melnick, Brandeis University; Paul Quirk, University of Pennsylvania; and James Anderson, University of Houston.

Michael D. Reagan
Riverside, California
August, 1986

CONTENTS

chapter five

SOCIAL REGULATION   85

chapter six

PROCESSES OF REGULATION: WAYS AND MEANS   112

chapter seven

REGULATING THE REGULATORS: THE PRESIDENT AND CONGRESS AS OVERSEERS   154

REGULATION
The Politics of Policy

chapter one

REGULATION IN PERSPECTIVE

The directions of policy can change quickly. Starting in the late 1970s under President Jimmy Carter, and continuing with a quickened pace under President Ronald Reagan, the politically most active part of the regulatory arena of government has been the question of deregulation. There has been more talk about removing regulations than about adding or maintaining them. Yet, in the years 1968–80, we had the strongest continuous extension of regulation since the 1930s, and perhaps in all of American experience. That twelve-year period saw the creation not only of the Environmental Protection Agency (EPA), to which new programs have been added as recently as the Superfund in 1980, but the Occupational Safety and Health Administration (OSHA), the National Highway Transportation Safety Administration (NHTSA), the Consumer Products Safety Commission (CPSC), and the Office of Surface Mining (OSM), plus a host of statutes establishing even more programs to be distributed among these and other agencies. To achieve an understanding of the political-economic dynamics of the intertwined, seemingly contradictory trends of deregulation and new regulation is a major objective of this book. We will start with the most basic proposition: regulation is political.

REGULATION IS A POLITICAL PROCESS

In a classic study of business regulation, Marver H. Bernstein wrote that the "determination of regulatory goals does not result inevitably from the logical analysis of certain economic facts, nor is it automatically deduced from a set of propositions concerning the nature of the political state and the proper boundaries of political action in a democratic society" (1955:258). In light of the rise to prominence in regulatory affairs of highly complex scientific and technological dimensions—as in air and water pollution, or toxic and radiological waste disposal—we should add that regulatory goals cannot be deduced from scientific principles, either.

1

It is not that economics, political science, and the physical sciences are irrelevant to regulatory policy-making. Rather, they are not decisive in themselves. Why is that? Since most regulation is directed at business behavior, can we not simply apply microeconomics? While writings occasionally imply that one can make policy by economic analysis alone, the more sophisticated presentations make it clear that what economic analysis—and other technical frameworks—can do is to illuminate choices, not decide them. To illuminate a choice is to explore its consequences and implications, both for the intended goal and any side effects it may have. If one has three options laid out as means for reaching an objective, any analytic process that helps to forecast the costs and consequences of each of the three will be helpful in reaching a decision.

Beyond such analyses, however, there are always judgmental dimensions and value choices to be made, and these are not reducible to programmed analysis (Lindblom and Cohen 1979). Judgmental elements enter because all the facts necessary to complete an analytic model are rarely available, and for some dimensions the value of experience may be greater than that of any formal framework. Value choices have to be made because the important questions in regulatory affairs are not simply instrumental (i.e., how to achieve a clearly specified objective), but involve differences of view, interests, and criteria regarding what is to be accomplished, not simply how. Even the "how" questions are complicated by the interrelationships within our physical and social systems: the means that may give us the most of objective A may do so by reducing what we can have in terms of objective B. A good example is the conflict between automobile safety and fuel efficiency: smaller, lighter cars look good in EPA mileage ratings, but are much less crash-worthy than the lumbering giants of twenty years ago. Regulators of fuel efficiency requirements should be aware of related accident statistics, but such knowledge cannot possibly settle the trade-off question for them.

Thus, regulatory decisions are at least as much political as they are technical, with political here meaning concerned with the allocation of values in the society. To allocate values is to make choices among values; since there is rarely total consensus on the values to be given primacy, there is almost always conflict over the allocation decisions. The conflict involves competing ideas, individuals, and often organized interests claiming to represent various values. Politics implies a struggle to see who will decide, who will win the contest of values. As a recent writer on the politics of monetary policy puts it, "for whom policy is good or bad is what politics is all about" (Woolley, 1984:185). In a democratic society, the policy struggle basically takes the form of competing efforts to persuade those in a position to make the formal (or authoritative; see Easton 1953:129) allocation of values; and majoritarian politics (even a majority consisting of a coalition of minorities) means bargaining and compromise. As Daniel Bell has written, "politics is haggling, or else it is force" (1973:365). Rarely does one position get carried to full fruition, for coalition building in a political system as open and diversified as that of the United States necessarily means giving up some of B to get more of A, or modifying how one reaches A to do less damage to B.

An example in regulatory politics is the process through which residential electric power rates are often set. The power company—a regulated utility—proposes a rate increase; the state Public Utility Commission (PUC)—sometimes called the Public Service Commission—applies engineering and economic expertise to an analysis of the justifiability of the request in light of legislatively-mandated criteria for rate-making; and often (in states having strong consumer advocacy groups; see Gormley 1983), a self-styled public interest or consumer advocacy group will challenge both the proposal and analysis as permitting too great an increase. The job of the commissioners (i.e., those having allocational authority) is to assess the competing presentations and to use their legal power to determine a rate that, if possible, will keep the power company financially healthy (i.e., able to interest investors in its securities) while minimizing the blow to the pocketbooks of electricity consumers.

At this point, one might ask: wouldn't it be a better world if such decisions were made on the basis of objective analysis and technical expertise—"on the merits," so to speak? The difficulty with this method, however, is that the preconditions necessary for making decisions on the merits are rarely present in public affairs generally, and even more rarely in hotly contested matters of regulation.

Let's look behind the phrase, using two concrete illustrations. In an extensive study of the interplay of economic, technological, legal, and political factors in shaping and enforcing the Clean Air Act, Melnick (1983) points out numerous anomalies in processes through which the EPA sets standards of allowable air pollutants. The legislation, he writes, "presents standard setting as a scientific investigation of the location of health effect 'thresholds,' " a threshold being a concentration "at which sensitive individuals begin to suffer adverse health effects" (243). This makes standard setting sound medical and scientific. But "few scientists now believe it is possible to identify non-zero health effect thresholds for most pollutants," and a congressional advocate of clean air programs admitted that the safe threshold concept was really "a necessary myth." Thus, asserts Melnick, "each time the EPA publishes or revises a standard, it must make a *policy choice* about what constitutes an 'acceptable' health risk. Standard setting is thus a political process, both in the sense that the EPA must make choices not dictated by medical evidence and in the sense that many political forces seek to influence its decision" (1983:243).

We should examine another example from broadcasting regulation. When the Federal Communications Commission (FCC) allocates a frequency for a new TV station, the statutory guidelines contained in the law that gives the agency its authority call for such decisions to be made in accordance with the "public interest, convenience and necessity." How is the FCC to make its decision on the merits? Would that mean awarding the broadcasting license to the applicant with the greatest experience, even if that firm has no roots in the community that the station is to serve? Or do the merits lie with an inexperienced group, but one with many local leaders among its board members? In fact, the FCC has made each of these criteria decisive, in different cases, but careful observers have assessed that fact as evidencing not choices on an objective, expert basis, but as rationalizations for choices made on grounds of political favoritism (Friendly 1962). Once a channel has been awarded, the FCC's problem at renewal time is greater: to compare the merits (performance) of the incumbent operator of the station with the merits (pledges of what it will do for the community) of the challenging applicant(s). Two FCC commissioners have called this problem "a riddle within an enigma within a conundrum" (Krasnow, Longley, and Terry 1983:206), and that is not how one would describe a situation in which decisions could be made on the merits.

FCC frequency allocations provide little basis for quantitative evaluation. Perhaps policy decisions that can be run through a quantified analysis are more likely to be made on the merits? Perhaps, in some cases; yet the respected Congressional Research Service studied the fashionable quantitative approach known as cost-benefit analysis, and found that the single most significant determinant of the outcome of the cost-benefit analyses covered was the factor of who conducted the analysis (*New York Times,* June 5, 1984:10): the results fit the preconceptions of the agency doing the analysis. In other words, political conflicts and questions of decision-making power seem to outweigh abstract merits.

The reason for this should now be apparent: to settle something on the merits presupposes agreement on what the merits are, which is the point of dispute in most public policy matters. Great national crises sometimes produce instant consensus on what matters most— as in World War II, or when the nation rallied to meet the challenge of Sputnik I in 1957. With such consensus, one can meaningfully contemplate deciding how to meet the objective on the basis of the merits; the goal is clear, as is its priority over other goals that may have to be partially dislodged or deferred. To decide on the merits, then, has a clear meaning: how to effectively reach an objective on which all agree to place overwhelming priority. Since such agreement hardly ever occurs, policy-making is almost always an exercise in political conflict, bargaining, and the search for acceptable trade-offs among multiple worthy objectives. This is true of regulation, as of most areas of national policy-making, and it is a basic perspective that permeates this book, in conscious contrast with the many non-political science studies of regulation that embrace the rationality of economic efficiency as the sole litmus test for assessing regulatory rule making.

To a political scientist, there is some irony, or at least a sense of deja vu, in recalling that before we achieved some sophistication regarding the realities of policy-making we had an earlier period— that of the Progressive Movement, 1900–1914—in which it was thought that the politics could be taken out of policy-making, and neutral expertise enthroned in its place (Vogel 1981). The peculiar regulatory structure that we know as the independent regulatory commissions (IRCs) is even today a living residue of that heritage, one whose operations have been much criticized by the same observers who assume that their kind of formal analysis can successfully substitute for the political process.

We can provide yet additional context for the proposition that regulation is political, by noting that all public policy can be seen as a combination of goals plus facts plus values, putting this in the form of

$$P = G + F + V$$

We mean to show that there are three necessary components of any public policy, but that none of them is sufficient alone to determine policy.

Some examples will illustrate the insufficiency of each of these factors, despite a strong tendency for all of us to ignore their interdependency in practice—which leads to what we call "jumping to conclusions." First, take the fact that highway safety programs save lives at one-tenth the "per life saved" cost of OSHA's health standards programs. Does that tell us, by itself, that we should cut the OSHA programs because they are less cost-effective? No, it does not, because a different value choice might suggest that we should keep both programs, but add budget support to the highway program (Mendeloff 1983:555). Or, we should start with a value position and see if it settles what policy should be—as so often seems to be the case in everyday political discussions. For example, take the proposition that regardless of income, all Americans should (*should* indicates a value statement; *is* indicates a factual one) have access to good quality medical care; therefore, government should regulate physicians' fees. The "therefore" really doesn't follow as smoothly as that statement makes it appear, because there are, factually, other ways in which the same value can be served (e.g., by national health insurance that pays a doctor's usual fees). Thus, a fact needs to be considered in light of varying value positions, and a value can usually be served through more than one factual arrangement.

Even when we have both the facts and the values lined up, the policy result may not be objectively or nonpolitically determined. For instance, the Carter administration and its regulatory agency heads strongly endorsed environmental protection and health and safety values. The facts of air and water pollution were clear enough, as were a number of major threats to worker and consumer health and safety. Did this combination lead to an unambiguous policy of maximum regulatory effort through the OSHA and the EPA? No, especially in 1978–80. Why? Because an even higher value priority was placed on economic stabilization, and the overriding goal became that of dampening the then-raging inflationary fires. In that same time period, another notable conflict was between environmental regulation and energy policy: reducing oil imports versus air pollution if use of coal was increased. These cases illustrate the basic political fact of a multiplicity of goals and values to be served at any given time. This combines with the basic economic fact of limited resources to create a policy world of difficult choices.

It is rarely a simple case of good versus bad in policy; usually it is a matter of competing good things, an improved physical environment, and a stable economy being two of the more stable goals of our time. Not only does the number of goals mean that value priorities need to be selected simply because we can't do everything at once, but the policy-making situation is complicated further by the interconnectedness of goals, such that increased pursuit of one diminishes (contrary to the policy-maker's intent) what can be achieved of the other, as with our earlier example of auto fuel economy purchased at the expense of decreased auto safety.

Regulatory policy (as any other policy) results from an interplay of goals, facts, and values. None of these is unidimensional; all are multiple and competitive—and generally have predictable consequences for specific interests. In turn, these interests are diverse, they cannot always be maximized by the same policy direction, and they are often aggressively represented in the political process by organized, articulate groups. The result of these factors: policy-making is first and foremost a political enterprise—before, during, and after it is an exercise in economic or technologic analysis.

A reflection of the political nature of much regulatory policy may be seen in the fact that regulation engenders controversy and public concern far beyond what its share of governmental activity would lead one to expect. Measured in personnel or budget dollars, regulation is, in fact, a very small part of the national government. The federal budget for fiscal year 1986 anticipated regulatory personnel (broadly defined) at 112,285 employees out of 2.5 million civilian employees (figures are from the Center for the Study of American Business, Washington University). (Such employment peaked at 131,462 in 1980, a clear measure of one way in which the Reagan administration's objective of deregulation has been met in substantial degree.) In dollars, the budgeted expenditure on regulatory agencies was $8.82 billion in 1986, compared with $6.78 billion in 1980, less than one percent of the total federal budget (and, taking inflation out, a lower *real* expenditure in the more recent years).

Why have the activities carried on with these funds and by these people generated so much political heat and newspaper space since the late 1970s? There are three reasons: (1) there was a several-fold increase in the scope of regulation in the 1968–80 period; (2) there was a reaction against some of that extension by the firms that had previously considered themselves to be within the unregulated sector; and (3) President Reagan came into office in 1981 with a philosophy of government that was antiregulatory.

While these factors help explain the extra attention recently given to regulation, the broader answer is that regulation has, since the earlier expansion of the 1930s, been an area of high political salience. It puts government and business into an adversarial relationship (unlike supportive intervention, such as investment tax credits, shipping subsidies, or aerospace production contracts). It also involves (in varying degrees) the intrusion of government officials (called "bureaucrats" when referred to pejoratively) into matters otherwise within the scope of managerial discretion, which sometimes have direct impact on the "bottom line."

Now let us take note of one additional factor in the political environment of regulation, the looseness of the American political system. In the oversimplified model of government once embedded in civics texts, the Congress legislated (in accord with majority will) a clear, specific policy, and a hierarchically organized executive branch implemented the policy (turned it into specific programs and carried it out through field offices). In the British cabinet government version of this ideal, which many American political scientists long sought to emulate as much as our separated powers system permitted, a disciplined two-party system linked government with the electorate, and the legislature with the executive.

Given these parameters, regulatory politics might be quieter, tidier. Each major political party would have a position on regulation; victory of one party would mean enactment of that party's program and its steady pursuit by the executive branch. Disputes would occur, but would be settled, and implementation would go on. In the actual U.S. context, however, these conditions are not met. Congress and the president share power, but are separate institutions (Neustadt 1980), each with its own policy outlook. They are not always of the same party (e.g., in 1983–85, a Republican president faced a Senate with a Republican majority, but a House of Representatives controlled by the Democrats. In recent years, a Republican president has faced a legislature entirely organized by the opposition party). When they are of the same party, there may still not be a working majority. Our parties are not ideologically very cohesive, and are hardly disciplined, in the specific political science sense that equates discipline with leadership control over the voting positions of the party's legislative members.

Because of the looseness and fragmentation of our political system, political struggle permeates policy-making at all levels and stages of the political process. The process is permeable by organized pressures, whether these come from regulated industry, consumer groups demanding more or stronger regulation, congressional subcommittee chairpersons acting either as surrogates for constituency interests or as policy "entrepreneurs" who see a chance to create an issue that will provide a favorable public image, or regulatory agency personnel themselves lobbying the White House or Congress for enhanced support. The result is a noisy, untidy, interminable political struggle—but also an open, visible system that the electorate can get to know and can, over time, cause to respond to at least the deeper currents of public philosophy.

Finally, a specific regulatory result of the loose, fragmented characteristics of the U.S. political process:

> The growth of regulation in the United States has not been the product of any farsighted plan or design, inspired by a general philosophy of governmental control. Step by step, whether in state or nation, it has been a series of empirical adjustments to felt abuses, initiated by particular groups to deal with specific problems as they arose. (Fainsod, Gordon, and Palamountain 1959:243).

Thus, regulation is political, but does not imply a planned economy, in either a democratic-socialist or a Soviet sense. Politically speaking, the U.S. system of regulated private enterprise stands as an alternative to socialism, not an equivalent.

REGULATION: THE HALFWAY HOUSE OF AMERICAN POLITICAL ECONOMY

It has been argued that regulation is the worst of all possible economic arrangements. Henry C. Simons states that a private monopoly is a "tolerable evil," since market forces would eventually stimulate a competitor, but that publicly regulated monopolies (e.g., railroads) are "cancers in the system" (1948:86). Given the deregulatory fever of recent years, one would guess that such sentiments would meet with strong favor among many microeconomists, and a sizeable number of attorneys.

There is, however, a case to be made for quite a different perspective: that regulation constitutes a peculiarly and appropriately American approach to political economy. Peculiarly, in the sense of uniqueness; appropriately, because it enables us to retain capitalism, yet have some social control over unwanted consequences of single-minded pursuit of the market system. At a time when regulation is under heavy attack, it may be a useful countercyclical exercise to lay out the basic case for this currently unfashionable view.

In the simpler ideological discussions, there are two kinds of economy: free enterprise (also known as a capitalist, competitive, or market economy), and socialist (also known as nationalized, politicized, or state-dominated economy). Citizens of the United States usually identify their own economy with the free enterprise model, and the Soviet Union or China (nondemocratic), or Sweden (democratic) as the socialist economies. In reality, it is not an either-or choice, but a continuum, a range. Within that range, the American system of regulation stands somewhere in the middle, between pure capitalism and pure socialism. We can, therefore, call the American system a "halfway house," if we remember that halfway indicates only a point on a continuum and not a movement toward either extreme. Let us take a look at the various dimensions of political economy and where regulation places us.

It will be useful to think of a purely private economy and a purely public economy as heuristic models; i.e., abstractions from reality that don't really exist, yet are useful in analysis (Lindblom 1977). The first dimension of the public and private models focuses on ownership of the means of production. In the classic institutional definition, capitalism is the economic system in which all productive property is owned privately, while pure socialism means that ownership is entirely in the hands of the government. In the one hundred years between Karl Marx and the middle of the twentieth century, much analysis (and even more rhetoric) was expended in attempts to extrapolate a particular government-business relationship that would flow from the form of ownership. If we have learned one lesson through more recent studies, however, it is the separability of ownership from control in any economy.

Within the large corporation such separation was first pointed to in a now-classic work, *Modern Corporation and Private Property* (Berle and Means 1932). More directly relevant to our purpose is another landmark volume, *Politics, Economics and Welfare* (Dahl and Lindblom 1953), in which the authors write of the "foolishness of the debate on nationalization vs. private enterprise." The book focuses on approaches to economic planning, which many would assume to mean exclusively a governmental activity; but one of the four modes of planning that is discussed is that of planning through the price system. Unfamiliar as a connection between planning and the price system may be, the concept is clear and it is accurate. Planning is a system of allocation and if there is one thing the price system does in what we call a market economy, it is allocate resources.

The interesting point, however, is that an economy in which ownership is predominantly or entirely private can, through regulation and macroeconomic planning, be one in which there is a very high degree of public control of economic resources. On the other side, in an economy in which governmental ownership of productive resources predominates, it is possible to let production decisions be guided largely by the market, within some very broad publicly set parameters. What we know as quasi-socialist democratic economies all, in fact, use market cueing as the day-to-day system of social control of economic activity. In other words, the relationship between private ownership and public control is *not* that of a zero-sum game: more of one does not always mean less of the other.

Further, we should note that if one has pure socialism then one will *not* have regulation, for regulation assumes a *private* organization to be regulated. Hence, regulation is in no way equivalent to socialism.

A second dimension of the free enterprise model (having the connotation of an economic system that can work sufficiently well autonomously to avoid a need for regulation) is a set of prerequisites that include the existence of a high degree of competition, perfect consumer information, an acceptable distribution of income and wealth, and what the economists call the internalization of third-party effects. Detailed argument is not necessary to suggest the limited extent to which such conditions exist in many sectors of the U.S. economy today.

For a third dimension, we note that current discussions of comparative political economy often focus on the share of Gross Domestic Product (Gross National Product minus the international dimension) flowing through government, which constitutes the financial rather than the productive measure of the public sector. Furthermore, while ownership and basic management of the means of production remain in private hands, there can be greatly varying degrees of public control over specific practices of businesses or other organizations, certain kinds of such controls constituting what we call regulation.

We will now briefly discuss each of these three dimensions. The postal service is the only enterprise owned entirely by government in all of the noncommunist industrialized countries. Telecommunications comes close, with Canada, the United States, and since 1985 Japan being the only countries in which private ownership is significant. The U.S. is the only country among the 12 covered in a recent survey (cited in Dolbeare 1982:86) that does not have some public-sector share of airline ownership, while the Netherlands and the United States are the only countries in which government does not own all or nearly all of the railroad assets. A chart of government ownership in France, Sweden, West Germany, Britain, and the United States contained in a political economy text (Andrain 1980:23) uses a point system ranging from one for complete government ownership to zero for complete private ownership in each of several industries. On this scale, the cumulative range is from France at ten and one-half to the United States at two and one-quarter. Even radio and TV are at least half government owned in the other countries. It is clear that on the criterion of ownership of industrial resources, the United States stands very close to the capitalist or market economy end of the spectrum. Further, there seems to be no trend in either direction; that is, we are neither substantially increasing nor decreasing the areas of government ownership, although we have recently decreased certain areas of government control, notably in transportation, telecommunications, and financial institutions (with the Federal Deposit Insurance Corporation's [FDIC] 80 percent ownership of Continental Illinois Bank an interesting aberration introduced in 1984).

We will look now at the public-sector share of Gross Domestic Product. In 1983, Japan, at 28 percent, was the only one of 11 industrial nations with a lower percentage than that of the United States (nearly 37 percent); Britain and West Germany stood at 44 percent, and Sweden at 62 percent, the top of the chart (OECD figures).

While 37 percent is more than a third of Gross Domestic Product, and far from negligible by any standard, it nevertheless leaves us at the low end of the spectrum, and still allows us to think of ourselves as a free enterprise economy. Actually, that figure is misleadingly high as an indicator of the government share of economic production, since it includes Social Security and other social welfare transfer programs, which simply circulate funds from those of working age to those receiving social security benefits for the aged (or, for example, from those who are healthy and paying taxes to those who are ill and receiving Medicaid). Whether there is a limit to the percent of national income that can flow through governmental coffers without endangering freedom and democracy has been much argued, but cannot be established by abstract reasoning; it seems clear that 37 percent does not even approach that limit, whatever it may be.

The third point on the private-public continuum is that of governmental decisions that impinge upon the freedom to manage within business firms and other organizations: i.e., government intervention and regulation. Ownership remains private; owners (or managers legally accountable to the owners) continue, as under unregulated capitalism, to decide what products to produce, and to make the bulk of managerial decisions. However, overlaid onto the system of private economic management is an incomplete patchwork of governmental interventions, some that affect particular industries and others that affect a wide range of industries, but only with regard to specialized activities. Until the recent deregulation took place, the airline industry was regulated both with regard to price and entry; i.e., the right of a firm to enter the airline business, and the allocated routes that it would be allowed to fly were set by a regulatory commission, the Civil Aeronautics Board. The FCC, which got its start at the insistence of radio broadcasters who could not agree voluntarily among themselves on who would have a particular broadcast frequency, allocates radio and TV frequencies, sets rates for interstate telephone calls, and is involved in various ways with other dimensions of the burgeoning telecommunications industry. Public utilities at the local level—natural gas for cooking and heating, electricity for lighting and power, and intrastate telecommunications—are the most tightly regulated of American industries; but regulation is performed mostly through state commissions, rather than by the federal government.

Although the trend has been to decrease regulation in the price and entry areas, there has been a more than equivalent increase in the totality of national government regulation in the United States since social regulation began to grow rapidly from the late 1960s through the 1970s. Air pollution, water pollution, toxic substances control, hazardous waste management, civil rights, and affirmative action requirements, occupational safety and health, consumer products safety—are all areas in which regulation applies potentially to all industries (indeed, beyond industry to other organizations, such as universities, community hospitals, and local government agencies), but only with regard to certain risks against which the public is to be protected. Because the reach of the newer regulatory pattern is so great, there is some truth to the comment that we no longer can separate the regulated from the unregulated sectors of the American economy.

Two more brief points will conclude this basic picture of regulation as the American middle way. First, within a regulatory system, we can sometimes use government *and* the price system (e.g., perhaps emissions fees), thoroughly mixing the public and private models and confounding the ideologues who populate each extreme. Secondly, note that there cannot exist a government that totally leaves the economy alone:

> If government really left the economy alone, there would be no system of competition but Hobbes's war of each against all. Without governmental enforcement of contracts, business men would not dare to make them. If government did not protect property, each firm would have to hire its own police force—or even an army. Without a money system backed by government, we would be reduced to crude barter or constantly subjected to ruination by extreme fluctuations in the value of private money substitutes. Without governmental mechanisms for adjustment of disputes between employers and employees, our industrial relations would be patterned on the bloody model of the coal fields of 1900.
>
> Government also provides organizational forms to fit business needs: proprietorships, partnerships, and the privilege of incorporation which vests the firm with immortality and the investor with limited liability. It develops procedures for bankruptcy and reorganizations to minimize the economic and social losses of business failure. It rewards invention by giving it privileged economic status through the patent system. It collects and disseminates knowledge in support of business operations, as in research reports on technological developments and market opportunities, and it establishes standards essential to common exchange: weights and measures, grading, and labeling.
>
> It is inconceivable that any economy could long endure in the absence of these governmentally provided supports. Certainly the modern, interdependent, complex industrialized economy could not. And businessmen recognize this, at least implicitly, for one does not hear them calling for repeal of the kinds of "intervention" mentioned to this point. What they object to is not intervention as such, but intervention which is regulatory rather than promotional. That is, it is not principle but self-interest which provides the rationale for their position. (Reagan 1963:159–60)

If the entire American Constitution is a great political experiment in free government—and it surely is—then perhaps we can equivalently describe the American halfway house of regulation not just as a questionable approach to allocational efficiency, but as a unique and worthy experiment in democratic control of economic resources.

DEFINING THE BOUNDARIES

Before going on, we need to build a more precise definitional base, clarifying both what regulation does and does not mean in ordinary political science and economics discussions. The diversity of academic definitions of regulation has led one pair of writers (Dubnick and Gitelson 1982:423) to describe the field as a "conceptual quagmire"; yet at least one common thread runs through most attempts to pinpoint the subject. This is the notion of government as an intervenor in the behavior of private firms. Thus, Christopher C. DeMuth, former director of the regulatory effort in the Reagan administration, writes that "regulation should be taken as the prescription by Government of the terms of private transactions" (1983:263). The authors of a recent study of regulatory reform identify regulation as "governmental legislation or agency rules, having force of law, issued for the purpose of altering or controlling the manner in which private and public enterprises conduct their operations" (Litan and Nordhaus 1983:5–6).

Both of these definitions convey the crucial point that regulation is an activity in which the regulated persons or institutions are directed by some political authority to take (or not to take) some specific action, to engage (or specifically not to engage) in certain kinds of behavior. But isn't that what law does? Does that equate all of government with regulation? No, it does not.

First, note that DeMuth discusses the "terms of private transactions." This means that it is not only the law applying to me (do not trespass), but something I have to do or not do in my transactions with some other person or institution (e.g., do not discriminate on the basis of race, sex, or creed in hiring employees; do not sell a toy that will endanger the children using it). In other words, regulatory requirements do not affect only the directly regulated entity, but also what it does in relationship to others.

A more important distinction between regulation and most other laws is the institutional arrangement for enforcement. Criminal law is enforced by police and prosecutors working through the courts, but they intervene on a sporadic, when-called basis, rather than through continuous, day-to-day supervision. Similarly, with most civil statutes, someone has to bring a case to activate the law on the books.

In the case of regulation, however, there is a government agency charged with continuous monitoring of the behavior that is to be regulated, and this feature is the distinctive characteristic of the regulatory process. The process involves an administrative agency in implementing in a continuing way various statutory mandates for insuring clean air and water, a proper handling of hazardous waste, and the provision of adequate information to prospective investors through the Securities and Exchange Commission (SEC). OSHA inspectors (or those of its state counterparts) make regular visits (at least in legislative intent) to factories in order to check on compliance with safety and occupational health requirements that fall clearly under regulation as defined here. The libel laws, on the other hand, although intended to proscribe certain behavior in the comments we make about others, have no administrative agency; instead, they rely on the person who claims to have been libeled to bring a suit. Although the libel laws are clearly regulatory in a broad sense, they fall outside the restricted scope of administrative regulation.

There is one other question of regulatory scope that we need to settle: does regulation apply only to the behavior of private persons or organizations, or does it include the behavior of subnational (state and local) public institutions? Traditionally, the definition is limited to private transactions, yet a growing body of writing covers what are called "intergovernmental mandates" and "regulatory federalism." These terms are used specifically to apply to requirements that the U.S. government imposes on state and local governments, sometimes when they are acting as agents of the national government, as when the states define water quality standards under the Clean Water Act, or decide on approaches to toxic waste cleanup problems in contemplation of receiving federal Superfund contributions to the cleanup effort. Although most regulation is directed at private parties, and most of our attention will focus on this type of regulation, some of the same prescriptions of conduct that apply to private parties also apply to public agencies. Questions concerning these processes are sufficiently similar in the case of some public-sector mandates that it seems reasonable to include intergovernmental regulation within our scope (see chapter 8).

To summarize, we are defining regulation as *a process or activity in which government requires or proscribes certain activities or behavior on the part of individuals and institutions, mostly private but sometimes public, and does so through a continuing administrative process, generally through specially designated regulatory agencies.*

This definition fits current usage reasonably well, with one notable exception: the field of antitrust and antimonopoly laws. The Sherman Act of 1890 did not establish an agency empowered to impose restrictions or penalties directly; instead, the Antitrust Division of the U.S. Department of Justice is charged with bringing cases in the courts when it perceives a violation. In this regard, antimonopoly efforts, although clearly intended to control business behavior in significant ways, are not part of the administrative regulatory world as it is generally conceived. The picture is complicated, however, by the existence of the Federal Trade Commission (FTC), established in 1914, which has an overlapping jurisdiction with the Antitrust Division in its enforcement of the Clayton Act of 1914, and several subsequent laws concerning competitive behavior. In some of its operations, the FTC issues cease and desist orders against behavior it feels to be in violation of the law, and it often engages in such administrative activities as the calling of trade conferences to agree on certain kinds of competitive practices. It sometimes investigates the competitive practices of a particular industry, and then issues rules to be followed by firms in the industry. A good example is the 1984 set of rules, which instituted a national requirement that funeral parlors provide a certain minimum of information concerning costs and alternative funeral arrangements to bereaved families making inquiry. The FTC also has some authority over fraudulent advertising, and in that regard acts as a continuous monitor, rather than a sporadic intervener. Finally, both the FTC and the Antitrust Division are quasi-regulatory because they both monitor merger proposals, sometimes negotiating with companies the limits of what will be accepted without challenge.

The areas of antitrust and competitive practices therefore constitute a borderline between laws enforced by prosecutors and courts, and those in which there exists continuing oversight by an administrative agency. (We will include the antitrust agencies within our scope only to the extent that they pursue a regulatory administrative process similar to that of the other agencies.)

The important point, and one that enables us to concentrate on the kinds of action that have made regulation a controversial term, is that the heart of the study lies in an area in which governmental representatives of an agency, charged with interpreting and enforcing statutory requirements and objectives, face across the table representatives of organizations whose behavior is being channeled and monitored (cf. Noll 1985:9–10). Ordinarily, we do not like to be told what to do or how to do it, and since the purposes of government are sometimes necessarily far from the purposes of the organization being regulated (e.g., the EPA wants cleaner streams, while the paper manufacturer whose processes may pollute the stream, wants lower costs), we have the basis for some inescapable antagonisms.

In clearing a path through the thicket of regulatory literature, there is one more distinction for us to make: to separate "economic" regulation from "social" regulation. (Our main discussion of these two types of regulation comes in chapters 3 and 5; here we provide brief definitions of the terms.) Economic (sometimes called "business") regulation is generally used to cover most of the older, traditional regulatory areas in which the price of the product or service and the authority to enter or leave the industry are the main objects of regulation; the public purpose is to protect the economic interests of consumers from monopoly exactions, and in terms of quality and quantity of service.

Regulation of electric, gas, and water utilities, which is mostly accomplished at the state and local levels, is the prototype of business regulation in this sense. Formation of the Interstate Commerce Commission (ICC) in 1887, marked the introduction of the national government into price and entry regulation, first pertaining to railroads and later extended to motor trucks, buses, and inland water ways. The Civil Aeronautics Board (CAB), formed in 1938, closely regulated fares, entry into business, and route allocations until the Airline Deregulation Act of 1978 began the process of moving this sector back into the world of unregulated competition. The CAB was eventually eliminated at the end of 1984. The Federal Energy Regulatory Commission (FERC), which is a 1975 reformulation of the older Federal Power Commission (FPC), regulates interstate telecommunications rates, interstate transmission of electricity, natural gas, and, until recently, oil. All of these are concerned directly with a product's price, or with the structure of the industry, which in turn may affect price. Because much of business regulation has been directed toward monopoly situations, and some of these industries (e.g., the railroads) no longer hold monopoly positions (and others never did), it is the area of economic regulation that has been seeing a vigorous push from political leaders of both parties, as well as economists, toward deregulation.

One further characteristic of traditional economic regulation is that it has taken place overwhelmingly through multiheaded collegial organizations known as independent regulatory commissions (IRCs), rather than through single-headed agencies of more direct political accountability to the president (see chapter 3).

Social regulation, on the other hand, is a recent arrival on the scene, pursued through single-headed line agencies that are clearly under presidential authority as part of the executive branch, and focused essentially on matters of health, safety, environmental protection, and social practices (e.g., employment discrimination), rather than on prices and conditions for entry of new firms into an industry. Social regulation is concerned not with the pocketbook but with the person.

The EPA is the prototype: while its requirements for lessening air and water pollution and for safe handling of hazardous wastes definitely have an economic impact (directly on industry costs, and indirectly on consumer purchasers), that impact is a side effect of its pursuit of legislated objectives. To a very considerable extent, social regulation may be termed risk regulation: much of the publicized activity of such agencies as the OSHA and the EPA—and much of the political controversy—revolves around the complex problems of defining socially acceptable levels of risk.

While these differences seem clear enough in a broad sketch, we shall see later that there are some important areas of overlap and a fuzzy borderline. Such areas as energy and health care regulation, for example, have simultaneously embodied price, entry, and nonfinancial public purposes under the same statutes and through the same administrative processes. Despite such exceptions, we will often find it useful to distinguish between business and social regulation as two arenas with some generally significant different characteristics.

Having defined our boundaries, we will now look at some major sources of regulation.

chapter two

WHY REGULATE?

POLITICAL ORIGINS

Before December 3, 1984, the EPA had been proceeding at a fairly leisurely pace in meeting the mandate it was given by the Clean Air Act amendments of 1970: to control hundreds of hazardous air pollutants that have a potential to affect human health. As of late 1984, ambient air quality indexes (i.e., limits on the percentage concentrations permitted in the open air) had been set for exactly 6 of the some 600 toxic air pollutants that have been identified. After December 3, 1984, it immediately became clear that major moves, administrative and legislative, would be made to quicken the setting of air pollutant limits, and to strengthen related safety controls on chemical storage tanks.

Why was that date so important? Because it is the day that the Union Carbide Corporation chemical manufacturing operation in Bhopal, India, released into the air great quantities of methyl isocyanate, killing 2,000 persons and blinding or otherwise severely injuring additional thousands.

Congressional subcommittees almost immediately started hearings, both at the town of Institute, West Virginia, where Union Carbide has a domestic plant manufacturing the same material, and in Washington. At the first hearing, subcommittee chairperson Henry A. Waxman and his associates excoriated both the EPA and Union Carbide, whose chairman, Warren M. Anderson, responded that it was "absolutely necessary" to restudy federal safety and pollution laws because of the Bhopal disaster. This assertion was ironically underscored in August 1985, when Carbide's Institute plant had a leak of aldicarb, a pesticide, that injured 135 people. In November of that year, the EPA issued a list of 403 toxic chemicals for which it urged municipalities to prepare emergency response plans.

Disaster abroad played a similar role in stimulating an expansion of the scope of Food and Drug Administration (FDA) authority to require that new prescription drugs be proven effective for the announced purposes. In 1962, the sponsor of such amendments, Senator Estes Kefauver, released information regarding what has been known ever since as "the thalidomide disaster." This was a widespread birth defect problem of truncated or missing limbs in babies born to European women who had used the sedative, thalidomide, while pregnant. Thalidomide had been kept off the U.S. market during the previous year only by the insistence for additional testing pushed by Dr. Frances Kelsey, an FDA staff scientist. Once the *Washington Post* (alerted by Kefauver's staff) broke this story, the senator's bill was a cinch to pass, and on October 10, President John F. Kennedy signed the Drug Amendments of 1962 (Nadel 1971:121–30). Thus do crises and scandals stimulate regulatory initiatives, and this includes new agencies as well as legislative programs.

Crisis and scandal are, however, by no means the only political origins of regulatory programs and agencies. The first task of this chapter is to sketch the great diversity of such origins. After that, we will look at both older and newer academic theories of regulatory sources. Then we will review economic, political, and normative rationales (i.e., arguments regarding why regulation *should* exist, and what are the conditions that justify it). (Note that actual sources and justifying factors respond to very different questions.) The chapter will close with an effort to articulate a political understanding of regulation's role in American society.

Abuses of Economic Power

Perhaps the most traditional source of regulation consists of the felt abuses of an economic nature—price gouging by monopolists or oligopolists (i.e., firms with substantial material power, although not sole suppliers of a given product or service). Thus, the first national regulatory agency, the ICC, was created in 1887 at least in part as a response to the complaints of grain shippers from the Midwest who were at the economic mercy of both railroads and railroad-owned grain storage elevators, who held monopolies for many shipping points and routes. The impact of the economic conditions was translated into politics through the Granger Movement, a revolt that took strong hold of midwestern state legislatures. (Contemporary scholars also suggest self-interest motives on the part of some rail carriers. See Fiorina 1984; Kolko 1965; but see Purscell 1967 for a critique of Kolko.)

Shortly after the turn of the century, the new technological developments of electricity and gas lighting produced an economic situation of franchised monopoly that led to the next significant regulatory development. The action was at the state, rather than the national level, through the creation of state public utility commissions (PUCs)—called public service commissions (PSCs) in some states. Most utility regulation remains today at the state level, although the Federal Energy Regulatory Commission has authority over interstate wholesale prices charged by electric and natural gas utilities. Because the retail distribution of electric and gas service (and local telephone service) is an area of high fixed costs and natural monopoly (meaning that it would be obviously inefficient to run several competitive sets of wires or pipelines down the streets), it is also a natural area for price gouging if it is not regulated. Interestingly, the development of the PUCs was not only a response to monopolistic abuse, but was also desired by some electric power companies on the basis that state regulation was the lesser evil when the alternative appeared to be government ownership (Anderson 1981).

Perhaps the most basic of all programs for social control of industry to develop in response to the growing economic power of late nineteenth century industrialization is that of antitrust and related efforts to restrict the development of monopolization and price fixing among otherwise independent firms. As with railroad regulation, antitrust statutes began at the state level in the 1880s. The environment of public opinion, stimulated by journalistic efforts, was one of concern over early manifestations of bigness in business, and the apparent contrast in power between the burgeoning corporations and individual citizens. Small businessmen and farmers were part of a populist coalition against the "captains of industry," and the Sherman Act of 1890 (outlawing trusts and conspiracies in restraint of trade, and attempts to monopolize) was the statutory result. Although ambiguity has surrounded its enforcement from the very beginning, there is little doubt that in origin the Sherman Act was an effort to use the power of the public sector to prevent perceived abuses of power in the private sector.

In addition to price gouging, fraudulent advertising produced another "pocketbook politics" issue. Section 5 of the Federal Trade Commission Act, as amended by the Wheeler-Lea Act of 1938, prohibits "unfair or deceptive" practices, and constitutes the statutory base for the continuing efforts of the FTC to regulate the more extreme forms of advertising—a kind of "felt abuse" that we sometimes find merely annoying, but at other times are seriously affected by. Representations made by used car dealers are the cultural prototype here, and the FTC recently came close to issuing trade regulations that would have required disclosure of known defects in an automobile. However, it backed down in 1985 under strong industry and congressional pressure, and issued only a requirement that dealers inform customers in writing of the limits of warranties. In 1984, the FTC did issue funeral home regulations mandating the provision of accurate and sufficient information so that bereaved families are not subjected to misleading sales pitches that can lead them to spend more than they can afford.

The Securities and Exchange Commission (SEC) provides another example of economic regulation initiated in response to marketplace abuses (McCraw 1984). After the Great Crash of 1929, postmortem investigations (including 12,000 pages of Senate hearings, 1932–34) revealed that the speculative fever of the 1920s had been worsened for thousands of small investors (and speculators) by chicanery in the touting of equity securities. Stocks were issued for worthless corporations without true information for purchasers; investment companies affiliated with commercial banks manipulated market prices to the advantage of insiders and the distress of outsiders; and fraudulent promoters had operated without constraints at the national level. Legislation in 1933 (information disclosure regarding new securities) and 1934 (regulation of securities markets) created the SEC and inaugurated a program that has become so extensive that charges are heard in the 1980s that the small investor is more overwhelmed than aided by "overkill" in the volume of required information.

Another institution created in response to a need for financial protection of the public, but of a different kind from that involved in cases of abuse of economic power, is the Federal Reserve System—what we know as "the Fed." The ups and downs of the business cycle, in the days before there was a theory of economic stabilization, or a set of institutions through which to pursue stability, were often accompanied by banking panics. With strong geographic and seasonal peaks and valleys in the need for money and credit (e.g., farming at planting time), and no national institution to move funds around in a temporary way to meet credit needs and to forestall "runs" on banks, commerce was frequently seriously disrupted. After the banking panics of 1893 and 1907, Congress created the Federal Reserve Board (now the Board of Governors of the Federal Reserve System) and 13 regional federal reserve banks to ensure smooth functioning of the money and banking system. Until changes were made by the Banking Act of 1935, the role of the Fed was more one of "accommodating" the financial needs of commerce than it was of stabilization through monetary policy in the modern sense. That change was, of course, also a political response to a given situation: that of the Great Depression, and a period in which economic activity so stagnated that unemployment reached 25 percent.

Health and Safety Hazards

To this point, the political catalyst cited as creating legislative majorities for regulation has been that of economic problems, whether through individual abuses or inadequacies of the preindustrial system to handle adequately the more complex, more nationally oriented, untamed corporations. Our next grouping might be summed up as regulations whose political origins lay in health and safety hazards. This area includes both some of the earliest instances of state (rail safety), and national regulation (the Pure Food and Drug Act of 1906), and many from the most recent regulatory growth period in the 1960s and 1970s: the Occupational Safety and Health Act (1970) and the Consumer Product Safety Act of 1972; the Nuclear Regulatory Commission (NRC), a 1975 spin-off from the Atomic Energy Commission; the National Highway Traffic Safety Administration (1970); and the Environmental Protection Agency (EPA) (1970).

The EPA was created by President Richard M. Nixon, through a 1970 reorganization plan, to provide an integrated approach to the administration of previously legislated clean air and clean water programs. The agency's tasks multiplied and became ever more complex as 1970 and 1972 clean air and clean water acts strengthened federal requirements, while also enlarging the mandated activities of the states, and as new acts were added to its charge: the Toxic Substances Control Act (TSCA) and the Resource Conservation and Recovery Act (RCRA) (both in 1976), and the Superfund of 1980, all concerned with chemicals and hazardous wastes; the Safe Drinking Water Act of 1974; and the Federal Insecticide, Fungicide, and Rodenticide Act (FIFRA) amendments in 1972—among others. The result is that the EPA has the broadest spread of responsibilities and probably the most difficult tasks among all health and safety agencies.

The focus of all these programs and agencies is not our financial protection, but the safety and health of our persons. As suggested in chapter 1, these fall under the heading of social regulation. Their political origins also differ from that of most instances of economic regulation. There, we had market power abuses, systemic problems, and interest group pressures. Here we had health and medication problems; broadly perceived environmental deterioration that at least threatened disaster, if action was not soon taken; a consensus of public opinion that amounted to a national environmental movement (symbolized by Earth Day, April 22, 1970); and an increasing practice of policy entrepreneurship in Congress.

Food and drug regulation was enacted in 1906 as a result of a combination of concerns—those of the American Medical Association (AMA), which wanted to get rid of quack medicines; some patent medicine firms that hoped regulation would give consumers confidence in the industry; and a crusading government chemist, Harvey W. Wiley, who acted as a catalyst to create a coalition against food adulteration and misbranded drugs. As is true of many regulatory intiatives, the original statute merely opened the door to largely symbolic government action; truly effective food and drug regulation had to await strengthening amendments decades later.

Clean air and water legislation had its political origins in physically visible and malodorous deterioration of air and water. The "killer fogs" of London, plus severe smog episodes in New York City (80 deaths), and Donora, Pennsylvania (20 deaths) in 1966 and 1948 respectively, stimulated significant concern for what we were breathing (Jones 1975:25–29). Disappearance of fish and plant life from Lake Erie and Lake Michigan, and the dramatic phenomenon of a section of the Cuyahoga River in Ohio bursting into flame as its oily pollution ignited, did the same for clean water politics. However, political action takes more than physical need. In the environmental protection case, the added agents were rapidly developing public opinion in the late 1960s (arguably a part of the activist, interventionist mood of the Great Society period), and the public and legislative policy entrepreneurship of such figures as Ralph Nader (self-appointed public interest champion), Senator Gaylord Nelson (organizer of Earth Day, 1970, which had its primary celebrations on college campuses), and Senator Edmund S. Muskie ("Mr. Clean" as far as air and water legislation were concerned in this legislatively fruitful period). One might also add the factor of party competition, for at one point President Richard M. Nixon and Muskie, a Democratic leader, got into a bidding match to see which of them could urge the stronger clean air bill (Jones 1975:179–183).

Even more clearly than in the case of environmental protection, social regulation to outlaw racial and ethnic discrimination (with sex and handicapped categories added later) had its political stimulus in a real political movement, the biggest of our time: the Civil Rights Movement that began with the Montgomery bus boycott, and was made convincing to the Kennedy administration (and to Lyndon B. Johnson, as Kennedy's Vice President and later political heir) by the Birmingham police assault on civil rights marchers in the Spring of 1963. Summer of that year saw the historic "march on Washington," with the late Reverend Martin Luther King's dramatic culminating oratory. The Civil Rights Act of 1964 then established the Equal Employment Opportunity Commission (EEOC), and included in its

Title VI the policy of withholding funds from organizations that discriminated in "any program or activity receiving federal financial assistance."

The Occupational Safety and Health Act of 1970 is an interesting example of the personal relationships factor that sometimes occurs in policy development. Although occupational safety laws had existed in some states for many years, and earlier federal proposals had included the late Senator Hubert H. Humphrey's Accident Prevention bill in 1951, congressional action in 1970 came only after President Lyndon B. Johnson included a call for new legislation in his 1968 manpower message. How did he happen to do that? The story (Kelman 1980:239) is that one of Johnson's speech writers had a research-oriented brother who worked in the Bureau of Occupational Safety and Health at the Department of Health, Education and Welfare. This connection had led to a number of references in presidential speeches to occupational safety and health issues. In the Department of Labor, fuel was added to the fire by an assistant secretary, Esther Peterson, who visited uranium mining lung cancer victims, and then took up the matter with Secretary Willard Wirtz, who had a draft bill readied and sent to the president in late 1967. Apparently, because of the fertile ground prepared by the earlier fraternal combination, the White House adopted Wirtz' proposal. Although hearings initially produced only a clear labor union-manufacturers disagreement, a 1968 mining disaster and political party competition in 1970 (Nixon worked hard that year at pulling blue-collar workers away from Democrats) gave the needed final push. The act creating the Occupational Safety and Health Administration passed both houses of Congress in the latter year.

A final crisis-response situation that produced a new regulation is illustrated by the "Tylenol rule," promulgated by the Department of Health and Human Services in 1982. The rule is so-named because the very direct and immediate stimulus was an incident a month earlier, when some deaths were caused by adulterated capsules of the analgesic, Tylenol. Only a small number of bottles had been tampered with, but shelf clearing was national and immediate, and public confidence could not be firmly restored until something was done that would provide visible point-of-sale consumer reassurance. The now ubiquitous tamper-proof seals and caps were the answer, mandated by the federal government with the generally strong approbation of the manufacturing concerns, whose products and packaging were subject to the same problem (and who preferred uniform national regulation to the variety of state regulations that were otherwise likely).

Business Demand for Regulation

We note two examples of business group demands as the proximate political stimuli for major regulatory initiatives of the New Deal period.

The first of these concerns the Federal Communication Commission (FCC). The FCC is an institution whose horizons have been enlarged with technological developments in telephones and other telecommunications, cable TV and satellite broadcasting (Krasnow et al. 1982)—although recent chairmen, Charles D. Ferris under Carter, and Mark S. Fowler under Reagan, have worked hard to diminish its role by purposeful deregulation (Fowler and Brenner 1982). In its earlier incarnation as the Federal Radio Commission (FRC), established in 1927, the commission was a direct response to demands from listeners and broadcasters alike—as well as to pleas from then-Secretary of Commerce Herbert Hoover. The problem was technological: the airwaves could not be split into enough clear channels to avoid direct confrontations of two or more stations trying to broadcast simultaneously on the same wave length. After valiant efforts at business-government cooperation were aborted in the courts, Hoover abandoned licensing efforts. Two hundred new stations arose in a few months. Broadcasting became useless; the multiple-station interference was great. The resulting "pandemonium" (Fainsod et al. 1959:388) produced the politically effective demand for a regulatory commission. In 1934, the FRC thus metamorphosed into the FCC, bringing telephone, telegraph, and broadcasting regulation under one agency.

Our other business-demand case is the Civil Aeronautics Board (CAB). The commercial airline industry had the misfortune (or perhaps the good fortune, from the viewpoint of the CAB's economic protection) to be an "infant industry" at the time of the Great Depression. The firms were dependent on airmail subsidies, and worried about the potential for "destructive competition" that could cause both safety problems for the public and economic problems for the existing carriers. With financial problems mounting after 1935, and Congress worried by near scandal in the question of the airmail subsidy standard, the demand for protection increased, producing the Civil Aeronautics Act of 1938 (Behrman 1980).

The Nuclear Regulatory Commission (NRC), created in 1975 as a spin-off from the Atomic Energy Commission (AEC) that had overseen the nuclear power industry since 1946, illustrates one additional type of political impetus to a regulatory program. In this case, the operative factors were a growing awareness (even before the Chernobyl disaster and the near-catastrophe at Three Mile Island in

1978) that nuclear reactors had severe (if remote) safety risks, as well as great potential advantages, and increasing recognition that the AEC's nuclear promotion role strongly inhibited its safety regulation role. (For the same reason, pesticide regulation was moved in 1972 from the farm user-oriented Department of Agriculture to the protection-oriented EPA.) Here, the basic reasons for regulation did not change, but a combination of publicity about nuclear plant accidents and technical problems, and the policy activism of the Union of Concerned Scientists led to legislation creating a new agency focused more clearly on one side of the regulation-promotion combination of governmental roles.

The difficulties of channeling strong economic forces through organization charts is evident, however, in the fact that although the NRC's authority calls for it to pursue nuclear power plant safety before licensing a plant, the desire to license often seems stronger than the desire to insure an extra margin of safety.

In summary, the proximate political reasons for instituting programs are as varied as the subjects with which the programs deal. What these capsule descriptions show is that the enactment of a regulatory statute (as with any law) requires some catalytic element— be it a person, an event, or an unfolding situation—that produces sufficient political support to overcome the antiaction inertia of the legislative process. This is true no matter what the underlying scientific or economic reasons for the regulation might be. Action takes both an intellectual justification or rationale, and a political rationale; i.e., reasons why elected legislators will find it advisable to vote for the proposed action. This applies as much to deregulation bills as to those that would impose new regulations, as the Reagan administration discovered. Too often, in current discussions of regulation, a world of pure economic rationality is assumed, and the necessity for political coalition building is ignored. The examples given here should give us a mental picture of the essential political element in the development of regulatory programs.

With this political context established, we will now turn from the actual historical question of why certain programs were enacted at certain times (which is what the political elements are most involved with), to the questions of why we should regulate and why we do regulate, in terms of explanatory theoretical models.

CAUSAL THEORIES OF REGULATION

Much of the literature on regulation distinguishes between "normative" and "positive" theories of explanation. The former are propositions of justification: reasons why regulation *should* exist, most often based on defined inadequacies of the private economy. The latter consist of "is" propositions: purportedly factual statements about social-economic forces that underly governmental regulatory actions. (Note: As used here, "positive" is not an evaluative term, as the opposite of "negative"; rather, it means empirically based. To avoid the confusion that often attends this use of the word, we will substitute "causal," to convey that the "is" theories are concerned with what actually produces political pushes for regulation, whether or not one thinks it should. Political dispute, of course, focuses on the "should" theories, but we will review both.)

Economists and economic principles so thoroughly dominate contemporary writings on regulation that today's students may find it strange that prominent earlier (1940s–1960s) books on regulation most often reflected a political approach, the primary theme being that the rise of regulatory programs could best be explained as a response to political demands from victimized groups for protection. In turn, these group demands were seen as the concrete manifestations of a very broad and basic societal adjustment to the realities of economic power, which developed as a function of the unfettered industrial capitalism of the late nineteenth and early twentieth centuries. Landmark political science writings in this vein included a historical analysis of the origins and organizational principles of the independent regulatory commissions (Cushman 1941); a 1955 monograph—*Regulating Business by Independent Commission* by Marver H. Bernstein—that established a lasting criticism of independence as equal to lack of accountability, which then produced "capture" (see chapter 3); and a very widely used text (that had its first edition in 1941 and its third in 1959) by two political scientists and an economist (Fainsod, Gordon, and Palamountain 1959).

Cushman largely took for granted the origination of such economic regulation agencies as the ICC, FTC, FCC, and CAB as responses to fairly specific economic problems. He specifically avoided the policy question of the appropriate scope of regulation, focusing instead on the organizational one of IRCs as neglected "cogs in the federal machine" (Cushman 1941:5). In his view, Congress acted with the intent of creating agencies that would find and analyze with neutral expertise the information needed to solve the identified problems.

More politically full-blooded than Cushman's technical-administrative orientation, Bernstein's 1955 monograph defined regulatory origins as a matter of group political struggle, with the presidency playing a vital supportive role. The struggle, in his view, pitted democracy against the excesses of private economic power, paradoxically saving capitalism from itself in the process. A quotation will provide the flavor of Bernstein's argument:

> In the American environment, regulation has been demanded by groups that seek the protection of public policy to prevent the continuation of harmful business practices. Regulatory policies adopted in response to those demands have modified the concept of private property; consequently, those who control the use of private property have often regarded regulation as an attack on the basic institutions of private economic enterprise. On the other hand, the effective demands for regulation of economic affairs have almost always come from groups which have been hailed as vital to the preservation of freedom and capitalism, namely small businessmen, farmers, and middle-class groups generally. . . . Regulation represents one way in which a democracy has attempted to modify economic relationships in a capitalist society without destroying capitalism itself. In terms of the long-run development of political and economic institutions, regulation is a conservative approach. . . . With the exception of industries like radio broadcasting, air transport, and trucking, which demanded regulation to restore order in a chaotic situation, groups subject to regulation have always fought against the adoption of public regulatory politics. *Regulatory agencies have usually been established during periods in which the forces demanding regulation have had the support of a strong president and have been able to find sufficient allies to command a political majority.* [emphasis added] (Bernstein 1955:250–51)

In Bernstein's model, the major problems that plagued the IRCs in the 1950s (and that continued later) derived in no small part from the failure of pro-regulation groups to keep up the pressure once the statute had been enacted, and of presidents to provide consistent, strong support.

The Fainsod, Gordon (he was the economist in the trio), and Palamountain text did not develop a set of explicit rationales, whether causative or normative, beyond the statement already quoted: American regulation was not the result of a theory at all, but of "empirical adjustments to felt abuses" (p. 21). Their prototypical example was the 1887 act creating the ICC—an act that had substantial support from agrarian forces normally distrustful of centralized power, and from industrial groups that usually wanted minimal government at any level; in this instance, however, they "found it necessary to strengthen government in order to remedy abuses which bore heavily upon them." To them, the ICC act ended a "century of expansion" in which "industry became national in scope . . . and new engines of wealth and power . . . threatened to evade all effective control," and began a new age in which uneasiness over the consequences of the earlier growth "crystallized in the creation of new instruments of national power to control and direct policy in important sectors of the economy" (1959:251).

These authors' academic conception of regulatory policy development differed sharply from the tendency in much writing of the 1980s to see policy as a simple application of microeconomic models. In their preface, they justified an emphasis on "the political forces which influence the formation and execution of public policy" by a "conviction that effective economic or other criteria of desirable public policy can be most fruitfully developed when there is a vivid realization of the potentialities and limitations of the political context in which they must be applied" (1959:xi). One could translate that into more contemporary social science parlance: political-institutional rationality regarding feasibility and implementation dimensions of regulation is a significant constraint on efforts to subsume all regulatory questions under the economic rationality heading of efficient resource allocation.

In the writings covered so far there are both explicit and implicit reliance on the proposition that industrialization created centers of private power, which were abused with sufficient frequency to stimulate political demands for countervailing use of public control. Power and its accountability were key concepts—an expected fact when political scientists are writing. What about the economists in the earlier period: what were their orienting ideas?

The "granddaddy" of all books in this field is *Social Control of Business,* by the late John Maurice Clark (1939), a distinguished economist (originator of the concept of "workable competition"), and social theorist of the business-government relationship. In this pathbreaking text, first published in 1926 and very substantially augmented in a 1939 edition that continued in wide use after World War II, Clark began by pointing to a "many sided movement toward control" of industry that had been developing since the 1870s, and which he thought could be guided but not stopped. Its primary causes, he asserted, were: "organized large-scale production . . . the growth of democracy, and . . . the growth of science." At a more concrete level, his description of the economy (from the perspective of the Great Depression) was of "a system of vast impersonal organizations in constant danger of being paralyzed by a deadlock of the interests involved," a system that could support the society's basic value of individualism in modern form only through "democratic and humanitarian control." It is clear that in Clark's intellectual framework, economic organizations and market institutions were means toward larger societal ends: individualism and democracy. In a democratic state "of individualistic traditions," Clark thought that control would "become a piecemeal matter, dealing with one particular felt evil after another, and directed toward alleviating a succession of specific sore spots" (1939:4–5, 28–29, 51). His view of the actual historical origins of regulation is nearly identical with that of Fainsod, Gordon, and Palamountain, differing only in being more explicitly related to a larger world-view that transcended all disciplinary boundaries. With this perspective, he was clearly not one to see the pattern of regulation as simply a search for efficiencies of production.

Another prominent text by an economist, Clair Wilcox's *Public Policies Toward Business,* was first published in 1955 and has undergone repeated revisions (Wilcox 1960: Wilcox and Shepherd 1975: Shepherd 1985). Wilcox's sense of the basic causes underlying historical development of regulation focuses on growing complexity and interdependence:

> A century ago controls were few and simple. In the economy of that day they were all that seemed to be required. In relation to its great resources the population of the country was small. . . . Productive activity centered in agriculture. . . . Enterprises were organized, in the main, as individual proprietorships or partnerships. They were managed by their owners; employers dealt directly with employees. The scale of industrial operations was small; the production of goods and services was scattered among many firms. Economic independence was the general rule. Now all of these conditions have changed. The population has grown; the land has been settled, and its natural wealth exploited. Agriculture had declined in relative importance; manufacturing, transport, and the public utilities have grown. The individual proprietorship and the partnership have given way, in many fields, to the modern corporation. Ownership has been divorced from management, and labor has been organized. . . . The scale of industrial operations has grown; production, in many industries, has come to be concentrated in the hands of a few large firms. Economic relationships have steadily grown in complexity. Interdependence, rather than independence, has come to be the rule.
>
> These changes have brought with them a host of new problems, and as these problems have arisen solutions have been sought through the extension of public controls. (Wilcox 1960:6).

Wilcox usefully supplements the group politics origins of regulation by pointing out these changes in the demography, technology, and social organization of productive units and markets as the underlying causes. When he turns to the political side, Wilcox's view is of a very reluctant dragon: "Government . . . intervenes only when it is forced to intervene. It acts reluctantly, deliberately, and tardily, in response to overwhelming pressures" (1960:9).

In sum, the academic interpreters of government regulation of 25–40 years ago were in broad agreement across the economics-political science boundaries. They explained the enlarged governmental role of the twentieth century as a response to industrialization and its corollaries of power concentrations, impersonalization of economic relationships, and a more complex, interdependent socioeconomic structure. In explaining particular regulatory program and agency origins, they agreed that organized group pressures acting in reaction to perceptions of economic power abuses were the causative factor. Theirs was a broadly institutional framework.

The most cited work in a newer and very different analytic framework for causal explanations of regulatory origins, is a 1971 article by University of Chicago Nobel Prize winning economist George J. Stigler (1971; 1975). The theoretical task Stigler was set was to ask, "Who will receive the benefits or burdens of regulation?" His central thesis was that "as a rule, regulation is acquired by the industry and is designed and operated primarily for its benefit." The explanation he proffers for this outcome involves treating political parties as governmental "sellers," to whom industries go with "demands" that they try to purchase with votes and resources ("educational" campaigns, campaign finance contributions, and so forth). Legislators are seen as having very broad discretion because voters "must eschew direct expressions of marginal changes in preferences," yet (somewhat contradictorily) they are assumed to vote in exact concert with their party, which is viewed as a political "firm" selling regulation as its product (1975:114–26). In 1976, Stigler's demand-oriented model was supplemented and generalized by economist Sam Peltzman (1976), who argued from a "supply side" position: government officials offer regulation where they see a good "payment" in votes.

The generic notion that legislators and other government officials have rational self-interests, and respond to incentives that serve those interests—which is the core behavioral idea in microeconomic modelling—is widely accepted also among political scientists. However, this is hardly an original position; political scientist Harold Lasswell long ago defined politics as *"Who Gets What, When, How"* (Lasswell, 1936). As Stigler wrote in 1975, when responding to a critique of his 1971 article, his theory "tells us to look, as precisely and carefully as we can, at who gains and who loses, and how much, when we seek to explain a regulatory policy" (Stigler 1975:140). That is, the "rational man" approach makes psychological sense in an individualistic society, and constitutes a useful corrective to the more naive version of an earlier approach that takes elected officials to be altruistic seekers of some disembodied public interest. As Stigler and many of his followers in both economics and political science apply the group demand approach, however, the result sometimes approaches an equally naive and extreme cynicism, which fails to allow for diversity of motivations or policy-making environments (see Derthick and Quirk 1985:245; Levine 1981:189–90, 193). At the least, can't a person see his or her self-interest as lying in gaining plaudits for "statesmanlike" behavior? Are we to totally deny independent governmental conceptions of public needs—the "autonomy of the democratic state," in the title phrase of Nordlinger's recent provocative study (Nordlinger 1981)?

With regard to Stigler's particular 1971 formulation, we must mention that his model of American politics is seriously deficient in its overstatement of the significance of parties, its assumptions about legislator-party and legislator-constituency relationships, and in its failure to consider (or even to recognize) the substantial policy role of appointed regulatory officials who are not directly reachable through the votes-and-resources incentives system he posits. And, while conceding that policy issues are never decided entirely on the merits, objective analysis of broad societal interests does occur and does form part of the effective political environment. His article, and similar writings that extrapolate directly from private economic power to governmental actions, are also deficient in ignoring the often significant variable of the internal organizational incentives of the regulatory agencies (McCaffrey 1982). Finally, Stigler's assumption that the effective "demanders" of regulation are always the producer groups reflects only a limited number of older economic regulatory instances. It is very strongly belied by the growth of social regulation measures, which have often been strongly opposed by business groups that one would expect his theory to dominate. One could say that Stigler published too soon: many of the counter examples were just coming into legislative being about the time he wrote—Clean Air (1970), Clean Water (1972), OSHA (1970), Consumer Product Safety Commission (1972), and Surface Mining Control and Reclamation (1977). On the other hand, he could already have considered FDA protective amendments (1962) and auto safety regulation (1966).

More importantly, a more sophisticated conception of the incentives concept changes the picture from whether or not producer groups dominate regulatory policy origins, to that of the conditions under which a variety of outcomes may occur. Such a typology has been developed by political scientist James Q. Wilson (1980:367–72), and is sketched in the section on capture of IRCs in chapter 3.

We can now say that both older and newer, economic and political, explanations of regulatory origins are needed to provide a rounded picture. Self-interest and economic power are important, but so are broad-based public interest groups and political entrepreneurs with their own, autonomous conceptions of what a situation demands—conceptions that will sometimes gain votes and some-times cost them. The particularities of regulatory programs—and perhaps especially the vigor with which, and ways in which, they are implemented—will often reflect group demands. The existence of some regulatory statute that calls on government to end an abuse, or prevent a disaster, more often than not (and here one is thinking primarily of what in chapter 1 we called social regulation) results from a good-of-the-society perception of a problem and a proposal for solving or (more often) ameliorating it, with substantial public support.

Recall the picture of increasing complexity and social interdependence that we gleaned from Wilcox, and we might end this section on a supplementary note in the same vein. Larry Reynolds has written of implicit and explicit nonmarket controls over social behavior, the former including private systems of ethics and conceptions of justice in the use of markets. He suggests that:

> As a social group grows and becomes more complex, the efficiency of nonmarket implicit controls declines. The group becomes more heterogeneous, and general agreement on ethical values and other institutional arrangements decreases. . . .This condition has been one of the by-products of the Industrial Revolution. . . .The response to the declining effectiveness of implicit regulations is the growth of explicit regulations. (1981:650)

In short, the rise of public regulation is, basically, the response of humane values and social analysis to situations in which older informal social controls have proven inadequate.

HOW IS REGULATION JUSTIFIED?

The line between reasons why we do regulate (causative or descriptive theories) and reasons why we should regulate is a fuzzy one. In fact, the two areas, although analytically distinct, overlap in the real world of political response: the underlying economic and social changes that have led to regulation, are also used to justify that regulation. (When the system is working well, they do and they should run together.) The connecting link is the application of our values to the situational facts. When a situation changes so as to produce results we don't like or that disturb our values, we feel justified in taking steps to change those results. As we pointed out in chapter 1, public policies always involve a mixture of facts and values.

We suggest, therefore, that the most basic rationale for regulation lies in the combination of those factors of complexity and interdependence engendered by industrialization, with increased democratic expectations. By the latter we mean both the more egalitarian, participative aspects of democracy, and our recognition that public authority must sometimes be used to control the concentrations of private power that industrialization has produced.

Another passage from Wilcox illustrates this point. Keep in mind that Wilcox saw the price system as "one of the greatest achievements of civilization" and governmental action, even when necessary, as "at best a poor substitute" (1960:x). His values also include consumer welfare and the control of power, so his normative response to the facts of the modern industrial economy is to justify much economic regulation in the following way:

> It is not always safe to leave business to its own devices; experience has shown that its freedom will sometimes be abused. Investors have been defrauded by promoters, corporate insiders, and market manipulators. Men, women, and children have been put to work under needless hazards, amid unhealthful surroundings, for long hours, at low pay, and without assurance of future security. Competitors have been harassed by malicious and predatory tactics, handicapped by discrimination, excluded from markets and sources of supply, and subjected to intimidation, coercion, and physical violence. Consumers have been victimized by short weights and measures, by adulteration, and by misrepresentation of quality and price; they have been forced to contribute to the profits of monopoly. Water and air have been polluted with the wastes of industry; the nation's resources have been dissipated through extravagant methods of exploitation. These abuses have not characterized all business at all times, but they have occurred with sufficient frequency to justify the imposition of control. Regulation is clearly required, not only to protect the investor, the worker, the consumer, and the community at large against the unscrupulous businessman, but also to protect the honest businessman against his dishonest competitor. (Wilcox 1960:8)

The view expressed so cogently by Wilcox is also the position found—generally only by inference, rather than explicitly—in many of the government regulation texts of the 1960s, especially those by political scientists (Cotter 1960; Dimock 1961; Redford 1965). Authors of that period did not see a need for an explicit theory of justification; they assumed, as a proposition self-evident to the reader, that power should be controlled and consumers protected, and that the positive use of government toward those ends was an appropriate application of the coercive authority of the state.

By the late 1970s, and continuing even more strongly into the 1980s, strong doubts were being expressed about regulation:

>   about its effectiveness, by economists who doubted that it could be effective, and by environmental advocates who thought it could and should be stronger.
>
>   about its costs, mostly by business firms and their spokespersons, but also by a number of economists concerned about the possibly negative impact of regulatory costs on productivity.
>
>   about its necessity in many of the traditional areas of economic regulation, where the microeconomic theorists developed strong arguments that the competitive market could provide adequate social controls without government intervention.

On the basis of such doubts, newer writings, of economists and public choice theorists, have emphasized an approach different from that of Wilcox or the earlier political science writers. Also, the abuse of power justification covered only part of the regulatory ground; the reasons used to support economic regulation are not the same as those used to support social regulation; and much regulation is justified by situations that arise even in the absence of excessive economic power. We will now spell out the rationales that have become standard in the economics-based literature, continue with other specific justifications, and conclude with some comments on the general pattern of normative reasons why we regulate.

Economic Rationales

Three major categories are cited in the standard economics explication of regulatory justifications: natural monopoly, inadequate information, and externalities. Some treatments add a fourth: the inability of competition to maintain itself. These can all be subsumed under the heading of "market failure," which means that there are instances in which one cannot expect the desired social results to be achieved by the autonomous workings of the competitive marketplace (economists see this as conditions in which resource allocation by the market will not be optimal). Income distribution problems are sometimes added for discussion, but largely rejected for technical reasons as being an adequate justification.

Natural monopoly is the term used for such situations as local distribution of electric power, natural gas, telephone connections, and cable TV. The meaning is that the competitive running of wires and pipes above or below the ground in duplicate, triplicate, or more would be so obviously inefficient and costly a use of resources that we "naturally" permit monopolistic supply of such goods with decreasing average costs. However, price gouging of the consumer will not be prevented by the classic workings of the competitive elements, and too little electricity will be produced and consumed, so regulation substitutes for the missing competition.

Inadequate information has grown as a regulatory justification, and will continue to do so as a clear function of increasing technological complexity in the products we consume. Prescription drugs are a standard illustration: as a consumer, I lack the ability to judge the appropriateness or the safety of any of the thousands of antibiotics and other wonder drugs. To some extent, such a lack also affects my physician—we are both protected by the FDA's regulations. When purchasing a refrigerator, I cannot tell by visual inspection which make or model is most energy efficient. In California, state regulation requires that the manufacturer provide an energy use comparison on a tag attached to each refrigerator. Sometimes the competition will give the consumer the desired information: a low-tar brand of cigarette will advertise that fact. Sometimes this does not work, however: automobile manufacturers at one time advertised their safety features, but later apparently decided that it was collectively inadvisable to call the consumer's attention to that dimension of the product.

Sometimes all the government need do is require that the producer supply information, and let the consumer decide whether to buy the product with the knowledge in hand (which is what we do about saccharin); in other instances, where the harm of acting from ignorance is seen as more certain to occur, government may require that the product be modified to remove the risk—as with accordion style baby gates that had caused at least eight deaths, leading to a 1985 Consumer Product Safety Commission rule, negotiated with the manufacturers, to cease production of such gates.

Does regulation of this kind amount to paternalism? Some would say it does; others argue that whatever term one may use, such regulation is justified in terms of the severity of consequences if the consumer is unaware of the information, or doesn't take the warning seriously. Take another example: auto seat-belt use is now the law in several states, and is under discussion in others (in good part because the Department of Transportation has said that it will require air bags on 1990 model cars if three-fourths of the population is not covered by mandatory seat-belt rules before that time). Is that justified only as paternalism? No, it is justified by the external impact of auto injuries and deaths on third parties: the impact on my family if I am killed because I fail to protect myself with a seat belt; the collective impact of higher insurance rates. Many rules that appear to be paternalistic at first glance are really justified by social consequences, while paternalism is usually defined as restriction of choice where only the person restricted is affected. (For a good discussion of the paternalism issue in regulation, see Kelman 1981a).

The third, and most frequently cited, economic argument for considering regulation, is that of externalities—also known as spillovers or third-party effects (Rhoads). As the very word implies, an externality is a consequence of a transaction that is felt by someone "external" to the transaction; a "third" party on whom the transaction has "spilled over." A standard example is that of a person owning property on a stream, and enjoying fishing and swimming. If a papermill upstream discharges effluent into the stream that kills the fish and fouls the water, our downstream owner is a third party suffering from a negative externality produced by the transactions between the paper mill and its customers, the first two parties. In other words, externalities refer to situations in which the private costs (benefits) do not equal the social costs (benefits). For example, if I have to pay to treat the water before I can swim at my spot on the stream, this is a social cost beyond the private costs embedded in the papermill's costs or the price paid by the paper purchaser. Putting this in terms of external benefits, the social gain from universal education accrues to the entire community, not only to the children educated in the public schools; regulations that save energy costs for an individual consumer also aid national security by making us less dependent on imported oil.

The externalities rationale applies mostly to the social regulation areas. It covers many of the most controversial areas of recent regulation: prevention of environmental pollution of the air, the water, and the ground; occupational safety and health protection, which the market relationship between a factory producer and the retail store buyers will not provide as a market result; protection against health hazards from toxic chemical production; provision for coal mine safety; required rehabilitation of strip-mined land, and so forth. In all such areas, the prima facie case for regulation is made by asking two questions:

1. Is the negative externality one that it is important to avoid? (e.g., factory deaths, air and water pollution?)
2. Can we reasonably expect competition (i.e., the operation of the normal private market system) to take care of the problems?

The answer to question 2, unfortunately, is that the more competitive a market, the less likely a producer will be to attend to the side effects of production: economic pressures militate against greater expenses than those that cannot be avoided.

In other words, the market system operates on the basis of self-interest incentives, but, from the viewpoint of the producer, the externalities we worry about are by definition other-interests rather than self-interests (Rhoads 1983). The task of regulation, then, can be put in terms of compelling the private parties to a transaction to "internalize the externalities," by making the producer and consumer, who are direct parties to the transaction, include in their costs whatever is involved in preventing the unwanted third-party effect. This might be electrostatic "scrubbers" on power plant smokestacks to remove harmful emissions passed into the air, for example, or the costs of installing protective safety guards on machinery in a factory. To the extent that costs of handling negative externalities are borne by the government and the taxpayers, then the externalities are "socialized" rather than internalized.

The prima facie (on the face of it) case for regulation is not by itself conclusive. If the cost of regulation clearly outweighed the benefits—assuming the measurability of both components, which is a big assumption—then one may take the position that it is better to live with the side effect than to use government to clear it up. Presumably, such a conclusion would be more likely if the externality is merely aesthetic, than if it is a matter of saving lives. Alternatively, one might suggest an educational campaign aimed at voluntary internalization of the costs involved in protecting the environment. Or, one could argue that a sense of social responsibility will lead corporations to act appropriately once alerted to the externality problems. However, few of those subjected to externalities would accept the latter approaches, because they lack incentives. Finally, when we are subject to the power of others, which affects our lives in important ways, our concepts of democracy and accountability argue against reliance on the self-restraint of others as our protection. Therefore, if the externality is significant in our scale of values, and we cannot find a way to build its avoidance into the market system of private incentives, then the case for regulation will be a strong one in the minds of most citizens.

These rationales are derived from the disciplinary models of microeconomics. When economists say that these are the only grounds for regulating, they logically mean (but sometimes neglect to state explicitly) that these are the only economic rationales—which says nothing one way or the other about other possible justifications that may lie outside of the discipline's theoretical structure. Real-world problems are never reducible to academic disciplines, which are mental constructs to aid in analysis, and should not be either reified or deified. Since regulation is a real-world activity, noneconomic justifications may be of at least equal importance.

Noneconomic Rationales

The most traditional of all regulatory justifications is the legal concept of a business "affected with a public interest." Derived from the English common law (law enunciated in the case decisions of judges, rather than statutes enacted by legislative bodies), this doctrine was used by the United States Supreme Court in the 1877 case of *Munn* v. *Illinois* to justify a state law regulating grain elevator prices, asserting that this business was "a thing of public interest and use." The core idea seemed to be best explained by what had been included over the years: roadway inns, toll roads, toll bridges—services that were somehow deemed essential, and in which a proprietor was perceived as offering his service to all comers, often in a situation where the consumer might have little competitive choice. At any rate, this decision paved the way for some regulation by the states in a period otherwise best known for adherence to the laissez-faire doctrine that government must leave business alone. A second legal landmark in regulatory development came in 1886, when the Supreme Court's Wabash decision (*Wabash* v. *Illinois*) ironically stimulated a push for national government regulation by forbidding states from regulating railroad rates (even within the state) if the traffic was part of an interstate movement. Thus, all effective regulation in a rapidly nationalizing economy would have to be done by the national government.

For nearly 50 years, the Court tried, on a case-by-case basis, to decide which particular industries could be regulated and which could not. In 1934, it gave up the fruitless attempt at an impossible distinction, and declared in *Nebbia* v. *New York* that there was no specific class of businesses affected with a public interest, but that the states were free to "adopt whatever economic policy may reasonably be deemed to promote public welfare." It required only that legislation so enacted be seen to have a "reasonable relation to a proper legislative purpose." *Nebbia* thus took a big step toward the modern legal situation, in which the Constitution is perceived by the Court as not imposing any obstacle to regulation other than that it must not be arbitrary or discriminatory. The Court defers to the so-called "political branches": the president and Congress. The legal justification has been transmogrified into a political situation: if a majority of Congress can be persuaded and the president is willing to sign, it is justified.

A justification that political scientists find much more congenial than do many economists is that of regulation as a device for balancing social power, for the sake of a power equilibrium in its own right, and as an indirect means of affecting income distribution in a less unequal direction. Perhaps the best example is the regulatory body known as the National Labor Relations Board (NLRB), established in 1935 to undergird the Wagner Act's declaration of the right of workers to organize in unions, so that their collectivities of people could bargain with the collectivities of capital known as industrial corporations on a more equal power basis. Stone (1982:146–51) suggests that minimum wage regulation and occupational safety and health rules constitute additional efforts to use regulation to redress a bargaining power disparity. A major general formulation of this rationale is found in the doctrine of "countervailing power" developed by the iconoclastic economist, John Kenneth Galbraith (1952), whose writings have always explicitly recognized that economics must relate to social power as well as to market efficiency.

Equalizing power is an end in itself in an egalitarian society, and a means toward achieving social justice. Social justice is sometimes a direct focus of regulation, the leading modern example being the range of agencies and programs that regulate social interactions to prevent racial, ethnic, or handicapped discrimination. Affirmative action is the most controversial of such regulations, partly because the laws do not enjoy total consensus regarding the objectives, and more because some of the means—e.g., numerical goals for minority hiring—are seen by a significant portion of the population as unwarranted reverse discrimination. Affirmative action and nondiscrimination regulations have obvious economic ramifications, whether directly in hiring practices, or indirectly in terms of access to the educational opportunities that predetermine later economic chances. However, the primary justification is moral, not economic.

A related, often neglected, rationale is one for which no recognized label is conventionally used. We will call it the social services justification, and it covers a diversity of topics:

> In a 1982 congressional hearing on a controversial proposal to impose an "access fee" on local telephone customers as a way to keep long distance rates down, FCC chairman Mark S. Fowler responded to one congressional critic by saying that while he shared the critic's concern for low-income phone users, "it skews the economy when you have incorrect pri-

cing." Acting from a social services perspective, Congressman Al Swift rejoined: "And what I'm suggesting is that it's perfectly acceptable for the government to skew the economy in pursuit of an acceptable social goal like universal service" (*Los Angeles Times,* December 2, 1982).

"Lifeline" utility rates—special rates for a limited amount of electricity, natural gas, or even local telephone service for the poor—are a regulatory requirement imposed by some state public utility commissions. Universality of service is seen as a quasi-right of our technological society. Lifeline rates for minimum checking accounts have even been considered for banks because financial deregulation resulted in the imposition of substantial charges.

At the state level, California in 1984 legislated a package of regulatory nursing home reforms that included fines for negligent patient care and a prohibition against evicting patients when their ability to pay private rates ended and they had to go on the Medicaid roles. (The rules were sweetened by higher payments from the state to the homes on behalf of its Medicaid—called Medical in California—patients.)

The fairness doctrine in broadcasting regulation, which requires equal time for expression of opposed viewpoints under certain circumstances.

All but the last of these can be viewed as falling under an income distribution rubric, and most economists say that explicit subsidies or grants to the poor are a more efficient way of accomplishing the same objectives—more efficient than hidden "cross subsidies," when services to the poor are covered in part by higher rates paid by other income groups. Politically, however, such services are not sold to legislatures or PUCs as income redistribution; rather, they are perceived as matters of social justice in the sharing of ordinary services. The political fact is that they probably cannot be accomplished as outright cash grants, which would place them under the "welfare" cloud. It seems that symbolism is more important in politics than in economics.

Finally, a minor factor in the total regulatory picture, but one that is probably more controversial than most, is the aesthetic rationale. An example is the highway beautification requirements imposed as a condition for states to receive their full shares of federal highway funds. Another is a provision of the Safe Drinking Act that requires the EPA (with no fixed date specified) to establish standards governing the taste, appearance, and odor of drinking water, quite apart from the primary standards to be established to prevent chemical poisoning. Also, rules forbidding any deterioration of air visibility quality within range of national parks are taken very seriously.

REGULATORY JUSTIFICATIONS: A POLITICAL-ECONOMIC SYNTHESIS

In the writings of Cushman, Bernstein, and other political scientists of the 1940s–1960s, the outstanding problems of regulation (which was then almost entirely economic regulation through IRCs) were those of the accountability of power and the coordination of regulatory policies with macroeconomic stabilization policies. Economists such as Wilcox used consumer satisfaction as their litmus test, but often saw this, too, as a function of controlling market power through the political system.

In the late 1960s and throughout most of the 1970s, when we were busy enacting new social regulation programs, such academic writing as there was (Stigler, Peltzman) focused on causal theories, rather than examining the public purposes and normative justifications for regulation. By the late 1970s, and with enhanced vigor after the 1980 election of an avowedly antiregulation president 1980, the most heard voices began to contend that competition (which took on the somewhat ideological label of "the free market") could do more for consumer welfare, and began to assert efficiency in resource allocation as the first and only legitimate justification for regulation. Symbolic of the new skepticism is an article (Wolfe 1976) developing "A Theory of Non-market Failure": ways in which government programs to redress market failures may themselves display failures paralleling those of the market. This followed by a generation Bator's "The Anatomy of Market Failure" (1958).

The older, political science-dominated view stressed power and its accountability, but ignored the efficiency of regulatory programs—it implicitly assumed that the economic basis was sound or that it was unimportant. Equally, the newer, economics-dominated view has stressed efficiency, and either ignored questions of equity and accountability (perhaps as simply beyond the disciplinary ken?), or denied that there were sufficient concentrations of power to worry about, or that market power had any broader social or political dimensions.

Regulation and its study have suffered from this disciplinary bifurcation of concerns, for an adequate approach to regulation as a real world phenomenon requires a synthesis of disciplinary perspectives. The comments of the late Douglas Needham are appropriate:

To some extent, specialization is unavoidable. . . . However, special-ization causes problems. . . . Disciplinary specialization is particularly troublesome if one is interested in understanding regulation, because the voters, legislators, regulators, and regulated decision makers whose behavior interacts to produce regulation and its effects are often the subjects of study in different disciplines, such as political science, economics, and law. . . . Efforts to understand and improve regulation will be slower if the interdisciplinary nature of many regu-latory problems, and their solutions, are not recognized and ade-quately taken into account. (Needham, 1983:37–38)

One way that we, as students of regulation, can begin to put the political and economic perspectives together is to recognize explicitly two essential dimensions of that elusive but essential concept, the public interest, as necessary additional criteria to the economic effi-ciency test:

1. Economic activity is not always channeled to the optimal satisfaction of public needs by the very imperfect competi-tion among industrial giants, or by the narrow incentives that press on marginal firms in the most competitive sectors; and a free society will therefore sometimes find it advisable to use government as its instrument for making the econ-omy serve us, better as whole persons, not only as "eco-nomic man (or woman)."

2. Regulatory agencies are accountable to the electorate through the active participation of interested citizens as advocates of their preferred policies, and the overall governance of our elected president and Congress.

The recommended basic framework for thinking about regulation (doubtless reflecting my own political science background) is an awareness that regulation is a public, governmental activity. As such, it cannot be satisfied with market efficiency as its only goal. Plato and Aristotle—not to mention James Madison and the Found-ing Fathers—had something more than the most output for the least input in mind when they wrote about the polity. Justice and free-dom are more fundamental values than those embedded in market processes, although the latter can operate to support our pursuit of the civic virtues (Clark 1957:245–83). The dynamic tension that can join together a free market and political freedom requires the use of market mechanisms to maximize individual opportunity, and regis-ter our material wants for producers to respond to in noncoercive ways. It also requires that we supercede the market when necessary, to achieve broader and more basic social values that are not encom-passible in dollar terms.

chapter three

ECONOMIC REGULATION: THE INDEPENDENT COMMISSIONS

SCOPE AND MAJOR THEMES

Although a "life cycle" (Bernstein 1955:74–95) for regulatory agencies has been described, the Civil Aeronautics Board (CAB) is the only major federal regulatory agency to pass beyond old age into death. Its tombstone could read: "Born, 1938, died, 1984," and its epitaph might well read: "from industry development through capture to competition."

The life story of the CAB contains in microcosm most of the characteristics and problems identified with efforts from the 1880s to the present day to regulate business for the purpose of protecting the financial interests of consumers. Recall that in chapter 1 we defined economic regulation as regulation of the price of a product or service and of entry into the industry or the allocation of particular business rights, such as routes in transportation or broadcast channels in communications. Such regulation often carries with it, mostly in the case of those firms that we call public utilities, obligations to serve certain segments of the public that might not be served simply on the basis of prospective profit. Whatever the exact scope of activities regulated and means by which regulatory objectives are pursued, the overall function that has legitimized economic regulation is that of protecting the consumer financially in terms of avoiding monopolistic prices, guarding against marketplace fraud that would waste consumers' money, and (as in the case of the CAB) occasionally protecting an industry from what is alleged to be "destructive competition," in order to ensure the availability of that industry's services for the consumer.

In Table 3–1 we list the major economic regulation agencies with an abbreviated indication of the coverage of each. You will notice that all of the agencies are boards or commissions; that is, they are multiheaded. They also fall under the category known as indepen-

Table 3–1
Major Economic Regulation Agencies

Year Established	Commission Name	Scope and Activity
1887	Interstate Commerce Commission (ICC)	Price, entry, and routes for railroads, trucking, buses, inland and coastal waterways.
1913	Board of Governors of the Federal Reserve System (FRB)	Financial System stability (i.e., preventing banking panics by providing a flexible national monetary system); bank reserve requirements; macroeconomic stabilization through monetary policy (since 1935).
1920 (current form, 1930)	Federal Power Commission (FPC)	Hydroelectric dam licensing; interstate electric and natural gas rates (since 1977, the FPC has become the Federal Energy Regulatory Commission [FERC].
1934	Federal Communications Commission (FCC)	Allocation of radio and television stations; regulation of interstate telephone rates; various other telecommunications regulations.
1934	Federal Trade Commission (FTC)	Monitors competitive practices, fradulent advertising, and certain dimensions of antitrust policy; focuses on consumer information designed to avoid wasting money, rather than protecting health and safety.
1934	Securities and Exchange Commission (SEC)	Consumer information regarding new securities issued; regulation of securities markets.
1935	National Labor Relations Board (NLRB)	Oversees procedural fairness of collective bargaining elections.
1936	Federal Maritime Commission (FMC)	Ocean shipping rates and subsidies to U.S. shipping industry.
1938	Civil Aeronautics Board (CAB)	Airline prices, entry, and route allocations.
1974	Commodity Futures Trading Commission (CFTC)	Protection of farmers and investors in commodity exchanges activity.
1977	Federal Energy Regulation Commission (FERC)	Successors to FPC.

dent regulatory commissions (IRCs). Before turning an intensive spotlight on the IRCs, we will briefly note some other characteristics of the economic regulation agencies that tend to distinguish them from social regulation agencies:

1. The techniques of economic regulation consist mostly of price and entry controls—entry both to the industry and to particular routes or markets.
2. They tend to be industry-specific, rather than functional across all industries. The CAB covered airlines; the FERC covers electric and natural gas utilities; the SEC concentrates on the securities industry. Exceptions include the FTC, which oversees competitive practices and antitrust problems throughout American industry, and the NLRB, which oversees collective bargaining elections wherever they may occur.
3. The economic regulatory agencies have tended toward broad and vague mandates, such as to allocate radio station licenses "in accord with the public interest, convenience or necessity."

Because the traditional economic regulation agencies all partake of the IRC organizational form, and have done so since the establishment of the ICC in 1887, issues of government regulation of business and issues of the IRCs have tended in the political science literature to be treated as one, although some new economic regulation (e.g., control of hospital prices for Medicare patients) is now done outside of the IRCs. The issue of organizational form, with its related issues of political accountability and regulatory effectiveness, continues to be important, because some of the newer social regulation agencies—CPSC, NRC, EEOC, and OSHRC—are IRCs, and calls have been heard to shift the EPA and the NHTSA in this direction. Two major systemic faults are traditionally alleged to result from the IRC organizational form: a lack of accountability, and consequent capture by the regulated industries. In this chapter, we will examine the structure of the IRCs, emphasizing changes since the major criticisms were developed in the 1950s; address the questions of accountability and capture; and conclude with comments on the mixed independence and dependence of the commissions today.

THE IRCS: REGULATION OF BUSINESS OR BY BUSINESS?

What are the different organizational forms that a regulatory program may utilize? Besides the multiheaded IRC with its substantial independence of administrative accountability to the present, the major one is that of a single-headed line agency, which means one that is in the line of command from the president down through the executive branch hierarchy. With the exception of the EPA and the Federal Deposit Insurance Corporation (FDIC), which are line agencies independent of any larger department and reporting directly to the president, the other line agencies are units within larger units. The OSHA is within the Department of Labor; the NHTSA is within the Department of Transportation; and the FDA is within the Department of Health and Human Services. In addition, there are regulatory activities in a substantial number of agencies that are not primarily regulation oriented. For example, the National Park Service regulates the activities of concessionaires, and the Department of Agriculture handles meat and poultry inspections—but regulation is clearly not the reason for the existence of these agencies.*

Why the IRC Form?

Whether one studies public or business administration, the conventional wisdom holds that a single executive pinpoints responsibility, while a board or commission diffuses and confuses it, and that executive vigor is much enhanced if a unit enjoys the support (and is subject to the discipline) of the chief executive, whether called CEO or president of the United States. Why, then, establish a number of agencies with significant roles in the economy along lines that strongly violate these primary canons of administrative hierarchy doctrine?

The answer may lie partly in simple historical precedent: the states used the commission form after the Civil War, and the national government's first regulatory effort, the ICC, took that form. When the next wave came in 1913–14, it was to some extent seen as "natural" to follow that precedent. Much more important, however, in the FTC and FRB cases and in the New Deal agencies that followed in the 1930s, was the impact of the Progressive tradition. The Progressive Movement (Croly 1914; Hofstadter 1948) was a "good-government" reaction against the machine politics of the turn of the century. Because politics was perceived by the Progressives only in its negative, rather than its positive senses, they

*In a category of its own is the FERC, which is located for housekeeping purposes in the Department of Energy, but which retains the substantial autonomy of other IRCs in making its decisions. However, the Secretary of Energy does have authority to place certain matters on the agenda of the FERC, and to make regulatory proposals on which the FERC must act within a specified period of time. Still, the final decisions in these instances are the FERC's, and cannot be overridden by the Secretary of Energy.

wanted to take regulation out of party politics. Equally strong was their positive faith in the concept of neutral expertise: the belief that there was an objective, knowable public interest, and that reaching it was a matter of applying "scientific" principles. Even outside of the Progressive Movement, we should recall that political science as an academic study had its own strong faith in the rather complete separability of politics from administration. Woodrow Wilson, a political scientist at Princeton University before he was elected president in 1912, wrote a classic essay on that theme (1887).

Although we no longer adhere to the rather quaint notion of turning important matters over to neutral experts, and although the modern search is for ways by which the policy makers can hold the administrators accountable, there is still a strong belief in the value of agency independence of the type provided by IRCs. Now, however, the rationale is that such independence makes sense for the kind of quasi-judicial decision-making that the regulatory bodies engage in when setting a particular price or allocating a particular frequency or airline route, and for ensuring due process for individuals (whether individual persons or the corporation). This argument is, as one would expect, put forward primarily by spokepersons for the legal profession. In developing a case for the Consumer Product Safety Commission (CPSC), a justification was found in the visibility that an independent agency would have, as compared with a bureau "buried" in the bowels of some large executive department. Finally, and much more importantly, U.S. Congress seems to enjoy keeping these agencies out of the hands of the president, even though it sometimes finds reasons to object that these "arms of the Congress," as members call them, become more independent of their legislative parents than the legislators always want to see. Whatever the mix of historical reasons, the starting point for us today is that we have a number of independent regulatory commissions (Hibbing 1985), and that substantial questions are raised about their effectiveness, efficiency, and accountability. Before proceeding to questions raised about IRCs, we will exam their component features.

What Is an IRC?

A number of organizational characteristics apply to all IRCs. The broadest and most fundamental is that once the members have been appointed by the president with the consent of the Senate, they operate outside of the presidential hierarchy in making their substantive decisions, although subject to the same budgetary review by the Office of Management and Budget as line agencies. The more specific components of policy-making and decisional autonomy include the following:

They are multiheaded, having five or seven members.

They are bi-partisan: no more than a simple majority of the membership may be of one political party.

Members serve for staggered terms. Thus, in a five-person commission, each serving a five-year term, one member's term will expire each year.

Members serve for fixed terms, ranging from five years to the extreme of fourteen, in the case of the Federal Reserve Board. The length of term is generally a number equal to that of the number of members of the board, except in the case of the seven-member FRB, where the term is fourteen years— double the number of members. The fixed term is fundamental to the political independence of IRCs, for it establishes their nonremovability by the president, except for "cause," which is a legal term for various kinds of official misbehavior. The inability of presidents to remove commissioners was further solidified by a Supreme Court decision, when President Franklin D. Roosevelt tried to remove one who didn't agree with him, but who had not done anything wrong. In writing to this member of the FTC to tell him of his removal, Roosevelt had put the dismissal clearly on policy grounds, saying "I do not feel that your mind and my mind go along together on either the policies or the administering of the Federal Trade Commission, and, frankly, I think it is best for the people of this country that I should have a full confidence." In deciding against the president when the ensuing case reached it, the Supreme Court cited the quasi-judicial and quasi-legislative functions of the FTC, and said that "it is quite evident that one who holds his office only during the pleasure of another, cannot be depended upon to maintain an attitude of independence against the latter's will"(*Humphrey's Executor* v. *United States*).

Commission chairpersons, on the other hand, serve at the pleasure of the president in most instances, the only clear exception being that of the chair of the Federal Reserve Board, who serves for a fixed four-year term, one that never quite coincides with that of presidential turnovers. Without going into great detail, we might observe the perennial, if sporadic, White House expressions of concern about Fed chairs going off in monetary policy directions inconsistent with presidential macroeconomic desires as continuing evidence that a fixed term helps to underscore the autonomy of the head of that particular agency. (Of course, the entire mysterious aura that tends to surround the central banking function in all countries also constitutes an autonomy-supporting factor for the FRB chairperson.) Since about 1950, legislative amendments, flowing from presidential study group recommendations, have changed the chairperson terms from fixed to service at the will of the president in most of the other regulatory agencies. The policy significance of this change has also been enhanced by additional amendments that have given the chairpersons stronger administrative authority than formerly vis-a-vis the other members. The original collegiality of IRCs has been substantially eroded by these changes during the past generation, which means that when we read about the views of a commission chair, we are likely to have a good idea of what the commission as a whole will do. One close observer of these agencies has expressed the view that the capacities of the chairpersons, with modest exceptions in a couple of agencies, "are probably little if any less than if they were single administrators" (Welborn 1977:139).

In the past decade, Congress has marginally increased IRC independence by requiring that a number of IRCs submit their budgets simultaneously to Congress at the time they go to the Office of Management and Budget (OMB), which permits congressional committees to see what the agencies themselves wanted, rather than simply finding out later what the president has recommended for them in the consolidated budget covering the entire government. Congress has also exempted IRCs from OMB clearance of their information-gathering requests, and has even exempted some of the financial regulatory agencies from OMB clearance of their legislative proposals.

In establishing the statutory features of the regulatory commissions, it seems that Congress is quite ambivalent about the degree of presidential control versus presidential independence that it wants to accord these agencies. However, it is less a matter of ambivalence than of the extended time over which these provisions have developed. In the earliest periods, Congress was very strongly pro-independence; criticisms of the "fourth branch" prior to World War II and in the 1950s produced a reaction in favor of presidential control for policy coordination and administrative symmetry; and then, after Watergate, another reaction moved it in the reverse direction. As we will see in chapter 4, there is simultaneous divergence of direction in the 1970s and 1980s, with newer social regulation agencies being mostly of the presidential control, line agency type, while Congress is also providing some exceptions from presidential control for traditional IRCs. To briefly summarize, one can say that the basic organizational form (being outside of the executive departments, fixed-staggered terms, multiple membership, and bi-partisanship) works toward independence, while the recent strengthening of the authority of the chairpersons, and their service at the will of the president, tends to work in the other direction, along with the most basic facts on the other side: the president appoints all the members (with the advice and consent of the Senate), and their official budgets are those that the president forwards to Congress.

The extent of present leverage over the operations of the regulatory bodies, whether IRCs or line agencies, by the president and Congress, will be given detailed consideration in chapter 7, but we will prepare for that discussion by reviewing the major lines of traditional and current criticism of IRCs, as well as the more supportive arguments.

Critiques, Political and Economic

In the modern history of the independent regulatory commissions, one charge stands out above all the other criticisms: that IRCs have been "captured" by the business interests they are supposed to regulate. Instead of regulation by government, according to this view, we have ended up too often with regulation of government by business. Capture, in turn, is derived largely from the lack of accountability inherent in independence. Nature abhors a vacuum, it is said, and so does political power. If an agency is set up to be outside the line of command from the presidency, and also beyond the day-to-day oversight of Congress, then it will be vulnerable to pressures from the regulated industry, whose representatives may be the only group of people with whom the regulators are in daily contact.

Besides the major problem of accountability and the charge of capture, other criticisms emanating primarily from political science observers of the commissions (most notably Bernstein 1955) include: inadequate coordination of IRC policies with the overall economic policy of the president at any given time; overly broad and vague mandates; and an emphasis on case-by-case ajudication rather than general policy development through a rule-making process. We will look at these first, and then give more attention to the accountability-capture question.

Under the best of circumstances, American governmental operations are characterized by great fragmentation. Subunits of units of bureaus of departments operate their small programmatic pieces of the entire governmental policy pie in substantial autonomy, at least on a day-to-day basis. Even at the bureau and departmental levels, the specialization and accompanying narrow blinders that seem to be endemic in large organizations make policy coordination one of the great perennial tasks of political leadership. Within the presidential "family," achieving a common direction at any one time among the Treasury, Commerce, Agriculture and Labor departments—all of which have substantial programmatic impact on the economy and are involved in matters of economic policy—is difficult enough. When one adds that independent commissions hold primary jurisdiction over major segments of transportation and communications, securities issuance and markets, labor relations, and the basic protection of a competitive economic system, then one increases the coordinative task by several orders of magnitude. Suppose that the president's economic policy at a given time is to dampen inflationary fires, and to restrict governmental stimulation of the economy. Suppose, however, that the ICC finds it simultaneously necessary to grant rate increases to railroad and motor truck carriers in the name of protecting the viability of existing carriers, or that the Federal Reserve Board disagrees with the president's analysis and sees unemployment as a lesser problem than inflation, and exercises its monetary policy leverage to restrict the economy through higher interest rates. In such circumstances, how is the president to execute faithfully the legislative mandate of the Employment Act of 1946, which calls for an integrated macroeconomic policy in the name of maximizing employment, production, and purchasing power?

We must concede the existence of a substantial coordinative need, although this is often also the case in regular line agencies. The traditional autonomy of the Army Corps of Engineers in terms of civil water projects; the inability of several presidents to rein in the late J. Edgar Hoover as head of the FBI; and the continuing difficulties in getting the armed forces to pull together in their procurement needs, rather than compete for duplicate equipment at the expense of the taxpayer—all suggest that the ability of top leadership to coordinate agencies under theoretical command depends more on a variety of pressures and circumstances in the political environment, than on organizational structure as such.

The most serious need for coordination in terms of the Employment Act goals, yet the one most unlikely to be achieved by a major change from independent status, is the occasional great gap between monetary policies of the Board of Governors of the Federal Reserve System, and those pursued by the president with the advice of the Chairman of the Council of Economic Advisors, the Secretary of the Treasury, and the Director of the Office of Management and Budget (Reagan 1961; Woolley 1983).

Another frequent complaint about IRCs concerns the vagueness of their mandates and policies. We have mentioned earlier that the FCC and CAB, for example, have had as their primary mandate that they permit entry and grant licenses and allocations in accord with the "public convenience, interest, and necessity." Conflicting decisions by such commissions in the award of particular franchises (Friendly 1962) are seen as an ineluctable corollary of such vagueness. Even at a slightly less abstract level, what policy could the CAB have followed in order to comply with the provision of the Civil Aeronautics Act of 1938, which called for "competition to the extent necessary to assure the sound development of an air-transportation system properly adapted to the needs of the foreign and domestic commerce of the United States, of the Postal Service, and of the National Defense"? Although some more recent statutory mandates in the environmental protection and health and safety areas have been much more detailed and specific—complaints are now heard about insufficient administrative discretion—the more vague mandates of the older statutes for IRCs have not been made more precise. Whatever problems flow from such vagueness continue today in a number of the agencies. The most serious charge here, however, concerns not the vagueness itself, but the related phenomenon that Lowi has termed "interest group liberalism" (1969, 1979): the tendency of government policy to be inordinately responsive to the demands of segmented organized interests without evaluating them in the light of overriding macro-objectives of the government, statutorily defined.

Whatever the problems with mandates may be, such problems are not the exclusive domain of the multiheaded regulatory agencies. Moreover, they do not derive from the independent form as much as from the legislature being unable to go beyond a coalition in favor of doing something to a coalition that is able to say exactly what should be done. Lacking the political integration to achieve this second level, Congress simply establishes an agency and provides a broad mandate that leaves the hot potato of specific policy definition in the hands of the commissioners. Latham put it vividly in describing the commissions as bodies that "carry out the terms of treaties that legislators have negotiated and ratified. They are like armies of occupation left in the field to police the rule won by the victorious coalition" (Latham 1952). We need only add that IRCs have to define the rule further before they can police it.

The criticism of excessive judicialization of procedures in IRCs does not derive directly from the multiheaded independent form, yet often seems to be related to IRCs. Perhaps this is because IRCs themselves owe so much to a lawyerly perception of the political universe, which sees the functions of regulatory bodies less in terms of governmental policy than in terms of actions (licensing, allocations of routes, setting of rates) that affect the rights of individuals and particular business firms. As a result of this emphasis on the quasi-judicial role of the commissions, rather than on the quasi-legislative-executive policy development and planning role, the economic IRCs have operated much more on a case-by-case approach than by the use of rule-making procedures. The former means that if there is any policy development, it comes in the same way as policies found in the common law: the precedents that are gradually established through a long line of cases. What government needs—and businesses dealing with government need it even more—is a clear sense of policy that can serve as criteria for what to expect as individual cases arise. While some legal observers (most notably Friendly 1962) believe that the commissions could determine policies by the case-by-case approach, they do unmercifully berate the commissions for failing to do so. Political science observers say the failure is not accidental, but a result of judicialization. The judicialized versus legislative modes of policy development will receive somewhat more attention in chapter 5, where we turn to how we regulate.

We will now turn to the most venerable and often cited criticisms of the economic regulatory commissions: lack of accountability, and capture by the regulated interests.

Does a Weak Structure of Accountability Lead to Agency Capture?

The most sharply worded criticisms of the regulatory commissions over the years probably have been those focusing on the extent to which independence has meant a lack of political accountability. The logic is simple enough: if Congress sets up a commission outside of the orbit of day-to-day presidential control within the executive branch, and does so in order to achieve detailed rules that it cannot find the time or political will to handle on its own, then such agencies have no direct accountability to any elected officials. If one takes such a picture at face value, ignoring for the moment limitations on independence that have existed from the beginning (e.g., presidential appointment and budgetary control), and the enlarged powers of the presidentially-appointed chairpersons (accomplished since the 1950s), then one may be led to the kind of judgments expressed by the prototypical critics.

The first of these was Louis Brownlow, chairperson of the President's Committee on Administrative Management, near the end of the New Deal period. In this group's report of January 1937 (U.S. President's Committee on Administrative Management 1937:36), we find the charge that IRCs "constitute a headless 'fourth branch' of the Government, a haphazard deposit of irresponsible agencies and uncoordinated powers." Brownlow's rationale for this harsh judgment lay in the proposition enunciated a few paragraphs later: "Power without responsibility has no place in a government based on a theory of democratic control, for responsibility is the people's only weapon, their only insurance against abuse of power" (1937:36). Writing almost a generation later, Bernstein's rhetoric was equally strong:

> The theory upon which the independence of the commission is based represents a serious danger to the growth of political democracy in the United States. The dogma of independence encourages support of the naive notion of escape from politics and substitution of voice of the expert for the voice of the people. . . . The commission has significant anti-democratic implications. (Bernstein 1955:293)

The theory of democracy on which such criticisms are based implies that the closer we can get to direct rule by the people the better, and that the only reasonable substitute is to see that those who operate the levers of government are clearly responsible to representatives over whom we retain direct electoral control. The heads of executive departments, such as the State Department of Agriculture or of such line agencies as the Veterans Administration or Environmental Protection Agency, clearly have accountability in this sense to a much greater degree than the multiple heads of an independent regulatory commission serving fixed terms, and not removable by the president for reasons of policy disagreement. The argument for executive accountability, however, does not focus only on the question of democratic legitimacy, as the quotations above might suggest. In practical policy terms, the problems perceived as deriving from inadequate accountability (i.e., inadequate presidential authority) include those of inadequate coordination with other economic policies, and vagueness of policy, in the statutory base and in the development of cases.

A more basic alleged corollary of the lack of presidential accountability, however, is the contention that an agency that does not follow the policy guidance of the White House will inevitably lack its political support. In this view, therefore, political isolation is the primary policy debility of an organizational structure that promotes independence at the expense of accountability. In turn, such isolation becomes the primary source of the capture of regulatory bodies by the supposedly regulated industries. A comment by William D. Carey provides a useful analogy:

> Cut loose from presidential leadership in protection, the agencies must formulate policy in a political vacuum. Into this vacuum move the regulated interests themselves, and by infiltration overcome the weak regulatory defenses to become the strongest influences upon the regulator. (Quoted in Bernstein 1955:138–39)

By what logic does the vacuum of isolation become filled by the regulated industry? Louis M. Kohlmeier, Jr., succinctly suggests the connecting link when he points out that those who regulate industry deal "occasionally with the White House, frequently with select members of congress and constantly with executives of regulated industries" (Kohlmeier 1969:69). Note the missing constituencies from this formulation: no consumers, no public interest groups.

The accountability gap in the structure of independent regulatory commissions is thus seen by political scientists as injurious to the body politic on two grounds: (1) because independence from control by those who are electorally replaceable is a violation of at least one form of the democratic ethic; and (2) because the lack of accountability leads to political isolation, which leads to capture—meaning, in a sense, regulation of the government by the regulated, rather than regulation by the government. We will now focus on the concept of capture in its own right.

The analytic concept of capture is strongly identified in the academic writings on regulation with Marver Bernstein's *Regulating Business by Independent Commission*. However, the phenomenon it refers to—domination of a government agency's policy decisions by outside groups, specifically those representing the regulated industry—has been around as long as regulation has existed at the national level. In the 1886 congressional debates on the legislation that was to create the Interstate Commerce Commission (ICC), Representative John Reagan of Texas, the House leader on the bill, argued against the use of a commission, and for a statute that would place the enforcement responsibility with the Department of Justice. The basis of his argument was "that the railroad interests will combine their power to control the appointment of the commissioners in their own interests," not because they would bribe the president, but because their control of "the best legal and business talent" would enable them to use such persons "to appeal to the President in the name of justice and on account of capacity to name such a man as would serve their purpose" (*Congressional Record,* vol. 17 (July 21, 1886) p. 7283). In 1892, Richard Olney, the Attorney General and a former director of several railroad companies, wrote to a friend who urged a drive to repeal the Interstate Commerce Act. The famous Olney response is a classic in the literature of what Edelman (1964) termed "symbolic politics":

> The attempt [at repeal] would not be likely to succeed; if it did not succeed, and were made on the ground of inefficiency and useless-ness of the Commission, the result would very probably be giving it the power it now lacks. The Commission, as its functions have now been limited by the courts, is, or can be made, of great use to the railroads. It satisfies the popular clamor for government supervision of the railroads, at the same time that the supervision is almost entirely nominal. Further, the older such a commission gets to be, the more inclined it will be found to take the business and railroad view of things. . . . The part of wisdom is not to destroy the commission but to utilize it. (Quoted in Mitnick 1980:181)

Suggesting that as the ICC got older it would become more busi-ness oriented, implicitly foreshadowed the life cycle model of IRCs that Bernstein articulated in 1955. This cycle—constituting more an impressionistic sketch than precise empirical data—had four peri-ods: gestation, youth, maturity, and old age (Bernstein 1955:74–102). The gestation discussion assumes a substantial period, perhaps a generation, in which there is "slowly mounting distress over a prob-lem and reform elements agitate vigorously for corrective legisla-tion." Eventually, a statute is enacted, but its mandate will usually lack clarity, and rarely provide clear directions. As the youthful phase begins, "the regulated groups are well organized" to protect their interests, but their pressures will be met by the "aggressive, crusading spirit" in which the regulatory agency begins its life.

As this hypothetical commission reaches maturity, it looks around and often finds no political support for vigorous regulation. The origi-nal crisis that called forth reform having passed, the consumer or general public groups supporting regulation tend to fade away, and the attention of the White House moves on to matters of greater urgency. The regulatory body settles down as "an essential part of the industrial system," "becomes more concerned with the general health of the industry, and with enjoying good relationships with the regu-lated groups." In the period that Bernstein labels old age, debility and decline are the descriptives. Being multiheaded and lacking continu-ing political support from the White House, IRCs, says Bernstein, "tend to lack dynamic administrative leadership. . . . Ignored or abandoned by an unorganized public, commissions tend to play for safety in policy decisions. Passivity deepens into debility" (1955:92).

For Bernstein, then, the phenomenon of capture flowed logically from a lack of political support in favor of regulation combined with organized pressures from the industry that has an immediate self-interested state in the proceedings.

Note that Bernstein assumes a broad and rather vague statutory mandate. Where this has been the case, the argument is that the greater the vagueness and the greater the area of discretion left to the commission by the delegation, the more open the agency is to industry pressures. When the mandate is to decide a regulatory case in accord with the public convenience, interest, or necessity, the commission has difficulty proving that a policy direction objected to by the industry is required by the legislators. However, sometimes industry leverage is provided by a very specific provision; for example, one that requires the agency to perform a cost-benefit analysis and show a net dollar benefit (see chapter 6).

Another element that seems to correlate closely with instances of alleged capture, is whether the regulatory body has authority over a single industry or if its authority extends to many industries. The thesis here is that a single-industry IRC is more susceptible to capture. On issues for which there is an industry consensus, a single-industry commission will face strong pressures from only one group. It is then not in a position to demur from the regulated group's demands on the basis that it needs to compromise in order to take into account the demands of others. The CAB, FCC and FMC are among the single-industry bodies to which such a generalization has often been applied. The FTC, on the other hand, is an across-the-board agency, but has on some occasions had its decisions clearly dominated by the group that its regulation is affecting (e.g., used car dealers, organized medicine). If the agency has not been captured in the full sense, the equivalent has occurred in particular decisions. While the connection of a single-industry commission with openness to industry dominance seems reasonably strong in at least anecdotal evidence, the rather mixed evidence of multi-industry regulatory agencies suggests that some other factor is also at work.

That factor may well be the way in which the distribution of burdens and benefits is structured, as James Q. Wilson has argued. As presented in his collection of regulatory case studies (Wilson 1980:366–72), the typology for the distribution of costs (which includes non-monetary burdens) and benefits has four categories, all relating to how broadly or narrowly the burdens and benefits are distributed. These categories, with Wilson's labels, are as follows:

1. Majoritarian politics: most of society is expected to benefit, and most of society is expected to pay. The benefits are broadly distributed on both sides, as with the Social Security program.
2. Interest group politics: both the costs and the benefits are narrowly concentrated, with the general public having a sufficiently small stake so that it lets the opposing interest groups fight it out. Shipping regulation, which is largely a tight little world of steamship lines and major shippers, provides an example.
3. Client politics: here the benefits go to a small group, but the costs are widely distributed. The Civil Aeronautics Board illustrated this category to the extent that the CAB protected the airlines from competition and let them charge higher than competitive prices to the traveling public. Various agricultural price support programs would appear to fit this category very well, also.
4. Entrepreneurial politics: in this case, one finds widely distributed benefits, the costs of which are born by a narrow group. Much of the recent health and safety and environmental regulatory programs fit this model rather closely. [Wilson's use of the term "entrepreneurial" as the label here simply refers to the fact that programs with this distribution of costs and benefits normally must be stimulated by political entrepreneurs in Congress or by leaders of public interest groups.]

We see that the interest group and client politics distributions of costs and benefits create much greater opportunities for capture than do the other two types. Of these two types, client politics is the most vulnerable to capture. The reasoning is fairly simple: if a small industry group has much to gain or lose from the pattern of regulations that an agency develops, then it has a very strong incentive to work hard on persuading the regulators of the virtues of its demands. However, in client politics the burdens are distributed over a large number of persons, with rather small costs per person. Little consumer incentive, therefore, exists for taking the trouble to organize and lobby on behalf of, say, a lower airfare between Los Angeles and New York, if one is likely to make such a flight only sporadically. In this situation, then, the regulatory body will be expected to face strong industry representatives across the table, but rarely will it see a consumer representative—at least, this is the classic expectation derived from the psychological proposition that we all organize more around our producer interests than our consumer or general public interests (Truman 1951). As Truman states in his classic study of interest groups, "the regulated groups will have more cohesion than those demanding regulation, . . . they can therefore keep close track of the work of the commission, . . . consequently little will be done by a commission beyond what is acceptable to the regulated groups (Truman 1951:418). In the realm of the regulatory commissions, and prior to the development of the public interests groups and the new ethic of participatory democracy in the last twenty years, this conventional wisdom held true. In the more recently developed areas of health and safety regulation, entrepreneurial politics has been able to develop effective organizations to take advantage of new opportunities for participation, and it may be that the public takes more interest in regulation because it immediately affects our health, safety, and environment.

A recent article on the National Labor Relations Board (NLRB) by Terry Moe (1985) provides empirical evidence for the proposition that regulatory agencies are affected by a broad range of factors, including presidents, congressional committees, courts, agency staff, and economic conditions, thus supporting a multicausation picture that diminishes expectations of simple industry capture.

We have thus far covered structural and interest group pressures that create a likelihood of capture; the remaining significant factor to examine is that known as the "revolving door": a tendency for regulators to come from the regulated industries and/or to move from the commissions to the regulated industries. The specific proposition implied is that regulators who come from the regulated industry will tend to see things from the viewpoint of the industry, and sometimes also engage in conscious favoritism. Similarly, because a regulatory commissioner cannot count on indefinite reappointments as the White House changes hands, and because private industry jobs usually have salaries substantially above those of public servants, there is alleged to be a strong incentive for regulators to please the moguls of the regulated industry, in hopes of moving into good private sector positions when the term of office expires.

Although it is true that a substantial number of regulatory commissioners previously worked in the regulated industry, it is also true that for a number of the regulatory programs it is difficult to find persons with sufficient technical knowledge, and familiarity with industry problems from sources other than the regulated industry itself. The more important question, however, is not where the commissioners come from, but whether their decisions as commissioners are oriented toward the larger public interests presumably expressed in the agency statute, or to the narrower self-interest of the industry. On this behavioral question, the evidence is mixed.

In a study of FCC votes during a two-year period, 1974–76, Gormley found that there were cohesive voting patterns for former broadcasters, but also that party differences were generally more striking than those based on prior background (Gormley 1979). Contrary to both the independence and revolving door hypotheses, some studies found that there is a close relationship between some regulatory commissions and the policy preferences of overseeing congressional committees (Weingast and Moran 1982, regarding the FTC), or close adherence to presidential policy preferences (Moe 1982). Also suggestive of an orientation other than to the industry, is the indirect evidence that party partisanship is a stronger factor than industry background in determining who is appointed to the commissions. Graham and Kramer (1976) made a study of appointments to the FCC and the FTC over a period of twenty-five years, and found that partisan political considerations dominated the selection of regulators "to an alarming extent." Similarly, Kemp (1983) studied regulatory commission appointments made during the first two years of the administrations of Eisenhower, Kennedy, Nixon, Carter, and Reagan. She found that activity in electoral campaigns (different from *party* service) on behalf of a president was a particularly significant factor in gaining appointment. Kemp found this tendency most often under Carter and Reagan.

Quirk used a detailed set of interviews with fifty commissioners and top staff officials in four agencies, two of them single-headed and two of them IRCs, in order to ascertain the pattern of incentives toward an industry orientation that commissioners believed to exist. Regarding the question of whether people perceive pro-industry decisions as necessary to get good jobs after their regulatory terms expire, the answer was yes, in varying degrees, in the CAB, FDA and NHTSA; but in the FTC one interviewee said that the best way to get respect from prospective private sector employers was to be vigorous, tough, and aggressive. A respondent was quoted as saying "employers don't want to waste money on someone who won't be effective" (Quirk 1981:149–50).

All in all, it is difficult to find compelling evidence that the employment incentives of regulators have been dominant, retrospectively or prospectively, in determining their decisions. Party service seems most important in getting them appointed, and party partisanship or personal loyalty to the president seem to be stronger ties than those with one's industry. With both Carter and Reagan there has also been greater attention to the ideology and policy preferences of the regulatory appointees, in contrast with most earlier presidents, who paid surprisingly little attention to the policy views of their appointees, when using the positions largely for party rewards.

One final comment on the revolving door hypothesis is that a regulated industry source of personnel and pro-industry orientation does not seem more strongly correlated with IRCs than with line agencies. Rather, a presence or absence of such connections and orientations depends more on the views of the appointing president. One sees this fairly sharply in comparing Carter with Reagan: the former emphasized strong pro-consumer policy attitudes in his appointments, and the latter emphasized a combination of personal loyalty and pro-deregulation orientation, the latter sometimes being an apparent function of previous employment in the regulated industry. Available evidence, although partial and inadequate, suggests that the revolving door is not a significant factor in regulatory commission capture. While the quality of regulatory commission appointments is considered to be poor by most observers, this is different from industry capture, and seems to reflect primarily the lack of significance that most presidents have attached to these bodies. Perhaps the fact that they are multiheaded makes it easier to use IRC positions for political rewards, because an appointing president can say to himself that it will not matter much when there are four or more other persons sharing in the decision-making.

Now that we have dismissed the revolving door hypothesis as having any major significance in producing regulated industry capture of IRCs, how do we come out in evaluation of the other factors that are claimed to produce capture?

Fundamentally, the capture doctrine in its usual form oversimplifies a complex situation, and does an analytic and political disservice by substituting a quasi-conspiracy model of regulation for a more accurate focus on the diversity of factors involved in regulatory program decisions, and in the changeability of the regulatory and political environment over time. A "revisionist" view includes the following three major points about capture:

1. To the extent that some of the economic regulation IRCs have at times clearly followed an anticonsumer orientation favoring existing firms in an industry, this has been primarily the result of statutory mandates that encourage such behavior. The CAB mandate, for one, clearly reflected a Depression-era fear of competition.

2. Although the capture thesis was first described in connection with the economic regulation areas, and developed before most of the modern social regulation agencies (whether IRC or departmental) came into existence, recent use of the term seems largely to have ignored that crucial fact, and the limitations and contextual limitations that it logically im-

poses. In other words, capture's limited validity is almost certainly greater with regard to the Progressive and New Deal agencies than it is to those originated in the 1960s and 1970s. Yet, it is the newer social regulation programs about which most of the current political discussion revolves, certainly in the Reagan administration.

3. From an organized interest perspective—the intellectual locus of capture theory—the present-day situation is one of much greater variety and diversity of politically effective groups than was the case when the capture doctrine was developed. We cannot argue that a pluralist heaven has been achieved in which every potential interest has become an actual and organized interest, and each as effective as the other. On the other hand, a rise in the numbers, memberships, and economic resources of consumer, environmental, and other public interest groups (Walker 1983; J. Berry 1984; McFarland 1984), and the often-documented success of these groups in moving regulatory agencies (whether directly or through court actions) in directions not wanted by the regulated industries do require a modification of the older assumption that narrow, producer self-interest groups inevitably dominate public policy decisions.

Furthermore, the political environment of regulation has changed in other significant dimensions as well, particularly those of judicial standing; provision (mostly in short-lived experiments) for intervenor funding (i.e., having the costs of participation paid for by the agency itself for some impecunious interested groups); clear and more precise statutory objectives; a rash of consumer-oriented policy entrepreneurs in and out of Congress; and judicial oversight that often seems to clarify statutory interpretation on the side of regulatory positions more stringent than were actually intended by Congress. Although these multiple dimensions of the changed political context are perhaps most apparent in the social regulation areas (see chapter 5), they have clearly been at work in the traditional economic regulation arena as well. For instance, in the most traditional of all regulatory areas—the state public utilities commissions—an earlier industry dominance reflected the absence of other contenders. Such dominance has been much diminished by the rise of consumer advocacy groups and statutory provisions in a number of states for a governmental consumer advocate (Anderson 1981; Gormley 1983; W. Berry 1984). Adding insult to injury, the California Public Utilities Commission even tried to require that electric utilities permit certain consumer groups to include their mailings in the utility bill envelopes, until reversed by a 5–3 Supreme Court decision in 1986.

An example of the increased diversity in the regulatory area is the changing constituency of the FCC. Krasnow, Longley, and Terry (1982) point out that the broadcasting industry, as it existed in 1973, had only weak competition from cable television, but by the 1980s it had become "clear that broadcasting can no longer be understood as an industry apart from or unaffected by other electronic mass media" (viii). In addition to cable, communication satellites, teletext, video-text, video tapes and games, and home computers can be attached to TV sets, as Krasnow and his associates point out. Reflecting the broadened range of telecommunications technologies as an independent factor in diversifying the constituency of the FCC, is the rise of nonindustry interest groups, and the Krasnow text now devotes a number of pages to the activities of such groups, ranging from the National Citizens Committee for Broadcasting, to Accuracy in Media, the National Latino Media Coalition, and Action for Children's Television.

If the basic fact about the regulatory environment today is the relatively effective representation of a considerable number and diversity of interests and viewpoints, enhanced by enlarged judicial scope for administrative participation by citizens, then it presumably follows that the autonomy of the agency decision makers is increased because they can avoid "giving in" to any one interest by pointing to the clamor of competing interests. In this situation, a very significant determinant of policy may lie in the values held by regulators appointed by the president. One might then write of capture by the professional norms of the predominant specialists or "technocrats" in the various agencies. In the OSHA, this might be safety engineers and industrial hygienists (Kelman 1981c); in the Department of Justice it has often been the attorneys who push for the initiation of cases so that young lawyers can "earn their stripes."

More recently, the economists seem to have become the dominant professional group in the regulatory agencies. In the FTC, for example, recent chairperson James C. Miller, III, "suggested that the FTC should not be a traditional 'law enforcement agency' but an 'economic agency out to achieve an efficient working of the market place' "; he therefore modified the agency administratively "by giving economists a much greater role in the working of the agency than traditionally has been the case" (Harris and Milkis 1983). Because professional norms always embody value elements as well as technocratic doctrines, the role of professional staff from a particular common background may be a factor of considerable significance in at least some agency decision-making. Supportive material can be found in the studies by Katzmann, Kelman, Quirk, and Rabkin, all in Wilson, 1980.

THE POLITICAL DEPENDENCE OF THE INDEPENDENT COMMISSIONS

Now that we have looked at the rationale and structure of the independent regulatory commissions, the elements that encourage independence of operation, and those that provide leverage toward accountability or capture, where do we come out? What does it all add up to: are IRCs a bulwark of expert judgement and objectivity, or are they a danger to democracy? Is the IRC structure a very significant element in the total picture of regulation, or does it take a back seat to other political factors? We will organize our responses to these questions on three topics: (1) the actual extent of independence and political accountability, (2) the policy significance of such independence as it exists, and (3) the contending viewpoints from which one chooses to assess the legitimacy of IRCs in the light of the actualities we have found. (Before proceeding further, note that although independence is a sufficiently ambiguous term so that it has been used to apply to freedom from direction by the president and Congress, the dominant meaning is that of autonomy from presidential control. Accordingly, that is the focus we will use here, reserving discussion of the larger elements of presidential and congressional oversight over all regulatory agencies, not only IRCs, for chapter 7.)

First, it is clear that the IRC form does not in itself preclude significant opportunities for presidential leverage. Even in the heyday of the commissions (1900–50), the presidential appointment power, and the review of IRC budgets through the Executive Office of the president constituted meaningful control levers. Reforms designed purposely to strengthen political accountability by making the boards responsible to the president in greater degree were enacted in the 1950s, especially by strengthening the president's power to appoint and remove commission chairs, and strengthening the role of the chairs vis-a-vis commission colleagues. In short, independence was never as great as proponents asserted or opponents feared, and the structure is much less conducive to independence today than it was in the 1930s. As of 1977, Welborn's summarizing judgment was that "through the position of chairman, the regulatory agencies stand in relatively close association with the executive branch in various important respects, rather than being truly independent of it" (1977:141). A decade later, that judgment stands.

Other factors enhancing presidential influence include the role of the Justice Department in deciding what cases to bring and what legal strategies to follow, the politicization of the highest level of commission staff through civil service exempt positions created during the Johnson administration, the custom of respect for the president's economic coordination responsibilities under the Employment Act of 1946, and the seemingly ever-increasing policy role of the president's managerial arm, the Office of Management and Budget. All of these clearly provide the president with ample opportunity to intervene in basic policy matters; however, he should avoid intervention in the adjudicatory role of the commissions—the deciding of particular cases, rather than the making of policy.

Whether recent presidents have used the leverage available to them is doubted by a number of observers. (See, for example, Quirk [1981]: the discussion of presidential disinterest in the policy predilections of commissioners they have appointed.) However, there are now numerous studies that suggest there is a significant correlation between regulatory agency behavior and presidential preferences. Moe (1982) examined such relationships in the NRLB, FTC and SEC in the period from the Truman years through 1977, and found that regulatory behavior varies systematically with presidential partisanship.

It may be worth noting parenthetically at this point that agency accommodation to presidential preferences and policies assumes that such exist. This is, of course, not always the case. A good example is provided in the response of the Federal Power Commission (FPC) to the 1971 report of the president's Advisory Council on Executive Organization. The FPC asserted that with respect to coordinating its operations with national policy goals pertaining to energy, the problem was not that the commission organization "prevents effective response to industrial, technological, and economic change," but that "policy goals concerning the development and utilization of energy . . . are in a state of upheaval and crisis; national policy goals concerning the uses and need for energy are obscured by a panopoly of conflicting problems ranging from intense environmental pressures to sensitive questions of our national security needs" (quoted in Welborn 1977:145). In other words, an agency cannot be accountable to a policy that does not exist.

Having qualified the extent to which independence exists today, the questions remain: What is the policy and political significance of the degree of independence that continues to exist? Does independence mean that less presidential conscientiousness exists in the quality of appointments made to such agencies, as compared to equivalent positions in executive line agencies? One rejoinder concedes that such appointments have been "less impressive than desirable," but suggests that this is also true of appointments to executive department positions (Freedman 1978:69). If regulatory appointments are less qualified than equivalent departmental ones, the reason may lie more in the multiheadedness of the commissions than in their independence, as suggested earlier. In Bernstein's view, isolation from the presidency is believed to result in a lack of presidential support. This is a significant implication, but Freedman questions this too, pointing out that the NLRB received strong support from President Franklin D. Roosevelt, whereas the FDA has not received as much support from any president, even though it is a line agency. Freedman suggests presidential support "probably depends upon the President's political priorities of the moment and his own relationships to regulated industry and its critics to a much greater degree than it does upon whether the agency is independent of, or subject to, his formal control" (Freedman 1978:70–71).

The only safe generalization in this area is that the IRC structure does not in and of itself determine anything significant across the board, although it may be a factor when combined with more dynamic behavioral factors. We can agree with Bernstein's (1972) warning that the factors he wrote about in 1955 had perhaps been overplayed in the meantime. In the more recent year, he wrote that "while organizational form is relevant to an institution's vitality, it is only one among many factors," and that "the time is overdue to recognize that structural change in itself is unlikely to overcome such defects as unsatisfactory presidential appointments of regulatory officials, inadequate staffing of agencies, over judicialization, and weak responsiveness to technological and economic changes." The significant points, he suggests, lay less in structure than in "the political sensitivity of regulatory issues, the economic stakes involved, and the depth of presidential concern" (Bernstein 1972:24, 22, 21).

Given the present day macroeconomic responsibilities of the president for the entire government, the matter of achieving an integrated macroeconomic policy thrust is a significant one. Here, the independence of the Federal Reserve Board is the most important single element in the problem of agency independence. Monetary policy is the necessary counterpart to fiscal policy in pursuing economic stabilization. In the mid-1980s, with fiscal policy largely straight-jacketed by horrendous deficits in the federal budget, the significance of monetary policy is overwhelming, making it more difficult to defend the autonomy of the Fed. Periodic, but carefully aborted, efforts to scare the Fed into line by threatening to decrease its independence emerged from both the White House and Capitol Hill, and the Fed (which usually means the chairperson) always seemed to accommodate just enough and in just enough time to remove any real threat to its independence. In his study of the FRB and its varied constituencies, Woolley summarizes the Fed's esoteric rationale in the following series of propositions:

—The Federal Reserve is independent within, not of, the government.

—Congress, in its wisdom, has made the Federal Reserve independent, and Congress can abolish or restructure the System if it is ever dissatisfied.

—If the Federal Reserve ever tried to ignore national objectives, its independence would be removed or limited.

—The Federal Reserve is still here and independent; therefore, its policy must be politically acceptable. (Woolley 1984:10–11; see also Reagan 1961)

It is difficult to give a precise operational meaning to the phrase "independent within, not of" the government, but the political essence of the matter seems to be that the elitist ethos of an autonomous central bank, derived from British and European precedent, has established itself sufficiently well in the United States so that only occasional populists mean it when they argue for placing monetary policy as much under presidential policy-making guidance as is fiscal policy. But if the Fed were made a single-headed agency in the executive branch, it would probably retain nearly the same degree of policy autonomy that it has now. The decisive factor is not structure; it is the accepted (although false) view that monetary policy is a purely technical matter that only the experts should touch.

It is, of course, true that the independence of the commissions can occasionally be politically helpful to a president, and that includes even the Federal Reserve. In 1966, for example, the economic policy makers in the Johnson administration knew that restraint was needed, but President Johnson chose not to seek a tax increase on political grounds. Members of the administration were not displeased that the Fed took action independently (Okun 1970:69).

We can generalize this last point to suggest that a true advantage of the multiheaded aspect of IRCs, as well as of their existing degree of independence through nonremovability, is the base that this provides for well-informed insider criticism of a presidential administration (Welborn 1977:146)—especially when sometimes vital interests are at stake, but the presidential "establishment" is holding cards very close to its vest. Examples include the gadfly criticisms of Michael Pertschuk as a deposed chairperson of the FTC, publicizing in colorful ways from that vantage point what he alleged to be the anticonsumer orientations of the agency under his successor, Reagan-appointed chairperson James C. Miller, III (Pertschuk 1982). Another example, one of great potential significance in the social regulation area, is that of the Nuclear Regulatory Commission (NRC), and the criticisms of alleged inadequacies in the regulating of safety problems made by commissioners Victor Gilinsky and Nunzio Paladino at different times in recent years. While the earlier literature on both regulation and the presidency, particularly that of mainline political scientists and public administration scholars, tended to assume that the public interest was generally identified with presidential policy decisions, the "imperial presidency" has fallen out of favor sufficiently enough that it is easier now than a generation ago for us to acknowledge that there is value in a structure that provides a platform for critics whose governmental positions give them access to the information needed to become effective and sensible critics.

We will turn now to the more fundamental level of concern, the overall legitimacy of the IRC form. We can best present the choice that we, as a polity, face in terms used by James O. Freedman. In concluding his interesting defense of agency independence, Freedman contrasts the populism that he views as lying behind the charge that administrative responsibility must be directly accountable through the political process with the Madisonian proposition that

> simple majoritarian means cannot alone create governmental institutions sufficiently stable to impose coherence upon the fluid, often volatile, politics of a dynamic and heterogeneous nation. From the beginning, Americans have understood . . . that for many purposes reliance upon qualities such as expertise, professionalism, independence, seniority, continuity, and tenure is more sensible, more functional, than reliance upon pure political accountability. (Freedman 1978:74)

He then concludes that "part of the genius of the American political system has been the constant interplay it has encouraged between elected officials who are politically accountable and mediating institutions that are non-majoritarian in character," and he cites the cabinet, the congressional committee system, the political parties, and the Supreme Court as such nonmajoritarian institutions, which enables him to conclude that IRCs are "scarcely an anomaly in the American political system" (Freedman 1978:74–5). Operating on this set of premises, Freedman is therefore able to argue that the "question of whether the specific degree of independence that any particular agency enjoys is a virtue must be decided by pragmatic calculations" (1978:76), rather than by abstract principle.

My own view is that when one looks at regulation in both IRCs and the line agencies, and in both economic and social areas (see also chapter 5), one is hard put to make a convincing case that the independent form is necessarily inappropriate. (One exception, however, concerns the Federal Reserve Board, whose functions are too intimately a part of basic economic policy to remain even halfway outside the crucial presidential orbit.) In any case, a judgment made by Bernstein in 1955 remains true: "politically speaking, some regulatory agencies would probably not exist at all if they were not independent" (Bernstein 1955:149).

chapter four

DEREGULATION AND REREGULATION

As a 1980 electioneering slogan, "deregulation" was successfully used by then-challenger Ronald Reagan to mean that he would "get the government off the backs of the people." Once elected, President Reagan seized upon doubts that had been rising about regulation since the mid-1970s in announcing that Vice President George Bush would head a presidential Task Force on Regulatory Relief. By the end of March 1981, an initial "hit list" had been issued by the Task Force, and by the time it went out of business in the summer of 1983, the vice president claimed that its eliminations and reductions of regulations would save businesses and consumers $150 billion over the next ten years. This figure—presumably as much a result of "puffing" for political advantage as of close analytic calculation—was widely disputed. An array of consumer and environmental advocates contended that many of the savings were illusory, and that there would be severe costs in terms of health and safety through reduced regulatory protections to the extent that the savings were real.

In the first year of the new administration, much was made of the fact that the number of pages of new regulations in the *Federal Register*—the official publication for the announcement of new rules by an agency—came to 58,494, a substantial reduction from 82,012 in the last Carter year. Perhaps a better measure is an OMB report that the number of rules published in the *Federal Register* in the 40 months after Reagan came into office was 33,364, as compared with 43,247 in the preceding 40 months under Carter (West and Cooper 1985: 206). On the other hand, by spring 1982, Robert W. Crandall, an economist who had been a member of the preinauguration Reagan Task Force on Regulation, published a piece called "Twilight of Deregulation" (1982). The gist of the article is a complaint that very little was done "to overhaul the more burdensome and ill-conceived of the regulatory statutes," and an assertion that "movement toward

72

reducing the burden of regulation has slowed to a crawl" (5). Clearly, deregulation was a matter of much sound and fury in the first years of the Reagan administration, but what did it actually mean then, and what are its more lasting effects? With "planning" something of a dirty word in political ideology, and competition among and within varied technologies perceived as healthy both practically and in theory, the time was clearly ripe for economic deregulation.

THE SCOPE OF DEREGULATION

Deregulation—partly by statute, partly by administrative action—is most notable in three areas: communications, financial institutions, and transportation. Although it has received the most attention in the Reagan years, the intellectual seeds were planted much earlier (e.g., Stigler 1971, 1975), and the first concrete action took place under President Gerald R. Ford: abolition of fixed brokerage fees by the Securities and Exchange Commission in 1975. A listing of the major actions includes the following:*

1976	Railroad Revitalization and Reform Act
1977	Air Cargo Deregulation Act
1978	Airline Deregulation Act
	Natural Gas Policy Act
1980	Motor Carrier Reform Act
	Household Goods Transportation Act
	Staggers Rail Act
	Depository Institutions Deregulation and Monetary Control Act
	FCC deregulation of cable television
1981	Oil price decontrol completed by executive order
1982	Bus Regulatory Reform Act
	Garn-St. Germain Depository Institution Act
	Settlement of AT&T antitrust case

The lead case, the prototype, is transportation. Although most visible because an agency (the CAB) was actually established, transportation is actually a diverse set of cases, as the above list indicates. It covers airlines, rail carriers, motor freight, household moving, and inter-city buses (Derthick and Quirk 1985; Moore 1986). The extent of deregulation has also been diverse, being all but complete for the

*For case studies of deregulation in several areas, see Weiss and Klass (1981) on early stages, and Weiss and Klass (1986) for a current assessment of economic consequences.

airlines, but only partial for most other forms. Economics and politics apparently come together again in partial explanation of this difference: the Teamsters Union, a dominant force in the trucking industry, is the only major national union that supports Republican presidential candidates, notably Ronald Reagan. Reagan's first chairman of the ICC (1981–86), Reese Taylor, is a good example of the importance of the leverage over the IRCs that is provided to presidents through the appointment process, and the fact that the chair serves at the will of the president. A Utah lawyer with very strong connections to the trucking industry, Taylor espoused deregulation rhetorically, but quickly made it clear in practice that he would go much slower and not as far with trucking deregulation, as what the "true believers" had hoped for.

The CAB, whose Reagan-appointed chairperson was an eager deregulator, no longer exists. The agency has been disbanded, with a few remaining functions shifted to the Department of Transportation. The ICC is currently functioning, but President Reagan has formally proposed its dissolution. In an area—crude oil—where price controls were imposed not as a matter of regulatory theory, but as a reaction to the first oil embargo crisis during the Nixon administration, the decontrol began under Carter and originally set for completion in September 1981 was moved up to February 1981; and almost-complete natural gas deregulation has proceeded in accord with the Natural Gas Policy Act of 1978. In his 1986 *Economic Report*, Reagan stated that he would again press for total deregulation, but his first attempt in 1981–82 got nowhere in Congress.

From the viewpoint of the largest number of consumers affected, the most significant deregulation of this decade was determined by the courts: the break up of AT&T as a nationally regulated monopoly, with the creation of seven separate local telephone companies partially regulated by the state, and the freeing of AT&T to engage in unregulated competition with IBM, Xerox, and other computer and electronic communication firms. The Reagan administration's Justice Department did play a major role by reaching an out-of-court accord with AT&T on January 8, 1982, on the basic plan for splitting AT&T into two parts. Anyone exposed to TV commercials can hardly be unaware that AT&T has aggressively entered into its new competitive realms.

Also in communications—and also the result of a Reagan IRC chairperson appointment—the FCC under Fowler has removed long-standing controls over the content of radio programming that were previously used to ensure that news, religion, local activities, and the preferences of nonmass audiences such as for symphony and opera, would receive some air time. It is the FCC's contention that the number of stations in most markets is now large enough to ensure an adequate diversity of programming without governmental interjection of a kind that has always been subject to charges of cultural paternalism and interference with free speech. On the other hand, the FCC has also lessened regulation in a possibly anticompetitive way that makes it easier for existing radio and TV franchise holders—and therefore harder for potential competitors—to extend the life of radio licenses from three to seven years, and those of TV stations from three to five years.

The FCC has been moving in a more pro-competitive direction since decisions in 1968 and 1969 by which suppliers of telephone equipment and long-distance service were granted access to markets previously monopolized by AT&T. Another landmark event occurred in 1980, when the commission forswore regulation of the new computer-based data transmission services and abandoned regulation of all kinds of terminal equipment (Derthick and Quirk 1985:6–7).

In the area of cable TV, a recent study argues that the deregulation of 1980 has been largely reversed by the Cable Communications Policy Act of 1984, which "returns to the FCC many of the powers it relinquished in 1980," and has some provisions constituting a potential renewal of the regulatory framework of 1972, when highly restrictive rules were adopted (Weiss and Klass 1986:99–101).

Except for the 1984 legislation, the pattern of communications deregulation has been one of the FCC actions without legislative change. While supervising congressional committees have informally and effectively set limits on what the FCC can do, the law makers have not been able to forge a new majority coalition to redefine statutorily a total new balance of regulation and competition in this technologically volatile field (Derthick and Quirk 1985:7).

The world of financial institutions (banks, savings and loans, credit unions, brokerage houses, and insurance companies) is also one in which the pace of change in technology and business operations has kept the regulators scrambling to adjust to the changing environment, let alone to control it in the public interest. Deregulation legislation came later to depository institutions than to most other areas, and is still very much in a state of turmoil, with further legislative action likely. However, certain landmarks can be identified (Meier 1985; White 1986).

Foremost among these is the Depository Institutions Deregulation and Monetary Control Act of 1980 (DIDMCA), the result of hard bargaining between Senate and House bills under a court order to settle some questions regarding new kinds of services, which different regulatory groups were authorizing in their respective business sectors. The DIDMCA transferred authority over interest rates from several different regulatory agencies to a new Depository Institutions Deregulation Committee (DIDC) consisting of the heads of existing agencies—such as the FRB, the Treasury, the Federal Home Loan Board, and the Federal Deposit Insurance Corporation (FDIC)—with instructions to gradually lift interest rate ceilings in the interest of more equal competition among the various types of depository institutions. Complete rate deregulation was accomplished by the end of March 1986, at which time the DIDC no longer existed. Savings and loans institutions received additional powers to compete in the marketplace; they were permitted to become more like commercial banks (e.g., issue credit cards, make consumer loans), rather than being restricted to home mortgage lending functions as in the past.

The DIDMCA failed to create a new stable equilibrium in the money markets, and it was followed in 1982 by the Garn-St. Germain Depository Institutions Act, which authorized the super-NOW accounts and money market demand accounts, and permitted commercial banks to sell life insurance, but did not allow them to sell property or casualty insurance. The savings and loans could now offer corporate checking accounts and allow overdraft checking, which made them directly competitive with the traditional bank and trust companies.

Both of these acts are characterized by Meier as weak legislation that "failed to recognize that the old barriers to financial competition have been leveled by economics and technology" (Meier 1985:70–1). In his view, the technology of electronic funds transfers changed the financial system from a series of local markets to a national and even international system of almost instantaneous money transfer. A system that had been segmented into different types of institutions, and with a different regulatory agency for each type, was now well on the way—whether the regulators liked it or not—toward becoming totally intermingled. Not only are the traditional depository institutions getting into each other's areas, but the nondepository institutions—brokerage houses, real estate firms, and even Sears, Roebuck—are acting like banks, and banks are acting like other kinds of financial service corporations. Sears, which already owned Allstate Insurance Company, now owns Dean Witter, a major brokerage house, and Coldwell, Banker and Company, the nation's largest real estate broker; and it has issued its own equivalent of a bank credit card.

The business and technological stimulants toward making banking a "generic industry" (Meier 1985:71) are challenging two acts of Congress, which have in the past inhibited competition geographically and by industry type. The Glass-Steagal Act (Banking Act of

1933) prohibited commercial banks from engaging in investment banking, at least partly as a reaction to problems discovered after the financial collapse of 1929, which attributed some of the causation to overly-close relationships between banks and the stock market. The effect of Glass-Steagal has been to limit the competition that commercial banks might otherwise provide to investment firms. Geographically, the McFadden Act of 1927 forbade interstate branch banking. In recent years, banks and other financial institutions have found loopholes in both of these acts to permit substantial new intersegmental competition and de facto interstate banking—partly through the creation of the curious phenomenon called "non-bank banks" (White 1986:197–98). These are institutions that either make commercial loans or accept deposits—they do not do both because they would then be classified as banks.

Although these two statutes have not yet been erased from the books, Meier considers them to be "dead" and asserts that "the only issue that remains is whether or not all financial institutions will be allowed to participate under rules that treat all institutions equally" (1985:74). Not all observers would agree with this assessment, but it is clearly the case that financial deregulation is one of the stronger instances of an unfolding business situation outpacing the efforts of legislative regulators. In our highly technological and managerially sophisticated economy, this situation probably characterizes an ever increasing portion of the regulatory world, for the dynamism of entrepreneurial industry is faced by the inertia of governmental checks and balances, designed more to retard than facilitate action.

Finally, antitrust policy under the Reagan administration has undergone changes that are the analogical equivalent of deregulation. William F. Baxter, first head of the antitrust division of the Department of Justice under Reagan, did not accept the proposition that large corporations "by virtue of their size had something called economic power, and that such power could be a threat to consumers." In his administration of the antitrust laws, Baxter was concerned solely with efficiency rather than with the control of power. Although efficiency is usually seen as a result of strong competition, Baxter's boss, Attorney General William French Smith, asserted that competition was not synonymous with a large number of competitors. In Smith's view, reflecting ideas identified with the University of Chicago Department of Economics, in some industries competition would yield only a few competitors, depending on such factors as distribution costs and economies of scale. Smith and Baxter together presided over changes in the antitrust prosecution guidelines that made mergers easier than earlier rules had done. In the area of resale price maintenance—the setting of a retail price by the manufacturer, which discriminates against discount retailers—both the Antitrust Division and the FTC have expressed disdain for taking any action to prevent vertical price fixing of this kind, as their theory holds that such practices increase competition in some areas. This view is, of course, much disputed.

Contrary to suspended enforcement and eased merger rules relating to manufacturing companies (which the Reagan administration proposed in 1986 to write into legislation), in the area of services and the professions the FTC and Antitrust Division have become stronger regulators, beginning in the 1970s and continuing strongly under James C. Miller's administration of the FTC in the first Reagan administration. Insurance firms, city taxi cartels, and professional licensing organizations such as the American Medical Association (AMA) and the American Bar Association (ABA) have come under much closer scrutiny for anticompetitive violations in the 1980s.

The most crucial change in antitrust policy is one that has taken place gradually since the early 1970s under four presidents. Whereas antitrust at one time "reflected the deep-rooted and persistent American fear that concentrated private power could undermine democratic government," says Robert A. Katzmann, now "the fundamental question that antitrust students . . . focus on is not whether a particular judicial decision makes sense in terms of past cases, but whether it makes sense from the standpoint of economics" (Katzmann 1984: 24, 26). The economics used is specifically that of the Chicago school, that which most strongly abhors governmental intervention in the economy. In a curious but real sense, one can say that the FTC and the antitrust division of the Department of Justice were "captured" by the Chicago-school economists, who replaced attorneys as the dominant professional group in the establishment of criteria under which particular cases may be brought.

ASSESSING ECONOMIC DEREGULATION

Although some backwater areas of economic regulation—such as milk marketing and the Federal Maritime Commission; see Derthick and Quirk 1985: Ch. 6—have escaped the net, we can safely say that where competition can be reasonably expected to adequately protect consumers' pocketbooks, deregulation has already been accomplished. It is true, however, that some areas have not gone as far as the Reagan administration had desired and expected (e.g., trucking rates remain partly regulated).

A second political factor limiting deregulation efforts—particularly efforts geared to change social regulation statutes, as we will examine in chapter 5—is that a presidential administration can pursue only a few large battles at a time. In the first term of the Reagan administration, some efforts at deregulation lost out in the political competition with the higher priority given major tax cuts and the struggle to reverse domestic and national security priorities in the budget. Similarly, in the Reagan administration's second term, deficit reduction, tax reform, and arms negotiations left little room for a major investment of political capital in an area that has so little "pizazz," and so little political payoff.

Probing to a more basic level regarding the major deregulatory successes, Derthick and Quirk, in a major political study of deregulation, used the airline, telecommunications, and trucking industries as a vehicle for analyzing the "highly significant theoretical question of how particularistic, well-organized interests can successfully be subordinated to diffuse, far more encompassing, but ill-organized interests" (1985:13). They found three principal elements in the successful cases, summarized as

> the fit between a well-developed analytic prescription and the need of politicians for positions that were responsive to current public concerns (inflation and intrusive government), appealing on ideological grounds, and easy to comprehend and explain; the presence of leadership roles and institutions, especially the commissions and courts, that facilitated action; and the difficulty encountered by the affected interests, though mobilized in opposition, in converting economic resources effectively to political use. (1985:245)

The analytic prescription was, of course, derived from microeconomic theory, and it was made especially effective by a flamboyant academic crusader, Alfred E. Kahn, in the case of the CAB. Unlike social regulation matters, here the question was not one of externalities, but of the role of competition. By effectively demonstrating (with empirical evidence from a study of unregulated intrastate airline competition; see Behrman 1980; Derthick and Quirk 1985) that competition could indeed provide substantial consumer protection against predatory pricing, the political case for deregulation was strongly supported by academic analysis. Appropriate analysis and convergence of elite opinion are not always available, of course; Derthick and Quirk also briefly analyzed some instances—milk price supports, air pollution, and the maritime industry)—in which experts disagreed, political support was lacking, or microeconomics had no convincing rationale to offer (1985:207–36).

Thus, the deregulation movement has been uneven in application, and is no longer a "front burner" political issue.

Can we conclude that the economic deregulation accomplished to date is beneficial? Has it reached a new and stable equilibrium? These questions do not have a single, simple answer. There definitely have been clear gains (emphasized in Weiss and Klass 1986) for some consumers by replacing fixed, regulated prices with competitive pricing, and most microeconomists are professionally pleased because the good of the market has been served. However, there are also some serious criticisms of economic deregulation; some consumers have been losers rather than winners; and proposals abound for reregulation and new regulations. While not exactly at the top of the public's most serious issues, questions of economic regulation have not disappeared and will not disappear. Changing technology and a changing economy will create many situations potentially calling for new regulations.

The major criticisms of economic deregulation include the following:

Service cuts: with the CAB defunct and the ICC permitting abandonment of routes by rail and motor carriers more easily than in the past, some consumers, particularly those in rural areas, find themselves with fewer transportation options than in the past. In one ironic reaction, the city of Fresno, California, became an investor in a commuter airline, in order to maintain service to the community. Thus, deregulation led to local socialism.

Deregulated airline prices have risen substantially on the less competitive routes, somewhat diminishing the enthusiasm of those consumers whose travel is other than between major coast-to-coast stops. Also, as of mid-1986, concerns were rising about airline mergers that were proceeding at such a pace as to threaten oligopolistic pricing (i.e., private regulation of prices) in a number of markets.

Lifting of restrictions on entry may bring back some of what was called "destructive competition" in the 1930s. The first result of trucking deregulation, for example, was to increase the number of truckers substantially. Since the amount of goods to be carried did not increase proportionately, the second effect in the first few years has arguably been to produce a lot of bankruptcies among small truckers, and increase the concentration ratio among the remaining firms. The ultimate fear is that the long-term result could be the gobbling up of the small by the big until the point is reached at which so few firms are left that pricing becomes notably oligopolistic—and then the cry for regulation will appear again.

Universal access, not only to transportation services, but to local telephone service and to such taken-for-granted things as checking accounts, may be an indirect victim of deregulation. It is asserted that long distance telephone rates subsidized local rates; with the two types now being provided by different business entities, local rates have risen substantially. Financial institution deregulation means that banks and savings and loans have to compete with each other more strongly to obtain deposits; the costs of paying higher interest rates (or any interest on checking accounts that formerly carried no interest) has led to very sharp increases in some instances in service charges on checking accounts with small balances.

The most serious criticism of economic deregulation, however, is that it may undermine safety regulation in the transportation industries. The case has been most fully articulated by Fredrick C. Thayer in a book whose over-all theme is a case for regulation. He argues that "Social regulation of health and safety standards cannot be effective (or can become effective only at very high costs) unless it is accompanied by economic regulation" (Thayer 1984:73). The argument is essentially as follows: under competition, some airlines will become financially weakened (e.g., Braniff, Eastern). Financial weakness leads to cutting corners. Competitively, a firm will not cut corners where the customers see them, but in such less obvious things as aircraft maintenance. Also, the labor turmoil that has accompanied deregulation means that one will often have pilots flying routes with which they are not closely familiar through repeated experience, and that has perhaps been a factor in some crashes.

It is logically true that economic and safety regulation can be separated from one another, with the Federal Aviation Administration maintaining its obligations to impose safety standards even after the CAB has left the scene. But, says Thayer, this is "an organizationally naive argument." He contends that as the number of firms increases, more and more FAA inspectors and greater enforcement expenditures will be needed (1984:85–6). Recent air crash experience and large fines levied against major carriers for inadequate safety maintenance have increased the attention paid to such arguments (Nance 1986). Although experts agree that the spate of accidents was statistically random, the Air Line Pilots Association has recently told a House subcommittee of growing maintenance shortcuts, and points out that the number of airlines has increased 122 percent since 1979, while the number of FAA inspectors assigned to particular airlines has dropped 30 percent. Also, a GAO report contends that the air traffic controllers force has been "stretched too thin"

(*New York Times*, March 23, 1986; see also Meyer and Vartabedian 1986). In other words, a theoretically satisfactory separation of economic from safety regulation becomes institutionally suspect in a period dominated by budget cuts and an antiregulatory mood in the Executive Office of the President.

A similar argument is made with regard to motor carrier safety, and Thayer suggests a plausible explanation, which serves to illustrate his entire argument:

> The union driver for a large firm operates within a highly structured system. The truck he drives will be turned over to another driver at a fixed terminal, and violations of speed limits will accomplish very little. The independent, conversely, is likely to drive the same truck from point of origin to destination, and whatever time he spends resting will result only in later delivery of his cargo. With a huge number of independents on the road [increased under deregulation], safety inspectors cannot locate them all, let alone subject them to rigorous enforcement of safety standards. A strong union, by the same token, contributes to safety by making it difficult for firms to pressure drivers into violating safety rules. (Thayer 1984:91)

WHAT NEXT?

To many microeconomists there remains a substantial deregulatory agenda. For example, an asserted need to re-deregulate cable TV (Owen and Gottlieb 1986). Another example: Lawrence J. White lists seven kinds of regulation imposed on depository institutions (including state usury laws, and controls over entry into business of new depository institutions) that can be deregulated with "proper disciplining" of firms that make mistakes being left to the competitive marketplace (White 1986:200). Natural gas remains partly regulated, and the ICC still oversees certain rates; some observers would end both areas of control. There is even an academic discussion looking toward electric utility deregulation (Joskow and Schmalensee 1983). On the other hand, there were losers and winners in the process of deregulation, so it is not surprising that political regrouping is taking place and efforts are being made to maintain some economic regulation, re-regulate in some areas deregulated, and to initiate new rules in other areas.

A vestige of air travel regulation—one that seems likely to remain—is control over airport access: which carrier gets how many landing and take-off slots. Both the FAA and the Department of Transportation are involved in this thorny allocation problem (Kaplan 1986:68–9), which may be decided on an auction basis. Also in transportation, some elements of the trucking industry are lobbying Congress to again control entry of new truckers. The insurance industry, which is regulated only at the state level, and generally likes it that way, now wants the federal government to restrict the freedom of the banking industry to get into insurance. One of the currently active re-regulation campaigns is that of electric utilities to get the ICC to reimpose rate controls on railroads where only one rail carrier has a line from a coal mine to a utility. This campaign goes under the banner of an organization called Consumers United for Rail Equity.

We have already noted that financial institutions deregulation has proceeded far enough to stir things up a great deal, but remains in a very unsettled state. It is not surprising, then, that demands for further deregulation invite calls for new government action in this area. After all, it seems that inadequate regulation rather than too much regulation is at fault in the shock of the Continental Illinois Bank failure that led to an unprecedented $4.5 billion federal bailout in 1984. One business columnist has called for a return to interest rate ceilings, asserting that younger and poorer persons (e.g., those who wish to buy a first home) suffer as borrowers from the higher rates of recent years, while the beneficiaries are largely older and more affluent (Flanigan 1984). Another example: when home mortgage rates went over 17 percent a few years ago, the adjustable rate mortgage quickly came into widespread use, with great diversity, and even greater confusion in low initial rates and the amount and frequency of changes that could be imposed. Two years later, the Department of Housing and Urban Development was proposing new regulations designed to remove some of the risks associated with adjustable rate mortgages, ensuring that consumers had adequate information in digestible form, but also setting actual limits on the amount of change that could be made in a mortgage's rate in a single year.

When we add to the financial institutions picture passage by the House of Representatives in 1985 of a bill that extends regulation to all securities dealers handling government securities, in reaction to failure of a major secondary securities dealer, the sum of the developments suggests that some deregulation may have been accomplished too rapidly and without adequate analysis of side effects. As this becomes evident, calls for new policies arise to fill the gaps newly created in protection of consumer-investors.

Another hypothesis warranted by current developments is that the consumer protection movement may be on the verge of a new upswing. From high-priced art auctions to alleged price gouging connected with rental car collision damage waivers, new regulatory moves are under discussion. The very dynamism of the economy—its constant change in the entrepreneurial search for financial success—carries with it the creation of situations that may threaten consumers, and our political system continues to respond.

In a way, the most interesting of suggestions for new consumer oriented regulations is also in the financial institutions area. We have already noted that universal access to such a common convenience as a personal checking account for paying bills—a convenience that may often be necessity for the ill and disabled, who are immobile and often lack transportation—has been threatened by banking deregulation. A call for mandated "lifeline" checking accounts arose as a response.

The issue posed by the lifeline bank account concept is essentially whether banking should be treated as just another business, or whether it should be considered as more akin to a public utility; that is, a firm offering an essential service that benefits from special governmental treatment (e.g., public insurance for depositors' accounts) in exchange for an obligation to provide universal access. Economic regulation then becomes more than a pocketbook matter. Given the lifestyle significance of telephone and banking access today, the lifeline issue moves economic regulation into the realm of social regulation—the area we will turn to in the following chapter.

chapter five

SOCIAL REGULATION

Love Canal. Three Mile Island. Times Beach. Bhopal. EPA. TSCA. RCRA. CRCLA. FIFRA. OSM. CEQ. EEOC. *Silent Spring* by Rachel Carson (1962). *Unsafe at Any Speed* by Ralph Nader (1965).

What are all these things? Symbols: the places, agency and statute acronyms, and books that represent stimuli and responses associated with health, safety, environmental protection, and social ethics problems for which regulatory programs have been established in recent years.

In the New Deal period (1933–38), the alphabetical agencies of economic regulation (the SEC, FPC, CAB, and so on) represented the financial protections attempted after the Great Crash of 1929, and during the Great Depression. Today, the items listed above symbolize the efforts that began in the mid-1960s and peaking (for the first cycle, at least) in the mid-1970s to provide personal protection against the physical hazards of modern industry and technology, and the moral hazards of discrimination. The environmental protection arm of social regulation also includes the recent concerns—aesthetic and recreational, as well as nature-protecting—of the older conservation movement.

Our primary focus here, however, will be on the health, safety, and environmental concerns that have made agencies such as the EPA and the OSHA subjects of passionate partisanship. Governmental rules that deal with water and air pollution, toxic chemicals, workplace safety problems, carcinogeneity, and hazardous wastes are the primary areas that have made social regulation highly controversial. We will look at the scope and focus of social regulation statutes and agencies, at the specific features that differentiate it from economic regulation, and at the strongly adversarial relationships between industry and regulators. The Reagan administration's initiatives aimed at regulatory relief will also be discussed, and the beginnings of a counter-attack.

THE SCOPE AND GROWTH OF SOCIAL REGULATION

Social regulation can generally be differentiated from economic regulation by the former's concern with harm to our physical (and sometimes moral and aesthetic) well-being, rather than to our wallets. In physical terms, that harm includes, by way of illustration:

Safety at home or on the road: the Consumer Products Safety Commission required baby crib manufacturers to respace the slats to avoid a child's head becoming caught; the National Highway Traffic and Safety Administration mandates bumper strength and the provision of seat belts.

Safety in the workplace: guard rails and screens on moving machinery as prescribed by the Occupational Safety and Health Administration.

Health hazards in the workplace: the OSHA's rules limiting employee exposure to such substances as cotton dust, which produces debilitating byssinosis, or "brown lung," which induces pulmonary problems of great severity after prolonged exposure—it has afflicted at least 35,000 cotton workers (Tolchin and Tolchin 1983, 1985:111–23).

Water-related health hazards at home or on vacation: the Safe Drinking Water Act and the Federal Water Pollution Control Act are directed at ensuring appropriate quality of drinking water, and water in which we fish and swim. In addition to traditional concerns with fecal matter seeping into sources of home drinking water, there is now the major additional fear that hazardous industrial wastes—from small establishments like dry cleaners to major industries processing man-made chemicals—disposed of in leaky landfills may be contaminating a significant portion of our underground water supply, the aquifers from which nearly 50 percent of the population draws its potable water.

Air pollution health hazards: the Clean Air Act has been the bell-weather legislation of the modern environmental protection movement. However, federal water pollution legislation actually reached the statute books, but not the streams and lakes, much earlier, and is currently of greater concern.

Nuclear power safety: a special area of regulatory concern, dramatized with some lasting effect by the 1978 near-disaster at Three Mile Island, a Pennsylvania nuclear power plant that came closer to the ultimate tragedy of a meltdown than anyone associated with the Nuclear Regulatory Commission (NRC) or the power industry would acknowledge (Ford 1982). TMI's message was reinforced by the Chernobyl nuclear disaster in the USSR in 1986.

Another recent event that grabbed public and governmental attention is likely to be with us for a long time to come: the chemical toxicity (such as that which killed 2,000 people in the Bhopal disaster) that occurs in all media of transmission—land, air and water—and that we are constantly adding to as a byproduct of our scientific genius. Some 67,000 chemicals are in commercial use in the United States, with 1,000 new chemicals added annually, but complete health hazards analysis has been done on only 2 percent.

As of 1980, we used 35 times (350 billion pounds per year) the quantity of synthetic organic chemicals we had used in 1940 (Peterson 1985:62–4). Between now and when we devise effective ways of minimizing the unwanted byproducts and after effects of the chemistry-based products, which contribute much to our standard of living, the problems can only worsen. (For some recent estimates of the problems, and descriptions of the regulatory framework for handling hazardous wastes, see CBO 1985a).

Environmental regulation also includes protection for animals and plants (e.g., the Endangered Species Act of 1973), and for elements of the earthly heritage threatened by the "paving over" which is one of the costs of urban civilizations—thus the Wilderness Act (1964), and the Wild and Scenic Rivers Act (1968). These laws have two duties which help to build political support for them: recreational and aesthetic interests are served, as well as conservation of physical resources.

The aesthetic dimension is also reflected in provisions seeking to insure clean air in national parks; in the mandate to set secondary drinking water standards for taste and odor, apart from health hazards; and in the Noise Control Act provisions that serve both health and irritation-reducing functions.

Harm to our person is not always physical, however, and a significant dimension of social regulation focuses on the moral harm area of discrimination in education, employment and job promotion, and housing on grounds of race, creed, ethnicity, sex, and disability. While some aspects (e.g., voting rights) are handled through laws that require the filing of law suits to start action, others are pursued through regulatory bodies, such as the Office for Civil Rights, and the Equal Employment Opportunity Commission. (The U.S. Civil Rights Commission is not a regulatory body, but an investigative and interpretive office intended by its legislation to provide a continuing focus on the civil rights agenda.) Earlier social regulation legislation included the child and female labor protection laws of the

1930s, and the National Labor Relations Board (1935), which cuts across the economic/social regulation distinction: it provides governmental recognition for workers' dignity in a capitalist society, and it strengthens worker power to bargain for economic gains.

There are other examples of mixed economic and social regulation; for example, the fairness doctrine of the FCC does not sort out economic interests (although it affects them), but protects the marketplace of ideas; and the NHTSA's bumper regulations are based in part on congressional authority given in 1972 to protect consumers from economic losses as well as injuries.

Finally, the scope of social regulation is enlarged by what can perhaps be termed "morality regulation." Administrative enforcement of state laws limiting or forbidding use of government welfare funds for abortions is an example. Another example is one proposed by the Reagan administration, but abandoned after a public outcry and a federal district court injunction. It was called the "squeal rule," and would have required physicians and clinics providing birth control information to females under 18 to notify the client's parents. At the local level, various efforts to devise regulatory ordinances that would lessen the distribution of pornographic materials are intermittently proposed, although most have been defeated by First Amendment objections.

Therefore, social regulation has a broad scope. The term is used to cover all areas of regulation that are not subsumable under the rubric of economic regulation. Recall that the primary economic rationale for social regulation (chapter 2) lies in market failures of the externalities type, whereas economic regulation stems most often from fears of monopoly power. The exernalities approach does not fit the entire spectrum, but it does apply to our primary focus in this chapter.

Although the new social regulation is associated with protective laws passed in the 1960s and 1970s, railway safety laws occurred decades earlier, and the Pure Food and Drugs Act was enacted in 1906 with major strengthening amendments in 1938 and 1962. Airlines have been regulated for safety since the 1930s, although the Federal Aviation Administration (FAA) did not enter the field of aviation safety, both as a regulator and as the operator of airport control towers (a subsidy to the industry, as well as a safety program) until 1958. Also, the Atomic Energy Commission (AEC), created in 1946, handled nuclear power reactor safety regulation until the NRC was created in 1977.

These precursors did not amount to more than governmental oddities until protective legislation came into being in the mid-1960s, not receding until the election of Ronald Reagan in 1980. The initial push came in the Great Society years (1963–69) of President Johnson (Democrat), although the momentum then achieved carried through the Nixon and Ford (Republican) administrations (1969–77), and on into the Carter (Democrat) years (1977–81), particularly with regard to the latest scare on the agenda: toxic wastes.

A categorization by Vogel (1981:162) shows that 62 consumer health and safety laws emerged from Congress in the fifteen-year period of 1964–79, compared with 11 during the New Deal and 5 in the Progressive period. Similarly, regulation of energy and the environment was embedded in 32 recent statutes, but only 7 in the Progressive and New Deal periods.

While some of these measures were narrow in their scope (e.g., the Egg Products Inspection Act, the Wild and Scenic Rivers Act, and the Medical Device Safety Act), others have very broad potential impacts indeed (e.g., Clean Air; Toxic Substances Control Act). As a convenient reference point for our discussion of this category of regulation, we will list a number of the major laws and agencies that most strongly embody the spirit—(and the problems)—of contemporary social regulation:

FDA (Food and Drug Administration)	1906
(Began as the Bureau of Chemistry)	
EEOC (Equal Employment Opportunity Commission)	1964
FAA (Federal Aviation Administration)	1958
OCR (Office for Civil Rights)	1965
NHTSA (National Highway Traffic Safety Administration)	1970
NEPA (National Environmental Policy Act)	1969
CEQ (Council on Environmental Quality)	1970
EPA (Environmental Protection Agency)	1970
OSHA (Occupational Safety and Health Administration)	1970
OSHRC (Occupational Safety and Health Review Commission)	1970
Endangered Species Act	1973
CPSC (Consumer Product Safety Commission)	1972
RCRA (Resources Conservation and Recovery Act)	1976
TSCA (Toxic Substances Control Act)	1976
OSM (Office of Surface Mining; Surface Mining Control and Reclamation Act)	1977
Superfund (Comprehensive Environmental Response Compensation and Liability Act)	1980

This is mostly a list of agencies, which fails to reveal the full range of programs implemented by these organizations. Most notably, the EPA has a jurisdiction that ranges from clean air (major legislation in 1967, 1970, 1977) and clean water (laws in 1965, 1972, 1977), through noise control (1972), ocean dumping (1972), and the Safe Drinking Water Act (1974) to pesticides (moved from Agriculture in 1972) and hazardous wastes (two major laws in 1976 and the 1980 Superfund law for cleaning up abandoned toxic waste dumps). Acid rain is also an EPA responsibility, but current action has been limited to research, with regulation in need of stronger public demand or support from the White House.

Without a doubt, the EPA has the broadest responsibilities of all the social regulation agencies, as budget and staffing data suggest (see Table 5–1).

Budget and staffing data also reflect the fact that social regulation has moved from little more than half the dollar size of economic regulation in 1970 to five times the size of economic regulation in 1985, and almost three times larger in personnel. Having established the scope, rapid development, and size of social regulation, we will turn to the special characteristics of this significant part of the government-business scene.

WHAT MAKES SOCIAL REGULATION DIFFERENT?

The first, most basic way in which social regulation differs from economic regulation is that an increase in competition cannot remove the need for social regulation. This flows directly from the economic rationale for most health, safety, and environmental regulation: that the problems arise because of externalities. Remember that this means effects felt by third parties, who are neither the producers nor the direct purchasers of a product. The market failure here is not, as with monopolistic pricing, a lack of competition, but the fact that producers can ignore byproduct consequences of their operations (e.g., air and water pollution), and the costs of fixing up unless the government steps in. An increase in competition may actually increase the dangers of inadequate job safety or environmental pollution, because a firm with its back to the wall financially

Table 5–1
Selected Social Regulation Budgets, Fiscal 1986

Agency	Budget (est.), Fiscal 1986 (in millions)	Personnel (est.), 1986
EPA	$2,300	12,042
OSHA	213	2,280
CPSC	34	549
NHTSA	132	705

SOURCE: Press release, Center for the Study of American Business, Washington University, St. Louis, Missouri.

is less able to afford the cost of complying with good health and environmental practices, than one whose profitability may be enhanced by a less competitive market structure. Consequently, while economists may push hard for "reform" of social regulation techniques, few of them argue for "deregulation" in a literal sense.

Next, note that social regulation tends to be focused not on a particular industry such as airlines, securities exchanges, or interstate national gas pipelines, but on problems or functions: hazardous waste clean up, smog, safety, and so forth. This distinction is not absolute, since the FTC covers competitive practices and fraudulent advertising over a very broad front; the NRC is concerned with plant safety in a particular industry. However, the distinction holds over a broad range of agencies and programs. Because most social regulation statutes are not limited to particular industries, some commentators have suggested that such expansion has succeeded "in undermining much of the historic distinction between regulated and unregulated industries" (Vogel 1981:162). This point is valid to the extent that manufacturing—often taken as the prototype of all industrial segments—was not much touched by the alphabetical IRCs of the New Deal period, which focused more on what we perceive as public utility industries and services. On the other hand, there is a clear differential impact of some of the new social regulation programs on particular industries. Some examples include (Tombari 1984:232–35):

> Clean air regulations most directly affect the automobile and electric power industries, those being two major sources of emissions.
>
> Water pollution efforts have focused strongly on the manufacturers of paper, since paper mills have often been located next to streams that have been used for disposing of the residues of processing trees into sheets of paper.
>
> The construction industry has received extra attention from the OSHA because of a historically bad safety record.
>
> Chemical, primary metals, and petroleum refining industries account together for better than three-fourths of hazardous wastes, and therefore will be the most regulated under the Resource Conservation and Recovery Act (CBO 1985).

Social regulation is thus a bit like monetary policy, which has a heavier impact on housing than on other industries, because of the special sensitivity of housing to interest rate changes (even though the Federal Reserve does not single out a particular industry when seeking to affect interest rates).

Organizationally, Congress has generally—but not always—

avoided the IRC form when creating social regulation agencies, placing most of them instead in the regular hierarchy of the executive branch. The OSHA is in the Department of Labor, the OSM is in Interior, the NHTSA is in Transportation, and the FDA is in Health and Human Services. The EPA is in a category of its own: a line agency, reporting to the president, but independent of any cabinet department. The organizational features of these agencies are thus the opposite of major IRC features: agency heads are appointed by the president and serve at his will, rather than for a fixed term. Each line agency has a single head, rather than a commission, and there is no question of a bipartisan balance. In legal-administrative terms, the lines of authority and accountability are much clearer in the bulk of social regulation agencies than in the economic regulation programs of IRCs. However, as we shall see in chapter 7, legal-administrative authority does not always translate into effective political authority, and an executive line agency can sometimes have substantial independence despite its position in a hierarchic organization chart.

Since the IRC form is thought to make industry capture of an agency easier, does the reverse follow? Are social regulation agencies not subject to capture because of presidential accountability? Most observers agree that there has been little industry capture; in fact, some charge that they have been captured instead by anti-industry groups. (Because the question of capture is sufficiently important, it is given its own section later in the chapter.)

Much of social regulation focuses on eliminating or reducing health and safety risks, and is sometimes equated with risk management. While the concept of risk management (i.e., deciding what to do about a risk that has been identified, measured in probability and severity, and evaluated as to acceptability; see chapter 6) does not easily apply to moral or aesthetic regulation, in the physical risk areas it does provide a useful "handle" for analyzing problems and issues with some semblance of rationality. In an era characterized by acid rain, smog, ground water toxicity, and near meltdowns of nuclear power plants, any set of ideas that gets us beyond simple emotionalism in dealing with hazards to our persons would seem to have much to recommend it. Thus, the burgeoning technical field of risk assessment and its policy-related cousin, risk management, are increasingly permeating agency-industry-academic discussions of health and safety regulations (although, without much impact on newspaper and TV presentation).

As a mode of analysis that has at least the ambition of developing a capacity for objective—scientific measurement of the dangers that we create for ourselves—risk analysis is one sign of the scientific and technical complexity of many social regulation areas. While it is true that economic regulation also has technological complexities (e.g., telecommunications via satellites and computers), the physics-chemistry-biology complexities of regulating prescription drugs, hazardous waste, and carcinogenic health hazards on the job are several orders of magnitude greater. Ever-increasing complexity is one reason for regulation, of course, because of consumer ignorance; probably more importantly, it is one of the difficulties in determining what to regulate, how much to regulate, and by what means. That is to say, there is a scientific role to be played in establishing protective standards, but we are at the earliest stages of spelling out how that role is to be played, and how it is to interact with regulatory accountability to the nonscientific public at large. (See chapter 6.)

Yet another major characteristic of the new social regulation is citizen participation, which can occur at various levels and stages of the policy process. Legislative lobbying is the traditional prototype, especially for the major organized groups such as chambers of commerce and labor unions, and has been equally present for both economic and social regulation. The new development in the latter type is citizen participation in the administrative process at the implementation stage, and through the initiation of citizen lawsuits. Until about twenty-five years ago, there would have been little opportunity for these types of action. The rules of what is known as "standing" (i.e., who has a right to participate in a lawsuit) largely restricted court access to those who had an immediate, personal economic interest in the outcome of a proposed governmental action. By both statute and decisions of the federal courts themselves, however, standing has been vastly expanded in recent years. It now not only permits those claiming to act on behalf of a general public interest to be party to suits (e.g., the Sierra Club suing on behalf of members from all states to protect the purity of air in the Grand Canyon area), but also sometimes permits citizen groups to sue both polluters and the government agencies themselves, in order to obtain more effective enforcement of legislative standards. Under the citizen suit provisions of the Clean Water Act, for example, there were six such suits in 1981, 108 in 1983, and 87 in the first quarter of 1984 (King 1985:34). It is interesting to note that these suits can result in negotiated settlements that not only solve the pollution problem, but often provide for payment by the polluter of funds for environmental education or private conservation projects. Attorneys for private firms sometimes see this outcome as a perverse incentive leading environmental groups to sue specifically as a means of fund raising.)

Can one conclude from this kind of activity that organizations pushing the protective regulation side of health, safety, and environmental issues now dominate the regulatory political process? Hardly. It is clear that there is now representation on the consumer, labor, and environmental protection side of the fence to at least some extent, as compared with earlier days when it was estimated—(exact measures were not available earlier)—that industry had almost all of the organization, and most of the money when it came to representation processes. Walker (1983) has detailed the sharp rise of the public interest groups (PIGs) after 1960, and a number of observers have suggested that the data indicate that such groups have partially balanced the scales. For example, Berry wrote a decade ago that the PIGs

> are slowly changing the overall environment within which governmental officials formulate public policy . . . they are not a countervailing force in that they are always an equal power to those they must influence or compete with, but they possess significant resources and public support. The opinion they can arouse, the bad publicity they can generate, the lawsuits they can file, are all factors that are relevant to the deliberations of those who must make policy decisions. (Berry 1977:289)

And Yaffee provides this illustration:

> Twenty years ago water resources development planning in eastern Tennessee primarily involved the Tennessee Valley Authority (TVA), the House Appropriations Committee, local congressmen, and perhaps state and local government officials. Its objectives centered on navigation, flood control, electricity production, and pork barrel politics. Today, groups representing interests ranging from commercial development to white-water rafting, energy production to archaeological preservation, agriculture to protection of endangered species all participate in planning and implementation. (Yaffee 1982:8)

While not totally rescinding this hopeful view of broader interest representation in the policy process, the most recent studies are less sanguine. A recent examination of some seven thousand interest organizations active in Washington politics concludes that "the overall business share of the pressure system has been enhanced" because the rise of the PIGs has been exceeded by the massive corporate political mobilization of recent years (Schlozman 1984:1026). And Berry's updated evaluation asserts that business has used expanded advocacy "to regain its primacy in Washington" (1984:35–41). Although the rise of public interest groups may not have created a new regulatory "regime" (Harris and Milkis 1983), it is clear that the political environment of the new social regulation is considerably more diverse and complex than that faced by business regulatory commissions in the 1930s–50s. Citizen lawsuits and administrative hearings constitute important elements of the social regulatory process today. (For an argument that the public interest groups prevail at the statutory design stage, while the affected industries win more at the enforcement stage, at least with regard to air pollution matters, see Melnick 1983).

While broadened access to the courts and an administrative process open to public comments provide opportunities for public participation, effectiveness requires also a peg on which to hang one's case. This is provided by yet other special features of social regulation: specific mandates, specific deadlines, and specific technological requirements. These developments are in sharp contrast to the vagueness of the traditional "public interest, convenience, or necessity" mandate of the business regulation agencies.

If clean air and water legislation had been written on the same lines as the acts creating the CAB or the FCC, Congress would have created the EPA; set a nonspecific goal such as "it shall be the task of the EPA to set air and water quality standards as strong as the public interest requires"; and perhaps stated that these goals should be achieved as soon as possible. Given such a broad policy mandate, the EPA would have had nearly carte blanche to use whatever means it found most appropriate; to set whatever deadlines it thought reasonable; and to negotiate as it saw fit the balancing act between imposing antipollution costs on industry in order to maximize air and water quality, and minimizing and stretching out the regulatory requirements imposed on industry in order to maximize economic development and growth. However, the 1960s and 1970s were not characterized by the same political environment or intellectual assumptions as the Progressive and New Deal periods. Specifically, there was no longer a simplistic faith that neutral expertise could do away with politics and the making of hard value choices, and there was already a sufficient literature on "capture" of the earlier regulatory agencies (Bernstein's book was published in 1955), so that protectionist legislators and interest group advocates were unwilling to provide administrators with large discretion for fear that it would be subverted by industry pressures.

Therefore, the new social legislation became extremely specific, including details that even the most sympathetic observer finds surprising as matters to be embedded in legislation, rather than left to administrative discretion. For example:

The 1970 Clean Air legislation directed the EPA to set national ambient air qualities standards for pollutants found to be harmful to human health or to the environment. While the EPA was to develop its own list of such pollutants, it was given a specific starting point in that the legislation specified that standards would be developed for at least seven named pollutants, including nitrogen oxides, ozone, hydrocarbons, and lead; that is, Congress made its own priority judgment. A deadline of 1982 (since extended) was set for air quality control districts to meet the primary standards for the protection of human health.

For automobiles, the 1970 air statute specified that there was to be a 90 percent reduction in nitrogen oxide emissions by 1976, as against the 1970 emission levels. (This deadline, too, has been extended a number of times.)

Under the Federal Water Pollution Control Act Amendments of 1972, two specific standards were set for specific dates: (1) navigable waters were to become fishable and swimable by 1983, and (2) *all* discharge of pollutants into navigable waters was to be eliminated by 1985. These deadlines have been extended, and one doubts that the total termination of pollutant discharge will ever be achieved. The importance of the deadlines, however, lies in what we suggested above: they provide pegs on which advocacy groups can hang their claims to push both the EPA and polluters ever closer toward the goals.

The 1972 water legislation also provided for specific technologies and deadlines for their implementation. The best practicable control technologies were to be in place by 1977, and the best available technologies by 1983 (the dates later changed). While this was flexible in that the EPA had to decide what was the best available technology for each situation, it was very specific with regard to limiting the extent to which the EPA could take cost considerations into effect.

For both energy-saving and environmental protection reasons, Congress has legislated fuel economy standards for automobiles, starting with 20 mpg (not for each car, but as a "fleet" average for the year) for 1980, and legislated to reach 27.5 in 1985 (but amended for the 1986 and 1987 model years back to 26 mpg at the request of General Motors and Ford, over the protests of Chrysler, which was ready to meet the stiffer standard with its smaller cars.

By the mid-1980s, many social legislation advocates had two additional motivations for getting Congress to specify what it wanted the executive to implement. One was the Watergate history, which created something of a dilemma for those who saw the creation of line agencies directly responsible to the president as a way of avoiding the capture tendencies of multiheaded independent regulatory commissions, but who also saw President Nixon's "Imperial Presidency" and Watergate as reasons not to place too much faith in the White House. Secondly, President Reagan's appointees to head the EPA, the OSHA, and other major regulatory agencies, and his attempts to scuttle the agencies' budgets created a substantial backlash in Congress—as in the public at large, according to public opinion polls. (So strong has reaction been that some commentators are now ready to pursue their policy objectives by moving away from reliance on presidential power, and back toward protected agency independence. For example, Rosenbaum (1985:299–300) suggests a five- or seven-year term for the administrator of the EPA.) Accordingly, we find that the tendency toward detailed statutory specifications continues.

The 1984 renewal of the Resource Conservation and Recovery Act (RCRA) for the management and disposal of currently generated hazardous waste, imposed more than two dozen specific statutory deadlines for the EPA to meet in such areas as establishing regulations for small quantity waste generators (17 months), new toxicity testing procedures (28 months), standards for leak detection systems for land facilities (30 months), and a ban on land disposal of bulk liquids (6 months). In what have come to be called "hammer" provisions (i.e., provisions that trigger certain automatic policy actions), the EPA was directed in 1984 to review some 400 kinds of waste, with the provision that those it did not find entirely safe for land disposal, or that it had not evaluated within the time limitations, would be banned from landfill dumping in three stages, ranging from 45 to 66 months after the law was enacted (CBO 1985:36–40). Similarly, the 1986 renewal of the Safe Drinking Water Act specified 83 contaminants for which the EPA is to set standards within three years.

This general tendency toward greater specificity in regulatory legislation, although strong, should not be considered absolute. First, there are statutory exceptions. The Consumer Product Safety Commission (CPSC), for example, was given a mandate "to protect the public against unreasonable risks of injury associated with consumer products," leaving the specific definition of "unreasonable" to the administrative rule-making process—not an easy task. Secondly, no statute yet written and no language yet devised can be explicit and totally without ambiguity in covering multitudinous future circumstances. Thus, administrative discretion will always remain a substantial element in the implementation process. In a free society, regulation is never a matter of "command and control" (as one unfortunate and inaccurate phrase would have it). Rather, it is characterized by bargaining, negotiation, and compromise.

Another characteristic of social regulation is its strong federalist dimension. Whereas the traditional business regulations were administered through national agencies (with field offices), programs such as clean air and water, surface mining control, occupational safety and health, and hazardous waste disposal were written with provisions for day-by-day implementation by the states, on delegation of authority from the appropriate national agency. The system of partially pre-empting certain policy areas at the national level, and then returning some of the authority to the states, constitutes a major development in the politics of intergovernmental relations— sufficiently so that we will give expanded treatment in chapter 8.

THE CAPTURE QUESTION IN SOCIAL REGULATION

Capture of the regulatory agency by the regulated industry has often been alleged concerning the economic regulation agencies (as we saw in chapter 3). The safety, health, and environmental protection agencies, however, have been largely free of such charges. The major exception was the 1981–83 period of an antiregulatory head of the EPA, but such bowing to industry as was involved then was not so much a matter of capture as of purposeful presidential policy. Occasional charges that industry has had a "back door" influence on regulation through the hidden processes of the Office of Management and Budget come a little closer, and we deal with that dimension in chapter 7 under the heading of "Presidential Oversight."

What is different about social regulation? Why has capture not been such a problem there? Basically, the answer is not that the capture theory was wrong as described, but that the circumstances of social regulation are considerably different in the politics of program origin and operation, the interest group environment, agency structure, economic interest, and the values toward which the regulation is directed (Quirk 1981: ch. 6). We will briefly describe the differences, some of which are implicit in the characteristics of social regulation covered in the previous section.

The most obvious difference is in organizational structure. As noted earlier, most of the social regulation agencies are headed by a single administrator, serving at the will of the president and located in the direct hierarchic line of command from the president to the agency head (in the case of the EPA), or through the appropriate cabinet officer. Thus, these agencies do not constitute a headless "fourth branch" of government, and meet one of the calls of the earlier critics of IRCs.

We have come to realize during the past quarter-century that formal organization never completely constrains agency dynamics. Specifically, agencies in the line of command can sometimes have substantial independence from presidential accountability in a de facto way, while some that are formally independent have periods during which they closely follow a presidential line (the FTC in the Reagan years is a good example). We will look more closely at the presidential role vis-a-vis the social regulation agencies in chapter 7; here we will simply state that the formal organizational arrangement, while it does not encourage capture as the IRC form does, is probably the least important reason for the absence of capture in terms of real political dynamics.

In those terms, the different political environment is probably the most important factor. One dimension of this environment is the structure of incentives: social regulation, as noted earlier, consists of programs that have wide social benefits and narrow (immediate) costs. In other words, there are a lot of beneficiaries among the electorate, but a small number of industries bearing the direct costs involved in achieving higher standards of health, safety, and environmental protection. Therefore, there is less ambiguous public support than for programs that are desired, but whose cost the public has to bear in a direct way. Further, the proponents of social regulation have turned out to be not only a temporary coalition reacting to a scandal, and disappearing after symbolic legislation has been achieved. Rather, both greater sophistication developed through time and a more educated populace, plus the resources represented by the public interest groups that have developed in the past generation, mean that there is a continuing pro-regulation presence to an extent that did not exist in the pocketbook regulation areas. For example, public opinion polls continue to show a high and stable level of pro-environmental protection sentiment. Industry lobbying to weaken protective laws when they come up for renewal has run into strong counter-lobbies of the PIGs, the latter trying to strengthen the laws at renewal time as much as the effected industry sometimes wishes to weaken them. The 1984 renewal of the RCRA illustrates the continuing strength of the pro-protection forces.

Other safeguards against capture include the open hearing processes in the administrative implementation stage, provisions for citizen lobby suits, and (as noted above) the specificity of mandates and deadlines in social legislation, which gives administrators leverage with which to withstand weakening pressures.

A fundamental element of the difference in political environment, however, is the greater moral authority of the claim for improved personal protection of one's safety in the workplace and one's health, whether at work or in daily living, as compared with the claim to be protected against financial predators in the marketplace. Perhaps more than any other single factor, this explains why social regulation can never be totally reduced to the economic calculus of cost-benefit comparisons.

In a more business-oriented way, a separate protection of social regulation is that we have built up substantial vested business interests in maintaining major elements of social regulation. The pollution control equipment industry is not a small one. One estimate is that 170,000 jobs existed in 1985 as a result of environmental protection requirements. There are professional associations of industrial hygienists, air pollution control officers, and so forth. There are corporate safety officials. And there are competitive gains for some firms that feel they can afford regulatory compliance better than others, who may thereby be disadvantaged in the marketplace, as well as economic competition among regions of the country that is reflected in congressional politics. For all of these reasons, then, we are not likely to see industry capture of social regulation agencies in any significant degree in the forseeable future.

One final question about capture: since the pro-regulation groups have so often been successful in using legislative lobbying and court suits to obtain stringent protective standards, is it fair to suggest that these agencies have suffered what one might call "reverse capture"? The answer has two parts. First, success in the shaping of regulatory legislation has never been taken as evidence of capture, the term having been reserved for what happens between contending groups and the administering agency in the implementation stages. Second, it depends on how broadly one uses the term.

If capture, which orginally meant dominance by those regulated, were extended to include all situations in which a major concerned group so dominates the political environment of an agency as to (implicitly) set the agenda and supply the informal decisional norms, then one might say that clean air and clean water advocacy groups have partially "captured" the EPA's rule-making during some periods of time—and the same could be said about the OSHA and the NHTSA. However, such dominance was probably never as complete as that of network broadcasters with the FCC or the major trunk airlines with the CAB a generation ago. The reason is that in the latter instance the industry groups did not face any substantial organized opposition, while the PIGs continue to face very substantial industry opposition in the newer social programs.

Another answer to the question is that if one defines capture (as did the earlier literature) as the frustration of presumed legislative intent to serve broader interests than those of the regulated industries, then advocacy in the direction of persuading an agency to maximize the values of its organic statute would be more of an amicus curiae situation than one of capture.

WHY THE ADVERSARIAL RELATIONSHIP?

Another notable difference between social and economic regulation is the level of adversarial tension, which has been far greater between government and business in the health, safety, environmental, and personal rights areas than it was in the price and entry regulation areas. Indeed, the extent of regulator-regulatee animosity has been so great as to lead some scholars to write books comparing the assertedly adversarial approach of regulation in the United States, with the allegedly more cooperative regulatory relationship in various European nations (e.g., Kelman 1981; Vogel 1986). While the breadth of such characteristics in each country has not been fully ascertained across program areas, it seems safe to say that the relationship between regulators and regulated industries is more adversarial in the United States. Note, however, that this quality is almost always described with reference to the social regulation agencies of the most recent period, and rarely to the traditional business regulation areas. Presumably, this difference would help to explain why one does not find traditional capture in the newer agencies: capture implies a coziness that would clearly be incompatible with a strongly adversarial atmosphere.

Among the most basic reasons suggested for a better working relationship between government and the business community in Europe, is the fact that "a powerful and relatively independent state bureaucracy" existed in such countries as Great Britain and Sweden long before industrial capitalism and big business developed (Vogel 1981;1983). Thus, as industrialism developed, business firms faced governments that were already strong, and the basic political environment was one in which state authority was respected and expected. In the United States, big enterprise came before strong government, leading to the plausible hypothesis that the late rise of positive government encountered established industrial social power, and a climate in which the laissez faire ideology had taken stronger root than anywhere else in the world.

Whatever the validity of such interesting but hard-to-prove-with-finality propositions, they do not answer the question, "Why has social regulation in the past twenty years been so much more adversarial a process than traditional business regulation had been in the Progressive and New Deal periods?"

The high decibel level of complaint about social regulation that seems to have peaked in the 1980–83 period, surely derived in part from the fact that risk management and social values regulation affected a much broader segment of American business than did the earlier, industry specific programs. If the FTC filed a cease and desist order against a shaving cream advertisement, firms not in that business probably paid little attention to the action. Rigorous rate setting by public utility commissions did not raise the ire of the great bulk of industry that was free of price controls. However, hundreds of thousands of firms, including many small businesses that often find it more difficult than larger firms to accommodate to federal paperwork, felt the effects of clean air and water, and workplace safety, rules. Many more will be affected by hazardous wastes disposal requirements, because the 1984 RCRA amendments sharply reduced the amount of hazardous waste generation that brings a company into the regulatory system.

Not only have many more firms been affected by the new regulations but more importantly, many of the new programs require substantial out-of-pocket costs, and require taking a number of active steps (e.g., to design, install, and operate, with the EPA's approval and inspections, a filtration system for air pollution emmissions from a factory). Business regulation in the 1930s was much simpler, consisting primarily of forbidding the raising of a price, or refusing a particular airline route, although there were some positive action requirements, such as developing disclosure statements when issuing new securities.

While we can measure rather easily the governmental costs of running regulatory programs, we have at best wildly disparate estimates of the private costs incurred by firms in the process of compliance—in terms of equipment, personnel, or negotiating time on the part of executives. Federal agencies naturally produce low estimates of compliance costs when justifying regulatory programs. Equally, business firms report extraordinarily high estimates when trying to persuade the government that a particular regulatory initiative is not economically feasible in terms of industry survival.

Litan and Nordhaus (1983:18–27) provide a careful review of approximately 30 published estimates of the incremental resource costs of regulatory compliance. Their own resulting estimate range (it is not possible to pin it down more closely) was from $13 to $38 billion for pollution control (before hazardous waste became significant), $7 to $17 billion for health and safety (to improve the safety of automobiles), and $14 to $36 billion for economic regulation. The latter has decreased since then because of deregulation initiatives, but the environmental costs are increasing because of additional hazardous waste control programs, and ground water contamination problems for which we are only beginning to face costs. On the other hand, it is also reasonable to expect that there would be some compensating decrease in annual air and water costs as the capital outlays are accomplished, and savings accrue from the normal "learning curve" process. Even these dated, rough ranges are sufficient to show that the new social regulations must account for two-thirds of today's total regulatory costs, a figure that would understandably elicit groans from regulated firms fearing that they will have difficulty passing the compliance costs to consumers in the form of higher prices (although, this is the ultimate result).

Since about 1973, the nation's productivity growth has fallen substantially and by the mid-1980s had become a major concern of government and the business world, because of the relatedness of productivity rates and international competitiveness. Since the rise of social regulation came about at approximately the same period as the decline of productivity growth, it has been seized upon as the villain. However, the energy crisis that produced a ten-fold increase in oil prices, and movement in the economy toward services and away from manufacturing, are clearly larger factors. We are, again, indebted to Litan and Nordhaus for a careful commentary on the evidence, and their conclusion is that regulation has accounted for between 0.3 and 0.4 percentage points of the 2.0 reduction in productivity growth since 1973. This makes regulation a "significant but not dominant contributor to the poorer economic performance in the United States economy in recent years" (Litan and Nordhaus 1983:33). Furthermore, a recent Congressional Budget Office study found equivalent small effects of environmental regulation in Canada, Japan, and West Germany, and concluded that the "magnitudes of those measured losses are small enough and comparable enough to support the view that U.S. economic performance in general has not been reduced relative to other nations because of environmental regulation" (CBO 1985:77).

Not only is the costliness of social regulation a source of business opposition to government initiatives, but also the cost-ignoring quality of the statutory standards in some of the recent legislation period (i.e., provisions that direct the regulators to achieve certain benefit goals regardless of how much the achievement might cost, as compared with other provisions that would limit costs by permitting or requiring that regulators take into account "economic feasibility" or "practicability"). For example, the EPA is required under the Clean

Air legislation to set ambient air quality standards at a level "requisite to protect the public health" with an "adequate margin of safety." The mandate makes no allowance for trading off some degree of public health with some reduction in costs. On the other hand, the banning of pesticides that pose unreasonable risks is to take into account the economic, social, and environmental costs of prohibition. Total elimination of the kinds of risks involved in health and safety regulations is not possible (see chapter 5). Vehement opposition is understandable when a regulated party has analysis showing that, while there is substantial benefit in terms of the proportion of risk eliminated by the expenditure of the first $10 thousand, for example, but only a 1 percent additional margin of safety would be achieved by expending the next $100 thousand. In other words, statutes that actually forbid paying attention to the relationship between the cost of regulations and the benefits obtained, are inevitably a substantial source of business frustration, which emerges in the form of fights with regulators.

Although the adversarial encounters occur between regulated firms and executive agencies, the sources of conflict cited derive from the legislation rather than from the autonomous actions of regulators. One more problem of which this is also true occurred in the original OSHA legislation, which provided for unannounced inspection visits even in the absence of reasonable cause to expect violations (since changed by court action), and a provision (to guard against capture of enforcement) that any violations found on first inspection, no matter how minor, must immediately be cited, even if immediate correction was feasible and promised. The regulatory "bad guys" here were the members of Congress who let their staffs write such predictably provocative provisions out of intense distrust of both business firms and inspectors.

Beyond all the legislated sources of antagonism, the administrative agencies made their own contributions. The OSHA was the leading contributor, and became the favorite whipping boy for chamber of commerce speeches in the 1970s. Its biggest flap derived from what in retrospect seems clearly to have been a mistake of over-eager regulatory speed. The story is this. In order to get a workplace safety program going as expeditiously as possible, Congress directed the new agency to adopt as its own formal regulations voluntary safety standards that had been developed earlier through two trade groups, the American National Standards Institute, and the National Fire Protection Association. The OSHA was to do this within 24 months, allowing time for reviewing the standards, and eliminating those that did not have a meaningful impact on safety. The OSHA opted for speed over discretion, however, and blanketed in the bulk of these industry-developed standards, promulgating them as government orders within the first four months.

When they then began a rather rigid enforcement program—without apparently discriminating between those standards that could have a substantial impact on the safety of a large number of workers and those that might have very little impact on a few—the error of their procedures became evident, as enforcement brought out unrealized characteristics hidden in the thousands of pages of standards. Among the more egregious examples was a prohibition against ice in drinking water, apparently dating from a time when unsanitary ice from ponds might have been used, and a multipage, detailed set of specifications for ladders that had not been written for safety purposes. With all of these factors generating an atmosphere of regulatory backlash—which had already produced revisions of many of the "consensus" regulations while Carter was still in office—the national mood was ripe for President Reagan's regulative reduction thrust.

THE ATTACK ON SOCIAL REGULATION

Adopting a strategy of administrative changes intended to pave the way for more permanent and basic statutory amendments later on (but never reached), the Reagan administration initiated a four-pronged attack in 1981: budget cuts, personnel changes, eased rules, and increased delegation to the states.

In constant dollars, regulatory agency budgets decreased 8 percent, comparing the estimated 1985 budget with the actual 1981 figures, with the bulk of the reduction taking place in 1981–83, and in the social rather than the economic regulation areas—a bit surprising when one considers that only in the latter area was there actual deregulation, including the disappearance of the CAB in 1984. The impact of budget cuts is better seen in staff levels. Figures collected by the Center for the Study of American Business at Washington University showed a significant decline even in the portion of fiscal 1981 that Reagan inherited from Carter (Reagan came into office on January 21, and the fiscal year (FY) 1981 ended on September 30): from 90,495 in FY 1980 to 86,666 in 1981. The low point in the Reagan years came in FY 1983, at 76,918, and by FY 1985 there had been a small increase to 77,507. These cuts were not spread evenly, of course. The Consumer Product Safety Commission (CPSC), one of the administration's major targets, went from 871 personnel in FY 1980 to 557 in FY 1985, and was still falling. The OSHA had a similar pattern from 3,009 in FY 1981 to 2,332 in FY 1985, while the Nuclear

Regulatory Commission (NRC) increased from 3,029 in FY 1981 to 3,353 in 1985. The EPA, which had reached 10,678 employees in FY 1980, hit a low of 9,223 in 1983, but under Ruckelshaus's house cleaning and rebuilding, it was back up to 10,675 by FY 1985. (That brought the agency back to where it had been five years earlier, although its responsibilities had magnified considerably, particularly in the area of hazardous wastes. It takes several years to move a new program from statute to routine field operation, so that the workload implications of the 1980 Superfund for abandoned toxic dumps was actually just being felt by 1985.)

With fewer dollars and fewer people, agencies necessarily regulate less, either in scope or in levels of enforcement. This was clearly the intent of an administration that came into office promising regulatory relief to businessmen, and which did not bother to distinguish clearly between the economic area where increased competition might well substitute for government intervention, and social regulation where the nature of the market made that an inappropriate and ineffective solution.

Who one appoints to regulatory agencies is probably more significant than how many people one hires. One of the undeniable successes of the Reagan administration was to bring into several of the regulatory agencies people who became noted for their strong adherence to an antiregulation free-market approach. Eads and Fix evaluate the Reagan regulatory appointees as "an unusually uniform pro-business and anti-regulation" group, making the point that the administration focused in its early appointments less on improving agency competence and efficiency than on "sending a clear signal to the regulatory bureaucracy" (1984a:140–41). One negative effect of pushing symbolism over technical program knowledge as far as the administration did, was to create political snafus that backfired later, and helped to lay the ground for some successful counter attacks.

We should also note that President Reagan's close attention to compatibility of regulatory agency heads with his own governing philosophy presented the electorate with a clearer case of administrative accountability, and the carrying out of an electoral promise than is often achieved. In other words, Reagan used the appointment process strongly and effectively to create presidential control over the direction of policy in the regulatory agencies, which is exactly what traditional political science critics of the independent commissions have always wanted—although not with the kind of policy results that most of the proponents of a stronger presidential role had been seeking. Thus, governmental procedures can be used in more than one direction (Reagan 1985).

The second line of attack was to ease the rules to which states had to agree when they wanted to run their own programs on delegation from the federal government (see chapter 8). In the surface mining reclamation program, the administration changed the criterion for state programs from a requirement that they be "no less stringent" than federal rules to being "no less effective." That change of a single word made the standard both weaker and more ambiguous, and harder to enforce. The Carter administration had attached many strings to its surface mining delegations; the Reagan administration attached far fewer when it initiated new delegations and removed virtually all of the conditions that had been set by Carter (Eads and Fix 1984b:161). After some backing and filling with the courts, the administration eased the bumper impact standard for automobiles from 5 to 2.5 miles per hour, asserting that this would save automobile manufacturers and consumers some $300 million a year. (Insurance carriers who fought the change claimed that insurance costs to themselves and consumers might increase more than that.)

Along with these rules went eased enforcement. Eads and Fix point to "systematic reductions" in the EPA's enforcement activity, and in the severity of fines levied against violators, and they assert that this situation was "typical of regulatory enforcement in all agencies" during the first Reagan administration (1984:201). The OSHA, too, so reduced its inspections and citations in the early Reagan years that a health and safety specialist from the AFL-CIO charged that the OSHA "succeeded in gutting enforcement," to which Thorne Auchter, first head of the OSHA under Reagan, responded that the OSHA is simply targeting its activities better, and that its job, after all, is "not to issue fines; it's to reduce injury and illness." Another way of reducing the burden of regulatory rules is, of course, to write fewer of them. Toward this end, Reagan greatly enlarged the authority of the Office of Management and Budget (OMB) in overseeing what the agencies did, and in mid-1985 a controversy arose over congressional charges that the OMB had prevented the EPA from regulating asbestos exposures. Since the question of presidential oversight is a major topic in itself, we will not go into that further here but reserve it for chapter 7.

The final element in the Reagan attack on social regulation was to speed the delegation of program operational authority to the states, while simultaneously reducing the amounts of federal aid available to the states for the running program. The administration increased very substantially—although the extent varies among programs—the number of states with partial or full delegation of environmental and other social regulation programs. Since federal policy standards and state implementation to take account of local circumstances may be the best combination for effective social regulation, the accomplishment of more delegation might in itself have been widely applauded. However, it was accompanied by reductions in funds to the states, and in the staffing of the oversight function under which the federal agencies monitor the effectiveness of performance on the part of the states. While the purported objective was simply to move regulation closer to the scene, the predicted result of this combination would be less, rather than more effective, regulation.

Perhaps because intergovernmental relations is not, politically speaking, a particularly popular topic, the Reagan administration's efforts to lessen the national government's role in environmental protection continues to make some advances, despite critics' objection. In 1984, the EPA first issued a formal ground water protection strategy, creating an internal office to provide a programmatic focus for this area, and outlining a partnership arrangement between itself and the states. The EPA's plan calls for the agency to provide technical assistance, while having the states play the primary role in ground water protection. The director of the new ground water protection office has called it "a states' rights issue," asserting that the states "have responsibility because they have the laws that directly protect ground water. Land-use policies and resources are state-controlled" (Piper and Ladd 1985).

There's a close similarity in the EPA's approach to air toxics. From 1970 to 1985, the EPA managed to regulate only six toxic air pollutants out of hundreds of potential pollutants. Many state and local agencies have begun to regulate air toxics on their own. Finally, in 1985, the EPA announced a strategy that calls for ranking the risk from exposure to different substances, and then leaving to the states the regulation of pollutants with severe risks but limited to a specific location, while itself regulating those pollutants that it believes constitute national problems (e.g., acid precipitation). The EPA contends that its strategy is not one of dumping responsibilities onto the states, but of a flexibility that takes advantage of the ability of a state or locality to tailor programs to particular plant conditions. Critics, including prominent congressmen, question both the risk assessment approach that would ignore the pollutants seen as least severe in their consequences, and the good faith of the EPA in following through with effective research, technical assistance, and financial aid to underwrite the states carrying out their part of the effort (Stanfield 1985). Since the new EPA strategy can be put into place without legislation, it has a good chance of accomplishing the shift from federal to state responsibility that it envisages—at least until some new air toxic disaster occurs that provides legislative proponents of a stronger national role with the "handle" needed to make their case.

Perhaps the most positive move taken in terms of delegation to the states is the adoption of what are called "generic rules" for certain amendments of state implementation plans under the Clean Air Act. Specifically, in the area of emissions trading (bubbles, off sets, and so on—see chapter 5), hundreds of formal amendments to state plans were bureaucratically backlogged when President Reagan came into office. By establishing general rules that provide criteria that the states can apply themselves, the EPA is able to reduce very considerably the mutual burden of case-by-case review.

This is only one example of the kinds of reforms that economists have been advocating for years, in an effort to achieve what they define as a more efficient, and less obtrusive system of regulation that focuses on financial incentives rather than on administrative rules. Many economists, whether Republicans or Democrats, saw the 1980 election as creating a "window of opportunity" for pushing a microeconomics theory-based agenda. Unlike the administration's political attack, theirs was not aimed at getting rid of social regulation (which they acknowledged to be necessary because of externalities), but of achieving greater efficiency. Their efforts, apart from minor gains like the generic rules, were largely thrust off the stage, and probably set back for some time, by the backlash against the heavy-handed political attack that failed to distinguish between the economic situations of business and social regulation.

THE COUNTER-ATTACK

The regulatory world, evidence suggests, is today more pluralistic than the images of capture and iron triangles (i.e., mutual support among an agency, related industrial interest groups, and an overseeing congressional subcommittee) would lead one to expect. The citizen interest groups—such as the Sierra Club, the Natural Resources Defense Council, and Ralph Nader's Public Citizen—first were able to use the threat of Reagan attacks as vehicles for increasing their membership and fund raising, and then in turn used these bases for administrative lobbying and the filing of court suits against particular rule changes. Further, they were successful in a number of their court suits, from which the Reagan administration gradually learned that one has to follow the administrative procedures intended to ensure due process as carefully and completely when one is attempting to deregulate, as when one is originally regulating. Journalistic defenses of environmental regulation most especially, but also of health, safety, and social regulation more generally, appeared quickly and often as the Reagan regulatory program unfolded, and by 1984 the counter-attack took book form in such volumes as *Retreat from Safety: Reagan's Attack on America's Health* (Claybrook), *A Season of Spoils: The Reagan Administration's Attack on the Environment* (Lash, Gillman, and Sheridan), and *Dismantling America: The Rush to Deregulate* (Tolchin and Tolchin, 1983). Thoughtful evaluations, partly critical but also supportive of some Reagan efforts, appeared in such volumes as *Relief or Reform? Reagan's Regulatory Dilemma* (Eads and Fix, 1984), and *Environmental Policy in the 1980s: Reagan's New Agenda* (Vig and Kraft, 1984).

While the legislative arena was not much used by the Reagan administration, the counter-attack found strong support in Congress. A classic American government result ensued: stalemate. The Clean Air Act, the Clean Water Act, Superfund, the Safe Drinking Water Act, the FIFRA, RCRA and TOSCA all came up for reauthorization of their organic statutes during the Reagan years, and the administration had initial hopes of both weakening them and reforming their procedures to make them less burdensome. However, a combination of a higher priority for tax, budget, and defense objectives, and the initial ineptness of some Reagan regulatory appointees effectively foreclosed all efforts to achieve the changes sought. The counter-attackers, on the other hand, were not initially able to achieve the kinds of regulatory strengthening that they had in mind. The initial result was that as these acts expired they were not amended, but kept on as they were by the device of continuing resolutions, which permit a program to carry on at a given level pending reauthorization.

By 1984, however, the advocates of social regulation were able to achieve reauthorization of the RCRA (covering treatment and disposal of current hazardous wastes), strengthened by the addition of specific deadlines of the EPA to meet in the course of further developing the RCRA programs. In late 1985, staff agreement was reached between the chemical industry and major environmental groups in major revisions in FIFRA (pesticide regulation), and in 1986 the Safe Drinking Water Act was reauthorized in strengthened form, as mentioned earlier. Mounting national concern over the threat of ground water pollution constitutes an almost certain barrier against weakening environmental laws relating to water.

Health, safety, and environmental regulation are clearly areas of very considerable political volatility, as this review of the Reagan years illustrates. Nothing remains at the top of the public agenda list, whether measured in public opinion polls, in attention on Capitol Hill, or at the White House. However, the experience of the last few years demonstrates clearly that while these areas of regulation may pause and be set back a step, the long-term thrust over two decades has been to institutionalize them as parts of the accepted pattern of life in the United States, beyond effective partisan attack. The real questions for the future, therefore, are not whether to regulate for health, safety, the environmental protection, but how to do so—most effectively, least expensively, and with a minimum of adversarial squabbling.

chapter six

PROCESSES OF REGULATION: WAYS AND MEANS

Identifying a broad target of action and setting a basic policy goal are only the initial steps in any area of government activity. Operational strategies are needed to implement the broad policy goals, giving them concrete definition and deciding what techniques to use (e.g., how much of the carrot, how much of the stick; what mode of enforcement; and what incentives for voluntary compliance).

As the regulatory process moved from its back-burner status in the 1950s and 1960s to the front-burner attention it has received in more recent years, a major question has arisen regarding whether the strategy now in use—pejoratively called "command and control" regulation by its critics—should be replaced by one that relies more on market incentives, and less on government-specified requirements. The proposal to move sharply in this direction is the leading "reform" idea espoused by economists. Because economists have dominated recent discussions of regulatory problems (McCraw 1980), the market incentives proposal receives more attention than any of the other improvement proposals currently on the academic and governmental agendas. A major purpose of this chapter, therefore, is to describe the existing system and its proposed major alternative, and to compare the merits and demerits of both.

Regardless of which basic strategy predominates, there is an overall context of due process that sets the tone of regulatory combat, and there are two major techniques—risk analysis and cost-benefit analysis—that are used for evaluating which products and activities are worth regulating, to what extent, and at what cost. These determinations of the regulatory environment are in important ways prior to the matter of deciding on the regulatory techniques applied to whatever objects and level of regulation have been decided on. We will lead up to the major issue of market incentives versus rule enforcement as a major strategy for pursuit of regulatory objectives,

112

by examining the procedural context and the two major modes of evaluative analysis.

DUE PROCESS: WHO GETS HEARD IN THE REGULATORY PROCESS?

In reaction to the perceived increase in governmental powers through the New Deal agencies, and to a perception by industry's lawyers that client interests are better served by more formalized procedures than the new regulatory commissions had developed, Congress in 1946 passed the Administrative Procedures Act. The goals of this act have been described as ensuring that affected parties have a role in the decision-making; attempting to ensure fairness through such requirements as advanced publication of a proposed regulation in the *Federal Register;* separating those who prosecute a case of regulatory violation from those who make the decision; and providing for judicial review in which the courts can throw out regulatory actions that are not supported by "substantial evidence" (*Regulation* 1982:35, 43–46). As the trend toward more open government developed in the post-war years, the APA was amended by the Freedom of Information Act in 1966, and by the government in the Sunshine Act a decade later. The thrust of both was to open up the operations of government to broader citizen participation. As the act now stands, it creates a regulatory context that combines protection of the individual against arbitrary actions (the due process dimension) with encouragement of public information about and participation in the regulatory process.

Under the APA, agencies may use either of two decision-making procedures: adjudication (a case-by-case, trial-type process), or rule-making (a general statement of policy guiding future actions). The adjudicatory approach had its heyday when most regulation was of the public utility, rate-setting, and permit-allocation types in the economic regulation area. That is, the case-by-case method is used when the question is which applicants are to receive a particular government-distributed privilege, such as a licence to operate a TV station. Because such cases involve primarily the economically competitive rights of individual business firms, it was deemed appropriate (by lawyers writing the legislation) to impose a court-style formal procedure, including the adversarial process of developing the information on which a decision would be based by the presentations of the contending parties. Although economic regulatory agencies might have moved more expeditiously by using rule-making—e.g., to set forth a specific set of criteria for the allocation of an airline route, or for the award of a TV station—they tended to prefer the adjudication method.

Now that the emphasis in regulation has switched to health, safety, and environmental regulation, and to defining the specific meanings of the various civil rights acts, the regulatory function is more legislative-like than judicial: it is filling in the interstices of the necessarily nondetailed laws, rather than deciding who from among a set of competing applicants is to get the brass ring. The rule-making process (West 1985) consists essentially of gathering information on a given problem (e.g., the effects of cotton dust on workers' lungs), analyzing the degree of risk involved, and perhaps the cost of varying ways of reducing the risk. Then a rule may be proposed, constituting a requirement of the protections that factories are to give workers regarding cotton dust. The rule must be published in the *Federal Register*, with all interested parties being invited to submit comments and information by a specified deadline. It is a kind of written hearing process, and there may or may not be a supplementary oral hearing. (That is the general rule; certain agencies are required under what is called "hybrid rule-making" to hold public hearings. For the subtypes of rule-making under the APA, see Heffron 1983:231–51.)

The rules of evidence are looser than the adjudicatory proceedings, and there is not always provision for cross examination of witnesses. When the deadline for comments has passed, and any oral hearing has been held, the agency writes a final rule (perhaps with amendments resulting from the comments), and must explain in its publication why it has or has not acceded to major points made in the comments received. In most cases, affected parties with strong objections to the final rule may petition a federal appeals court for judicial reconsideration. This rule-making procedure is sometimes also called the notice-and-comment procedure, and its model is closer to a congressional hearing than a trial court.

Recall that the rule-making procedure is used more often than the adjudicatory in the social regulation areas. There are two good reasons for this. First, the nature of most problems faced in social regulation is to determine how to minimize or eliminate certain risks to people, and to the environment in which they live. A single regulation—say, one forbidding more than two parts per billion of a certain toxic substance in a water supply—can protect you, me, and everyone else from using that water supply. While enforcement has to reach individual violators of the standards set, the rule itself can be a kind of class action. Since Congress cannot specify in the basic statute every specific environmental rule needed to protect us (although it has tried to go surprisingly far on occasion), a protective statute would be nothing but "an empty declaration of intent" without rule-making (Schmandt 1984:23). Second, rule-making better suits the kind of information needed for making social regulation judgments than does the adversarial style of the courtroom.

The kind of information needed for deciding whether to permit the marketing of a new prescription drug, or to restrict the use of a pesticide because of toxicity, is not well obtained by asking interested business parties to make the case for what they want. Although citizen interest groups are sometimes able to play the equivalent role to a business "competitor," they generally lack the necessary financial and staffing resources. More importantly, the information needed is best developed by objective scientific research, most often of the physical and natural sciences, but sometimes of a social science character. The focus of regulation has shifted, writes Schmandt, "from industry's economic behavior to its use of technology" (1984:25). The new regulation therefore requires what Schmandt calls "regulatory science," the products of which are "summaries and interpretations of available knowledge, variously called science, exposure, health, hazard, or risk assessments" (1984:28). (For more on the APA and the differences between rule-making and adjudication, see Heffron 1983:85–96, 226–289; and Breyer and Stewart 1979:398–420.)

Part of the more democratized context of regulation in the 1980s, as suggested earlier, are the liberalized rules for standing to sue, which have enabled citizen groups to challenge agency decisions in the courts, as an addendum to the role they may play through comment and public hearings in rule-making procedures. Further, there has been some experimentation (now largely dormant) with public funding of citizen intervenor groups, to ensure that the superior financial resources of regulated industries do not dominate the processes of regulatory decision-making. Because this funding is no longer available at the federal level (although it does exist in a few state agencies), the ability of protective groups to supplement the information and viewpoints of regulated industries is almost entirely dependent on foundation grants and the success of membership drives, both highly variable sources of funding.

The final element of the due process context that we need to mention briefly is the role of the federal courts in changing the definitions of what constitutes regulatory due process.

American government is often described as the most lawyer-dominated government in the world. If we add to that the constitutional doctrine of judicial review that makes the Supreme Court final arbiter of the constitutionality of acts of Congress and the president, and the more frequent activity of all federal courts in interpreting statutes, it is no surprise that the context of regulatory rule-making is greatly affected by the doctrines of a given time in the federal courts. Here we use Shapiro's concise and compelling analysis (1982) to summarize the shifting tides among those doctrines in recent decades.

In the 1930s and 1940s, the courts deferred to the supposed technical expertise of administrative agencies, in obeisance to the Progressive doctrine of neutral expertise. Passage of the APA in 1946, with its provisions for rule-making, "wrote into basic law the transfer of law making power from Congress to the Executive Branch," writes Shapiro (1982:20). This, together with the political theory of group pluralism that became the fashion in the 1950s, produced two decades of judicial surrender to law-making in the executive branch. During this time, the public interest was effectively defined as a policy produced by a decision-making process to which all the relevant groups had appropriate access. In the 1960s and 1970s, then, deference to expertise became a less important touchstone of due process than group access. Despite the rather sparse procedural requirements of section 553 of the APA, which called for "notice and comment," the courts wrote into these vague prescriptions a number of specific requirements. They prescribed that the process of "comment" should include opportunity for each group to rebut evidence submitted by other groups, and that the agency's final publication of a rule must include substantive responses to every point made by the groups. Note that the courts still deferred to the agencies in terms of the substance, but enshrined citizen participation as a way of ensuring due process, and the consideration of a maximum range of views on determining the rules. Technocracy was thus democratized.

In the 1970s, suggests Shapiro (1982), a new political theory emerged, one that stressed substantive elements, particularly economic elements. By the early 1980s, the federal courts were demanding that all the significant questions be answered, rather than that all the groups be responded to (cf. Sunstein 1984).

Although this switch appears to limit the role of citizen participation simply as participation, it makes a considerable amount of sense as applied to health, safety, and environmental regulation. As noted earlier, these areas are ones in which the type of information is more technical and scientific than in most of the older economic regulation, and technical information is at least in principle objectively determined. In an FCC award of a television channel, the value of local ownership can be argued by one group against the value of previous experience by another. Group access provides all that is needed. When the regulatory question asks whether there is a specific threshold for carcinogeneity of a particular toxic substance, or the safety of a layer of clay under a landfill for protecting a ground water supply from contamination, then substantive rationality calls for technical data, not only for access. However, it is important to note—as hearings before the NRC, for example, have demonstrated more than once—that experts rarely agree in complex technological matters, and a group with a different value structure may be useful in providing alternative analyses by the use of a different set of technicians (Roe 1984).

What this leads toward, Shapiro speculates, is a return to expertise. One would expect that by the 1990s the courts would again defer to the agency experts, rather than second guessing them in terms of the adequacy in group access, and whether they have asked the right substantive questions in writing their rules.

The movement of the federal judiciary toward substantive rationality complements and undergirds the claims of the newer techniques of formal analysis, to which we turn in the next two sections of this chapter.

RISK ANALYSIS

One of the least controversial propositions to emerge from an exploration of social regulation during the past twenty years, is that the range of jobs to be done is far greater than the legislative fathers of environmental, health, and safety laws could ever have imagined in the late 1960s and early 1970s. Equally certain is the proposition that the choices to be made in establishing priorities among the overwhelming smorgasbord of problems will require much technical analysis to ascertain which problems are the most difficult, and which are the most amenable to treatment. It is also safe to say that the cost will be horrendous.

To attend to these considerations, two analytic approaches are urged upon us by scientists, economists, some courts, and some government officials. As we shall see, however, both approaches are also highly controversial and far from being publicly accepted. The first, risk analysis, is covered in this section, and is followed by a section on cost-benefit analysis.

The 1983 report, *Environmental Quality*, from the President's Council on Environmental Quality starts its section on risk management with this statement:

> Probably the most important and most difficult government role emerging in the 1980s is risk management—that is, deciding if and when and how human exposures to potentially hazardous substances should be regulated. (CEQ 1983:11)

Human exposures to hazardous substances include, of course, food additives, contaminations in the water and air, some pharmaceuticals, and many chemical products. The fields of risk analysis and risk management potentially apply not only to the EPA, but also to the OSHA, FDA, NHTSA, and some less known agencies.

The thorniness of the problems faced by the regulators is suggested by the peculiarities of our existing responses to risks: we are expending the major part of our present effort at risk reduction on environmental pollutants that are estimated to cause 8,000 deaths a year, yet the estimate for cancer deaths from tobacco consumption is 120,000 annually, and here we subsidize more than we regulate. Does the pattern of our responses make sense? By what criteria can one respond to such a question? The purpose of risk analysis, broadly speaking, is to move us as far as possible from ad hoc emotional responses to newly discerned risks toward factual, objective estimates of what we face, and of how one risk compares with another.

As a new area of professional activity (the modern classic of the field was published little more than a decade ago: Lowrance 1976), risk analysis does not even have a consistent terminology. However, basic components of it can be identified and described.

Risk assessment is the most scientific part of risk analysis, consisting of identifying a risk (which can be defined as a possibility of loss or injury), and measuring its extent in terms of frequency of occurrence and severity of the harm (e.g., how many traffic accidents are there per one million vehicles on the road, and how many deaths?). The second stage is risk evaluation, which means deciding what is an acceptable or an unreasonable risk. Lowrance defines "safe" as meaning a situation in which "risks are judged to be acceptable" (1976:8). Note that none of the latter terms is scientific. The acceptability of a risk is inherently a combination of knowledge of the extent of a risk, and value judgment about whether the risk is too great, or whether the benefits involved make the risk worthwhile. The evaluation can be informed by science, but not determined. The third stage is risk management, meaning what action to take: how much do we spend on reducing or eliminating the risk? Do we control it by ordering people not to take the risk, or by using science and engineering to remove the risk? Is our management goal the total elimination of certain kinds of risks (say, carcinogenic dangers), or risk reduction below a certain level? It is immediately apparent that risk management overlaps with evaluation, but it goes further because it is concerned with how we handle the action we decide to take, as well as with determining which risks are unreasonable.

All of this may sound quite straightforward, but that is an illusion. Controversies reported daily reflect the great gulfs that often divide the proponents of strong regulatory risk reduction efforts, from those who argue that certain benefits are worth the risk identified, or that cost is greater than the risk reduction desired. One fact is basic to all thinking about risk analysis: a no-risk society does not exist (Aharoni 1981).

Living with Risks

"Living with risks" is a crucial statement, for failure to accept its implications leads us into contradictions, makes difficult the setting of cost-effective priorities, and generally deflects us from effective pursuit of the risk reductions that are possible. Is that a strong statement? Possibly, but necessarily so, for public opinion poll materials and personal discussions with groups of serious students indicate that wishful thinking about the avoidability of risks plays a large role in our existing approaches to risk regulation.

Some of this is understandable because earlier technology for detecting hazardous substances in air and water, for example, seemed to indicate that one could eliminate many of the hazardous substances. When the best we could do was to locate one part per hundred thousand or one part per million of some unwanted chemical, then we could often sufficiently screen the material to produce a seemingly clear substance. However, instrumentation has so improved that we can now detect one part per billion, and in some instances even one part per quadrillion. [One part per billion equals 1 kernel of corn in a silo of corn 45 feet high and 16 feet in diameter, which seems very small. On the other hand, a part per billion also means 100 million trillion molecules of a carcinogen per liter of water, and a single molecule may be enough to start a cancer (Page 1978:222).] Now, therefore, we often find that there is no such thing as eliminating the unwanted chemical. In other words, we assumed that there was a threshold below which lay total safety. Now we find that the dose-response curve is often linear; that is, that there is no identifiable point at which the amount of a substance (say, carcinogenic or mutagenic) can be declared harmless and risk-free. We can measure the dose-response relationship (i.e., how many deaths per thousand exposures there are in rats that have been fed saccharin), but once we establish that saccharin is a carcinogen, we cannot establish dosage below which it would be true to assert that there is no risk whatsoever. We then enter the more complicated realm of asking how much risk will we accept.

Unfortunately, we have not accepted this basic truth in all of our policy-making. The resulting anomaly is that Congress has passed a law to violate another law that it had passed earlier, in response to public outcry over a threatened ban of saccharin. What happened is this: in 1962, the Delaney Amendment to the Food and Drug Act defined the acceptable risk for food additives as no risk whatsoever, asserting that if an additive "is found, after tests which are appropriate for the evaluation of the safety of food additives, to induce cancer in man or animals," then its use is absolutely prohibited. After public outcry over a proposed saccharin ban, Congress legislated an exception to the Delaney amendment.

Another example of congressional tilting at the risk windmill is the provision of the Clean Water Act that required reaching a no pollution level in navigable streams by 1985. Or take the most outstanding current health hazard concern, Acquired Immune Deficiency Syndrome (AIDS): reacting to the very remote possibility of a child with AIDS giving the disease to other school children, parents in some cities have demanded absolute assurance against risk—although, there can be no such thing. Once we recognize that a no-risk standard cannot be met, we can better focus our attention on the real problems: determining a rationale for defining acceptable and unreasonable levels of risks; analyzing the mixed bag of values that we wish to use in risk assessment and management; and applying these values in such a way as to set some priorities for the application of limited funds and organizational abilities to an almost unlimited series of health, safety, and environmental risks.

A second basic proposition is that the use of risk analysis to organize our thinking in these areas of regulation involves a choice that must be made on a policy basis rather than one of pure science. One of the recent (perhaps continuing) disputes between the EPA and some environmental groups is whether the EPA's toxics strategy should be based on risk assessment, or on an emissions control approach that calls for maximum reduction of pollutants by technological means wherever they are being produced (Stanfield 1985).

Data Problems

Once one adopts risk analysis—as both statutes and court decisions (Conservation Foundation 1984:300–301) now require of the social regulation agencies—the fundamental difficulty at the stage of assessment is the inadequacy of the empirical data on which the estimates of frequency and severity are to be based. Elizabeth L. Anderson, director of the EPA Office of Health and Environmental, said that performing such assessments "is almost like a circumstantial murder trial"; and another EPA official said that it might not be a bad analogy to accuse the agency of "drawing numbers out of thin air" (Peterson 1985:63).

To appreciate the problems, consider the case of a hypothetical chemical tested on rats and mice. Suppose the male mice developed tumors at a much higher rate than the females, and the rats did not develop them at all. Is a rat a better or worse analogy for human response than a mouse? Next, since human exposure rarely comes close to the very high doses used in animal testing, the mathematical models developed by the EPA must make some estimate of presumed actual human exposure; but firm numbers rarely exist. If, for example, the chemical being tested is one used as a pesticide on apples, what data can one use to determine the residue on each apple, or to estimate the number of apples the average person will eat in one year? What difference can it make whether the apple is eaten directly, in the form of juice, or in a pie?

Peterson suggests that the estimates resulting from such calculations amount to nothing more than "mathematics masquerading as science," the danger being that a very squishy figure, simply because it is a number, is likely to be seized upon as expressing an unreal certainty. And some policy makers, suggests a division director of the NRC, are subject to "terminal bottom line illness" (Kraft 1982:667), meaning that all they want is the final number, as subject to misunderstanding as that is likely to be if one is not sophisticated about how it was produced. Given these problems, why are the regulatory agencies placing an ever stronger emphasis on risk assessment?

> Like most human endeavors, risk assessment is as much art or philosophy as science. However, an explicit and quantitative assessment lets society see and weigh the limitations of the technique. An intuitive assessment of risk, based only on the instincts of the scientists, engineer, or decision maker, is likely to have more problems and limitations, and the problems and limitations would be less visible. (Conservation Foundation 1984:291)

Operational Values and Guidelines

If, then, we are to get the most out of the risk analysis approach as a tool to aid decision-making, rather than as a mindless substitute for human judgment, two further dimensions need to be specified. One is the value assumptions or conditions that we, the electorate, use to express our initial reactions and preferences when faced with risk-policy questions—recognizing, however, that information and public discussion may lead to revised judgments in place of initial gut reactions. Secondly, decision rules are needed. By this I mean something akin to what physicians and scientists call "protocols": standard procedures or value positions to be used as principles in making individual choices. Decision rules, or frameworks (Lave 1981), sometimes do and sometimes do not attempt to relate risks to the further factor of the costs of achieving a specified risk reduction. That type of framework we will consider in the following section, on cost-benefit analysis.

In the category of public values on which some apparent consensus seems to exist, public opinion shows a clear preference for the total elimination of risk, as suggested by the AIDS experience. Where that is not attainable, presumably the public preference is to follow a "worst case" approach: given a range of possible levels of risk, regulators should assume the worst and control the risk accordingly. One reported research study found that public rating of risks showed particular concern for those risks that were new, unknown, involuntary, and delayed in their effects, and for those "associated with events whose consequences are seen as certain to be fatal, often for large numbers of people" (Conservation Foundation 1984:274; see also Lowrance 1976:87–94; and Slovic et al. 1985). These findings help to explain, for instance, why there is more concern about nuclear power (where the risk may be remote, but the harm would be certainly fatal for very large numbers of people), and for pesticide residues in ground water (exposure being involuntary) than with dangers from driving a car or smoking cigarettes, these being known and in considerable part voluntary exposures. Even when the cost dimension is brought to people's attention, the verbal response (admittedly not likely to be the same in actual behavior if a tax increase became necessary) is to insist on a very high level of protection, at least with regard to unspecified environmental hazards.

In a study focusing on living with high-risk technologies, Perrow suggests as a decision rule that we be particularly cautious regarding the risks of nuclear power because its production process involves both what he calls a "tightly coupled" situation (i.e., if one part goes wrong, the rest follows quickly) and great complexity, which may lead to unexpected interactions (Perrow 1984). Protocols might include one in some use within the medical profession, which can set the exposure level to a known hazardous substance at 1 percent of the lowest level known to produce harmful effects. A similar protocol sometimes suggested defines an "acceptable risk" for cancer as not more than one cancer per million population annually from a given substance.

This is not the place to argue for a particular set of decision rules or public values. However, both the enormous complexity and some of the ways of dealing with that complexity should now be understood. Our society has reached a difficult point. Having eaten of the fruit of science and technology, we must now live with the goods and bads that result. While we want maximum safety, in the abstract, we also know that we are not going to cut the speed limit on our highways to twenty-five miles per hour, let alone to the zero level required to eliminate all moving vehicle deaths. Wrenching as it is to our dreams of a wholly positive world, we will have to accept some risks. The policy choice is how much, of which ones, on what criteria.

> Life's choices, after all, often come in bundles of goods and bads, which have to be taken whole. There is no sense in acting as if one can pick the eyes out of the potato of life, making entirely discrete choices, when it comes all tied up, and the bad with the good inextricably mixed. (Douglas and Wildvasky 1982:18)

COST-BENEFIT ANALYSIS

In the study of political science and the practice of public administration, a variety of techniques for assessing proposed solutions to public problems has been developed under the general heading of policy analysis. The Program-Planning-Budgeting System, MBO (Management by Objectives), and PERT (Program Evaluation Review Technique) are examples of analytic techniques— usually using quantitative data—for choosing among (and devising) options toward a given goal. Among the forms of policy analysis, most of which tend to emphasize concepts derived from microeconomic theory, perhaps the most prominent in recent years is cost-benefit analysis (CBA) (Smith 1984:43–85). This approach requires one to compare the relative efficiencies of different options in terms of dollar costs and benefits; according to its proponents, it can also be used in deciding whether or not to take any action toward the given goal. The decision rule is that benefit is to exceed cost if action is to be worthwhile.

The author of a leading text on CBA characterizes it as ultimately nothing more than a "logical attempt to weigh the pros and cons of a decision . . . a framework for organizing thoughts" (Gramlich

1981:3). If that's all it is, why is it a highly controversial and much criticized approach to regulatory proposal evaluations? Surely, one would reject a proposal with costs that were clearly greater than its benefits. Put that way, it's hard to argue with the concept, and certainly in some applications its use is entirely positive. But not always—as a few examples will begin to indicate.

Because CBA, to be applied in the strict sense, requires measurement of both the cost side and the benefits side in dollar terms, its most uncomplicated applications are in the private sector. Suppose the inventor-manufacturer of a better mouse trap finds that demand is outrunning the supply that his single plant can produce. He then asks his staff to prepare an analysis showing the costs of a second plant in another region of the country, and the benefit (i.e., dollar sales). Dollar valuation is appropriate and feasible on both sides of the equation, and there is a single, clear objective. However, note that even in a case of this kind, one could include as a "cost" the additional managerial effort and psychic strain imposed on the owner-manager who now has to supervise a distant plant, and worry about whether the resident manager is doing a proper job. That is not so easy to put a dollar value on.

If we move to the public sector, the difficulties are immediately compounded. Suppose now that the OSHA is considering a regulation to safeguard a set of factory workers from possible hearing impairment from some very loud machinery that they work with 8 hours a day. First, a risk assessment analysis is done—this will most often be the prelude to CBA, and forms the logical connecting link between the two approaches—perhaps in the form of how many cases of deafness, of what degree of severity, would occur per 100 workers per year, for example. With that assessment in hand, the OSHA must now do CBA on alternative ways of reducing the risk. One way would be the provision by management of ear plugs, ear muffs, or similar protective gear to be worn by the individual worker. The other, obviously much more costly, is an engineering approach that calls for redesigning the machinery and equipping it with adequate noise insulation to reduce the risk to an acceptable level. (This choice has been one of the major areas of contention in a number of discussions of the OSHA.)

Now let's look at some complexities of this example. First, the costs of ear plugs versus redesigned machinery are presumably accurately ascertainable. The benefits to the workers, much less so. What dollar value do we place on hearing impairment—at the 50 percent level? At the total deafness level? Do we take into account simply the cost to a worker, whose hearing impairment prevents him or her from promotion to a better position? Secondly, in comparing the personal protection with the engineering approach to the problem, how is the analysis to take into account the problem of compliance with the ear plug approach, versus the automatic protection of less noisy machinery? Or the distributional question: who should bear the burden of protection, the manufacturer whose machinery is noisy, or the worker whose ears are to be protected?

Cost-benefit analysis is the most formal and quantitative of the commonly discussed decision rules for policy evaluation. (For scholarly explication of the CBA technique, see Mishan 1976; and Gramlich 1981.) Where its fairly stiff data requirements can be met, it is an extremely useful tool for policy makers. However, these requirements are not often met, as suggested by Rourke's comment, "the numerical values assigned to both costs and benefits are more often the product of imagination than of mathematical skill" (Rourke 1984:176). Lave, in an excellent study of decision frameworks, even though generally arguing for greater use of quantitative analytic approaches, cites many "controversial aspects" to the application of CBA, "including putting an explicit value" on prolonging a life, modifying other benefits, deciding the rate at which effects on the future are discounted to make them equivalent to current effects, and redistributing income (Lave 1981:24).

As in the case of risk analysis, we should assess very positively the advantages of measuring with precision (i.e., reducing to numbers) all the factors of a situation amenable to that treatment. Objectivity is enhanced when facts take the place of both guesses and biases. The greater the proportion of aspects of a situation that can be objectively quantified, the smaller the number of dimensions that the decision maker must handle on the basis of experience-derived judgment or seat-of-the-pants estimates. Having acknowledged that much, let us now go on to note in greater detail some of the major criticisms and problems of cost-benefit analysis as used in health and safety regulation areas.

Problems and Criticisms

Problems of measurement loom largest in discussion of CBA. Particularly on the benefit side, many values to be protected consist of what economists call "nonmarketed goods," which means things that we don't normally trade for in dollars. How many dollars worth of pleasure do you get from seeing a beautiful sunset? How many dollars worth of benefit are there when regulation protects a worker from losing an arm in unguarded machinery, or a carcinogenic substance is removed from the environment, saving three lives per hundred thousand population annually?

The most emotional objections to CBA applications in the regulatory arena occur over life evaluation problems (for extensive discussion of the policy dilemmas, see Rhoads 1980). Since there is no "market" for lives, economists seek substitute measures.

One is to add up the foregone income derived from a worker's expected earnings in a given kind of employment, subtracting the years lost between the time of death and that of normal retirement. This is falling into disfavor as some of the obvious inequities have been pointed out: greater value is placed on the life of a younger person than an older one, on a white-collar than a blue-collar worker, and on the lives of men over women, to the extent that a sex differential still exists in average salary levels. The second, more commonly used, approach is to examine wage levels as related to risk levels in various occupations. While there are some clear cases (deep sea divers, skyscraper window washers, and test pilots), this is not very precise in many instances. Further, some people are more attracted to risks than others, and some may accept risky employment because it is the only thing available, rather than out of a personal calculation comparing wage and risk for a particular job. Would we want the general value of life to be fixed by either of those circumstances? Presumably not.

The difficulties of dollar-valuing lives are illustrated by anomalies among government programs. The OSHA has used a figure of $3.5 million dollars per life, while the FAA uses $650,000 dollars. A couple of years ago, the OSHA was in a dispute with the Office of Management and Budget, which wanted to use a figure of $1,000,000 dollars for the life of a construction worker, against the OSHA's $3.5 million. In the spring of 1985, EPA officials and members of a House subcommittee listening to them questioned the morality of a purported OMB instruction to dollar-value lives when considering how to regulate asbestos, and to do so by discounting that value by 10 percent a year. While discounting is a normal procedure in economic analyses designed to compare present with future values on something that takes place over a period of time, a 10 percent discount of human life in the case of carcinogenics would, of course, mean that the life value would approach zero long before cancer would appear. Strangely, some economists nevertheless explicitly endorse this approach (Seligman 1986).

There are other measurement problems, too, particularly those of how to handle intangibles and second- and third-order effects of acting or nonacting. For example, an analysis of cotton dust disease done by White House economists was said to ignore the costs of inaction: "increased illness, lower productivity, and increased medical expenses over the long term" (Tolchin 1984:214). In the area of automobile safety, where there has been a battle of competing cost-benefit analyses concerning the value of seat belts and air bags, a 1983 NHTSA study of the effects of auto crashes on American families found that "financial costs paled in comparison to victims' continuing pain, disability, and psychological stress, other family members' emotional strain and added burden of care. . . . the quality of life deteriorated markedly for at least a year, and in some [families], accident-related problems have persisted for much longer periods and may affect succeeding generations" (quoted in Claybrook 1984:179). Cost-benefit analysis, as generally practiced, often seems to ignore nonmonetary costs and benefits. It is exactly because such factors constitute nonmarket priced goods and bads that government has to intervene in the first place. Finally, with regard to measurement problems, it is worth noting that the disciplinary focus of economics has overwhelmingly been applied to the elaboration of costs with little measurement of benefits. Notable exceptions are Ashford and Hill (1980), and Kneese's short study (1984).

A second kind of problem with CBA is that government programs generally involve a multiplicity of values to be served, while CBA lends itself best to application in a single-value context. Environmental regulation, for example, can very often be pictured as environmental protection versus economic development (and it is often in the interest of the potential regulatee to so pose the issue). Even with the best information in the world (and there are many incentives for industry not to supply accurate information in these matters), at some point there simply are value choices to be made between how much development and how much protection, as illustrated by the case of protection for an endangered species of fish, the snaildarter, delaying the Tellico Dam in Tennessee a few years ago (Gramlich 1981:146–48).

Broadening the criticism of CBA from a values perspective, Kelman has written a provocative ethical critique in which he argues with illustrative materials that in some areas of safety and health regulation, certain decisions may be right even though the perceivable benefits do not outweigh the provable costs. He suggests reasons why we should oppose efforts to put dollar values on nonmarketed factors, one being that placing prices on nonmarket things is to reduce those things' perceived value. More positively, the argument is that refusing to dollar value something is a way of announcing that it is not for sale . . . it signals a thing's distinctive value to others and helps us persuade them to value the thing more highly than they otherwise might. It also expresses our resolution to safeguard that distinctive value. (Kelman 1981d:38–39)

The Mix of Mandates

From an explicitly political viewpoint, there are two additional criticisms to be made of CBA. First, it is useless on distributional questions, which are often at the heart of the politics of policy-making. CBA shows us the aggregate benefits, but not their distribution among income groups. On whom the burden will fall is often as important as how great the burden is. Secondly, anyone with a sense of the politics of organizational incentives will be somewhat suspicious of a mode of analysis as susceptible to manipulation of the data to be cranked through the formula as is CBA. In fact, one study of a substantial number of analyses found that the best single factor for predicting whether an analysis would show a favorable ratio for action was the identification of the wishes of the sponsoring organizational unit. Given the extent to which economics, particularly in its public choice manifestation, stresses self-interest motivations for organizations as well as for individuals, one might expect its practitioners to be more sensitive to how such incentives might skew the workings of the CBA.

Given the putative advantages of cost-benefit analysis and its practical problems, it is not surprising to find that in writing health, safety, and environmental protection statutes Congress evidences mixed reactions to the concept. While the national legislature rarely uses the term cost-benefit analysis as such, it does in some statutes require that the regulators balance the intended benefits against "economic practicability" (as with fuel economy standards), or "taking into consideration the cost of achieving such emission reduction" (as in the new source emission standards under the Clean Air Act). Sometimes such balancing is required by a court action when the legislation is not itself entirely clear, as in the case of the Consumer Product Safety Commission (CPSC), which is required by court decision to balance the likelihood and severity of injuries against the cost of risk reduction (Viscusi 1984:37). At the other end of the spectrum, Congress sometimes writes into its regulatory laws decision frameworks that forbid the balancing of costs and benefits, such as with the setting of primary ambient air qualities, or the attainment of fishable and swimable status for navigable waters, the first of which is to be done "to protect the public health" while allowing "an adequate margin of safety," and the second wherever "attainable." In yet a third category fall statutes that permit balancing of cost and benefits while not specifically requiring them, such as the OSHA standard on toxic substances—employees will not suffer "material impairment of health or functional capacity" to the extent feasible, feasibility being defined partly in economic cost terms. (For additional examples in each category, see Litan and Nordhaus 1983:192–94.)

There is indeed great inconsistency regarding the role that cost considerations are to play vis-a-vis the extent of the pursuit of regulatory benefits. The reason is clear enough: we did not pass a single set of regulatory principles before enacting the various protective laws. Rather, each is the result of its own legislative process, meaning in part its own vector sum of forces playing on the legislative volleyball. After two decades of experience with these statutes, there is something to be said for attempting a legislative formula that would provide a more unified set of guiding principles—something that would be equally desirable in the case of risk analysis provisions.

We should note here that congressional prescriptions requiring an agency to consider costs when proposing regulations are mostly written in terms of economic feasibility, which is a far looser standard than one that would specifically require a positive ratio of benefits to costs in a formal quantitative analysis of both factors. Economic feasibility does not necessarily mean that the regulation cannot cost a firm a substantial sum to comply with the regulation— although, it would probably be held in a judicial test to forbid an agency from driving firms of average or better efficiency into bankruptcy—but plain congressional politics would stop an agency long before it reached that point, in any case.

Cost-Benefit Analysis and the Reagan Administration

Among the earliest tone-setting actions of the Reagan administration were the creation of a Presidential Task Force on Regulatory Relief, chaired by Vice President George Bush, and the closely related Executive Order 12291 of February 17, 1981, giving strong regulatory review authority to the director of the OMB, and requiring regulatory agencies to undertake and submit to the OMB a cost-benefit analysis on every major proposed rule (major equalled having an annual effect on $100 million or more, or likely to result in significant cost or price changes), and not to undertake any regulatory action "unless the potential benefits to society for the regulation outweigh the potential costs to society." It would seem then, that an analytic approach long endorsed by academic economists and other policy analysts was about to be given a vital position in the regulatory operations of the national government.

In fact, the cost-benefit initiative turned out in practice to be at best a bit of rhetorical symbolism, at worst a false front (although probably not intentionally so) on a rather unsophisticated scatter-shot approach to reducing regulatory cost burdens on business, as perceived by business, with little or no attention at all to the consequences for benefits along the way.

Cost-benefit analysis would constitute regulatory reform to the extent that it was actually used to strengthen the fact-based analyses on which proposed regulations were promulgated. But regulatory relief, the word of the task force title, more accurately describes the intent and the practice of the administration. Cost relief and CBA are not, however, synonymous.

When the Bush task force wound up its work in the summer of 1983, its claims of success were based on money ostensibly saved for consumers and business firms, and not on an improvement in net benefit ratios resulting from hard-nosed CBA. The extent to which the emphasis was on relief rather than analysis is illustrated in FDA actions regarding sodium as a food additive. A high proportion of sodium intake comes from processed foods, and Americans have been advised for several years now that we consume too much sodium from a hypertension perspective. A congressional subcommittee in 1981, considered requiring reductions of sodium in foods, or the labeling of sodium content in foods so that the consumer had the information on which to make a personal choice. The commissioner of the FDA in a 1982 hearing objected to both approaches, asserting that they might "only serve as road blocks to a good faith effort on the part of industry to deal with this problem." This position was advocated despite the FDA-funded study by a private enterprise consulting firm that estimated an extremely high positive benefit ratio, with a sodium labeling program costing the food industry $50 million dollars annually, but producing possible benefits in excess of $1 million a year (Claybrook 1984:34–35).

While such anecdotes are only suggestive, broader evidence that the administration was not really upgrading the serious use of CBA is the fact that research budgets were cut in the regulatory agencies (as elsewhere in the government) at the same time. As Paul Portney of Resources for the Future commented,

> if the Reagan administration wants to see good cost-benefit regulatory studies, then these research budget cuts . . . make it virtually impossi-

ble to do it . . . you will not get the enhanced analysis the administration says it wants if at the same time it slashes the research budget needed to do it. (Mosher, 1981)

Analytical tools are often put to political ends, and the major actual use of CBA in the Reagan administration, on the evidence, has not been as an objective tool to help select the most beneficial among competing regulatory proposals, but as a weapon employed by the OMB in its generalized crusade against social regulation. The major use, therefore, has been as a part of White House oversight of the regulatory agencies (see chapter 7).

Cost-Effectiveness: Better than Cost-Benefit Analysis?

Can some of the policy-making advantages of cost-benefit analysis be preserved in situations where the intangibility or difficulties in measuring the benefits make the full framework unsuitable? Yes, by using an alternative approach known as *cost-effectiveness.* This is a concept that compares two or more options as means for reaching a particular objective in terms of maximizing the amount or the quality, as the case may be, per additional dollars spent. Initiated in the Department of Defense back in the Kennedy administration as a way of getting a handle on the relative merits of expenditures on competing weapons systems, cost-effectiveness analysis "offers a major advantage over benefit-cost analysis in that it does not require an explicit value for the social cost of premature death" (Lave 1981:20).

An example will help. Suppose the goal is saving the maximum number of lives in highway accidents for a given additional expenditure of $100 million a year beyond present funds. The question is: will the most lives be saved by seat belts, air bags, or stronger bumpers? The analysis then determines how many lives could be saved by an additional expenditure of $100 million on each of these techniques. That would be cost-effectiveness analysis. Cost-benefit analysis, on the other hand, would require placing some value on the lives saved, in order to determine whether the ratio of lives saved to additional expenditure was positive or negative for each of the three techniques. Since there is no objective measure of the value of a human life, we would reject that approach and turn to the cost-effectiveness. (Economists would want us to note at this point that the essential comparison is "at the margin"; that is, what the additional dollar spent will accomplish in this area as compared to what it might accomplish in another area, rather than the accomplishments of the average of all expenditures. Since budgeting is normally incremental, it is the marginal difference that counts rather than the totality.)

Because of the life-valuation problem, and the multiplicity of intangibles and nonmarketed goods involved in many social regulation programs, as well as other nonhardware public sector areas, such as the value of wilderness enjoyment or the preservation of the California Condor, cost-effectiveness is not simply a "backup position" in relationship to cost-benefit. Rather, in social regulation and human resources areas of policy-making and program evaluation, cost-effectiveness should be the dominant technique for laying an analysis before the policy makers. It can provide a quantitative basis for comparison of the utility of various dollar expenditures in selected program areas, without as much false precision as CBA; and it is more open to the plurality of values that the political system embraces.

The basic point in all of this is that we do not think as cost-benefit analysts, and we do not let any single set of values, particularly those of efficiency, determine our views on public policy. Does this mean that we are not rational? Not necessarily, as Mendeloff points out:

> Rationality consists in undertaking actions so that more rather than less of the things one values are attained. If a person derives satisfaction from thinking of himself as someone who will not "reduce" human life to economic terms, it may be rational for him to dismiss the costs of life saving as irrelevant. If such views are widely shared among citizens then rational action may require that collective decisions eschew the guidelines that economic analysis provides. (Mendeloff 1979:69–70)

REGULATION BY PUBLIC OR PRIVATE DECISION?

When a problem has been analyzed from the standpoints of risk, cost, and benefits of governmental action, only the preliminaries of regulation have been accomplished. The next question of regulatory strategy is whether to act directly on the regulated entities by telling them what they are to accomplish and how, in terms, say of reducing a specified risk; or to act indirectly by establishing certain market incentives that regulated entities will hopefully respond to in such a way as to achieve the public interest objectives as a byproduct of pursuing their private interests.

In fact, in the United States this choice has almost entirely been made in favor of the first type, which we will call directives or standards regulation. The second type, called the market incentive approach, is the pet regulatory reform espoused by economists in recent years. In the social regulation areas, it is a partial analog to actual deregulation in such business areas as transportation and communications. (As with almost everything else, these are not mutually exclusive types, and certain market-like approaches already operate as modifications within the directives strategy, as we will see in the next section.

(A note on the terminology used in this text: advocates of market incentives often use a derogatory term, "command and control," as their pejorative label for regulation by directives. A rejoinder might be to use the term, "profit-oriented regulation," as a label for the market-incentives approach. To avoid even inadvertent bias through terminology, we will use the phrases directives regulation and market-incentives regulation in the materials that follow.)

The existing (directives) system puts the decision about how much and by what means to reduce a given risk or other social regulation problem in the hands of government officials; therefore, this approach constitutes regulation by public decision. Since economic regulation came first, the classical techniques of regulation (see Redford 1952) were licensing (e.g., an airline to operate); allocation of desired but scarce business resources (e.g., a broadcasting channel, an airline route between Los Angeles and New York, or a taxi franchise); rate-setting (interstate rail traffic); trade practice negotiations (an FTC device to achieve "fair" competition); and imposition of sanctions in case of violation of directives. In the social regulation areas, other regulatory techniques are dominant, especially the setting of standards (e.g., ambient air quality, or water pollution discharge limits), combined with follow-up inspections, requiring that specific technologies are installed (e.g., as factory safety devices, or for emission control on a coal-burning power plant); and negotiation over the extensiveness, severity, and cost of all kinds of controls.

In the market-incentives reform proposals, the government's role is to set certain fees, taxes, or prices for rights to engage in certain behavior (i.e., it creates a market structure), and then hopes that regulated entities will respond to these incentives by finding it more economical to reduce targeted risk than to pay taxes, fees, or buy a right to produce more of the given risk. The point-of-action decisions are, therefore, made by the regulated entities, so we call that regulation by private decision.

With an understanding of these preliminary topics, we will now describe each major strategy and then compare their respective advantages and disadvantages as modes of public policy implementation.

Public Decisions for the Public Interest: Directives Regulation

Regulatory directives often consist of setting a specific standard for what protection is to be achieved, or specifying the means to be employed. Examples of several types will best explain regulatory directives.

Under the Clean Air and Clean Water acts several types of standards are used. First are the standards setting the quality of air or water that is to be attained. Water legislation calls for navigable waterways to be fishable and swimable, which are imprecise qualitative standards, requiring further translation into specific maximum levels of pollutants. A primary portion of the Clean Air Act calls for the EPA to establish ambient air standards for seven specified pollutants (e.g., ozone, carbon monoxide, and nitrogen dioxide), and for other "hazardous air pollutants" that the EPA may identify as contributing to death or serious illness. While it is generally the EPA's responsibility to decide the specific levels (expressed, for example, in parts per million limits), sometimes Congress decides what level of protection it requires, as when it specified that automobile emissions of carbon monoxide be reduced by 90 percent of the 1970 level by a fixed date.

Deciding what concentration of pollutants one will allow requires also that one identify the sources of those pollutants, and then impose a second set of standards: emission standards. This often involves extremely difficult problems of data gathering and scientific analysis—usually done today by computer modeling—to determine how much pollutant emission from each of many sources can be permitted, while still attaining the amount of reduction required to achieve the specified ambient air quality.

Quality standards are not just used in environmental protection. We can, for instance, speak of the affirmative action goal of a work force that reflects the ethnic composition of its surrounding population as a quality standard in the civil rights area. Following the analogy further, the "emissions level" target is the guideline established during the Johnson administration, which required a work force to be challenged as prima faciae not meeting its "quality standard" if its percentage of specified ethnic minorities or of women was less than 80 percent of that category's availability in the area's labor pool, in terms of the requisite skills for particular positions.

In addition to quality and emissions standards, health and environmental regulations frequently involve technological requirement standards. Among the controversial ones is the EPA requirement of "scrubbers" (electrostatic filters) on smoke stacks from electric power plants, which the utility managers and other critics say is an excessively costly and inefficient way to reduce emissions, particularly when the use of low-sulfur fuel might accomplish the same emission reduction. Under the Clean Water Act, the EPA is required to impose the "best practicable control technology currently available" at one stage, and the "best available technology economically achievable" at another point in time. These are technology standards at the level of principle, which the EPA must then operationalize by specifying what pieces of equipment will be deemed to meet the applicable technological standard for particular firms. Obviously, this is an extremely complicated and time consuming way to regulate, and involves much negotiation between EPA officials and representatives of affected firms.

In the OSHA's jurisdiction, technological standards have an added dimension of controversy because the technological requirement for plant safety can be imposed either on the machinery or on the workers, although a powerful argument for the former is that "collective measures are more likely to save lives than are methods that require repeated individual decisions" (Keiser 1980:489–90). Consider excessive noise as an example of the problem. The risk of hearing impairment can be reduced or eliminated by engineering controls on the machinery creating the noise, and this is the route always recommended strongly by safety engineers; but it can be very expensive to the firm, particularly when it involves retro-fitting an existing plant. Or, personal protective equipment such as ear plugs, can be mandated at an insignificant cost compared to engineering solutions, as mentioned earlier.

From the viewpoint of regulatory agencies, technological requirements are not only a way of accomplishing a targeted emissions or quality level, they are also perceived as an independent standard in themselves. That is, specified risk-reducing machinery, its performance measured and deemed reliable, can serve as a surrogate for emissions and quality controls. The considerable advantage, from the viewpoint of the agency, is that one does not need to inspect as frequently to be certain that the machinery is working according to standards, as one does if compliance requires specific measurement of an emission level—or, to return to the OSHA example, wondering if the ear plugs are worn on days that inspectors are not at the plant. From the viewpoint of the regulated firm, on the other hand, imposition of the more costly technological standard constitutes a negative externality of the regulatory process: a cost that the agency is willing to impose because it is not drawn from its own budget. [To round out the noise example, the workers' viewpoint should be mentioned: hearing protection worn for a number of hours produces a difficult kind of psychological isolation and may produce headaches or ear infections. Also, there is a moral resentment that the burden of compliance is on the worker rather than on the employer whose machinery is causing the problem (Kelman 1981c:22–3).]

Finally, risk assessment can be used as a form of standard, as well as an analytic tool. For example, the EPA's strategy for toxic air pollutants, announced in 1985, is to rank the risk from exposures to different substances, and then to regulate itself only those that it terms national problems, leaving to the states those where the risk is limited geographically, and ignoring those that they see as posing only a minor risk. This turns assessment into a standard for action. It has been described as in competition with a congressional view that if a compound is shown to be dangerous, then its emissions should be reduced through a technological standard of best available technology for emission reduction. A third position is taken by the Chemical Manufacturers Association, which would like the EPA to use an ambient air quality standard with the readings taken specifically where people live and work (Stanfield 1985).

One more complexity of the standards should be mentioned: the choice of a technological specification for reducing a risk, or the use of a performance standard, which means stating the level of risk reduction to be reached, and leaving it to the regulated entity to find the least costly way that it can comply. The value trade-off is again between a cost factor that argues for the performance standard approach, and the degree of certainty that the risk will be reduced by the mandated amount, which argues for the more predictable approach of specifying the means to be used. (For concern that performance standards may require a level of technical sophistication that is not generally to be expected, see Eads and Fix 1984:228–30.)

Simultaneously one of the most innovative and controversial of directive regulation techniques is known as the "technology forcing" concept. This is a conscious strategy of demanding levels and timetables of risk protection in regulatory legislation that are known not to be feasible at the time of enactment. The Clean Air Act requirement for drastic automobile emission reductions provides a major example. Initially, Detroit noted that the technological obstacles were too great to meet the goal within the time specified. However, when the California Air Resources Board introduced effective smog devices that independent manufacturers were able to offer, and was ready to mandate use of them on cars sold in California, car manufacturers announced that they were able to comply on schedule, with devices they would manufacture.

Applied almost exclusively in the area of environmental pollution control, this technique's deadlines have often been extended. For example, the water quality standards still cannot be met because of inadequate technologies for controlling nonpoint pollution sources, such as run-off from pesticides on farmlands, or hazardous wastes from construction sites, and even from homes. Compliance delays have led to extensive litigation and, some critics charge, have greatly diminished the credibility of EPA programs. Yet Congress, pressed by environmental groups that show continuing political clout, continues to use the technology-forcing strategy, as in the 1984 RCRA amendments that set specific deadlines for the elimination of dumping specific chemicals in landfills. One suspects that some of these new deadlines will be extended as they are approached, for lack of feasible alternatives.

Why does Congress persist in trying to force technology, when the results have been very mixed, at best? As the example of automobile emissions showed, it can be effective and keeps the polluters' "feet to the fire," bringing forth "a faster pace of pollution management and greater innovation and emission control and technologies than might occur without such persistent pressure" (Rosenbaum 1985:9). Clean air and water laws have aptly been termed "aspirational" statutes, but that need not be taken pejoratively. Democracy itself, after all, is an aspirational goal; a standard for which we strive. Since organizational inertia, and the understandable reluctance of business firms to add to their costs (and prices) might inhibit prompt antipollution actions, there is a strong rationale for continuing to force technology. After all, we are proud of our technological ingenuity as a nation, and while technology forcing is a cost to some manufacturers, it is also a potential source of new products, markets, and profits for other firms.

Having looked at some of the major characteristics of the existing systems of standards and directives, it is time to turn to the alternative area of the market incentive reform proposal.

Private Decisions and the Public Interest

In areas of the economy, where there are effective competition and no significant externalities, Adam Smith's famed "invisible hand" enables the individual private pursuit of gain to achieve the public interest. No governmental directives are necessary to insure that food markets exist with a wide range of products in every place that there are enough customers. Wonders of coordination are achieved by the market in the process of making many products available to us. Take this example of the manufacture of a wooden pencil:

To produce it people must cut down trees, and this alone requires saws and trucks and rope, which in turn require the mining of ore, the making of steel and its refinement into saws, axes, motors; the growing of hemp and bringing it through all the stages to heavy and strong rope; the logging camps with their beds and mess halls, not to mention the thousands that have a hand in every cup of coffee the loggers drink. And still to come is the millwork to convert the logs to slats, the graphite from Sri Lanka that much later becomes pencil lead, the brass made from zinc and copper that holds the rubberlike eraser, which is made by reacting Indonesian grape seed oil with sulphur chloride. (Rhoads 1985:64)

The quotation provides a good example of complex coordination accomplished by market incentives and without overhead direction. The perennial problem of governmental overload can be substantially reduced if market incentives work as well as in the social regulation areas. Of course, the reason we have governmental regulation is because the market does not work well enough by itself to protect health, safety, and the environment. Can we purposefully create new kinds of markets for previously untraded goods (and bads) through governmental action, thus enabling us to draw on the market system for regulatory purposes? That is the question to which the discussion of market incentives is directed.

Types of Market Incentives

The overwhelming bulk of writings on regulatory market incentives focuses on environmental pollution applications as alternatives to the existing system of directives in the implementation of the Clean Air and Clean Water objectives. However, the generic concept of market incentives has a considerably broader application. Three examples follow:

1. When commercial air traffic increased in 1984, the Federal Aviation Administration (FAA) faced problems of substantial delays as the deregulated airlines concentrated take-offs and landings to fit traveler demand patterns. Air traffic waiting to land also created an additional safety problem. One way to handle such a problem would be to allocate take-off "slots" through directives regulation. Another was to suspend antitrust laws long enough for the carriers to agree on voluntary changes in peak-hour schedules—a temporary solution. The third, which was considered but not adopted, would have permitted airlines to buy and sell their existing

peak-hour slots. Presumably the higher cost of peak-hour service would be passed on to passenger fares, as a second level of market incentive to balance the airlines' traffic loads.

2. So-called "bottle laws" (returnable beverage container statutes), such as those in effect in New York and Oregon, have created a new market incentive for the recycling of glass and can containers. The scrap value was not enough to prevent people from throwing them away, or to entice others to collect the throw aways and turn them in—which is what the bottle deposit laws accomplish. (This may work best when supported by the directive regulation of an enforced antilitter ordinance.)

3. Workplace safety regulations—an area in which the OSHA's early efforts created particularly strong negative reactions to directives regulation—could be approached through an injury tax, once proposed by the Council of Economic Advisors. (For pros and cons, see Mendeloff 1979:24–31.)

The major market incentive proposals emanating from almost all microeconomist commentators on the regulatory scene, focused on two types of financial incentives oriented specifically to environmental problems: emission fees or taxes (also called effluent discharge fees, when water rather than air pollution is being discussed), and marketable rights (also called tradeable rights or tradeable permits).

Emission Fees

In this system, the governmental role is to impose a tax or fee on the source of pollution, setting such fee at a level that analysis shows will lead polluters to reduce emissions to a level that will attain the ambient air or water quality sought in a governmental standard. The essence is that the individual polluting entities will be led by their own financial calculations to reduce pollutant emissions and/or to sanitize those emissions at a lesser cost for control devices and processes than they would impose by paying a larger fee.

From the viewpoint of its advocates, the benefit of emission fees is that once the government determines the required level of air or water quality, and the appropriate fee, then it gets out of the way, with the exception of monitoring emissions. In the abstract model, bureaucracy is reduced, flexible response to circumstances is enhanced, the regulated firms are free to find the least expensive ways of meeting public objectives, and the air and water are cleaned up more efficiently than through direct regulation.

In the tradeable permits system, on the other hand, the government actually creates a private market in pollution, structuring it so that its private operation will produce the proper pollution controls through the invisible hand of competition. Specifically, as applied to air quality, the government analyzes the air quality level desired; analyzes the total amount of emissions compatible with the desired quality level in a given airshed; and then distributes permits to the polluting entities in the airshed area. Each permit allows a specific amount of pollution emissions—the total summing to the level analyzed as the maximum consistent with achieving the quality objective. Once the permits are distributed, they become a marketable "product" that can be bought and sold. Thus, when a new firm wishes to build a plant in a given area, or when an existing firm seeks expansion, the company is required to buy emission rights from another firm—which could be one that has decided to move out of the area, or that is ready to modernize its own pollution equipment.

From an environmental improvement viewpoint, tradeable permits are preferred over emission fees for a number of reasons (Oates 1985:33–36). The most basic is that the governmental role still includes setting the maximum limit on total emissions in a given area. With the fee system, government hopes that the level at which it has set the fee is enough incentive to achieve the required emissions reduction—a difficult calculation. It is, therefore, not unlikely that an unhappy situation could develop—one in which emitters are paying substantial fees at the same time that the total pollution reduction is not enough to achieve the quality levels sought. In the case of navigable waters, for example, this could mean that a stream becomes not quite fishable and swimable. In other words, the technical outcome becomes a function of uncertain economic decisions. While there are other problems with tradeable permits, they are at least not subject to that fundamental disability.

These are the two major market incentives, with tradeable permits being emphasized for air pollution, and effluent discharges for water problems. For substantial discussion of the philosophy, and many of the specifics of these incentives, see Crandall 1983; Graymer and Thompson 1982; Kneese and Schultze 1975; Schelling 1983; Schultze 1977; and Wenner 1978.

In principle, these market alternatives to directive regulation sound enticing in terms of their advantages in greater bureaucratic simplicity and reliance on market freedom. But remember, "the advantages in principle of anything usually outweigh the advantages in practice of anything else" (Krier 1982:152). Regarding fees or taxes, overhead policing by governmental personnel (i.e., bureaucrats) must still occur, "perhaps more closely and unforgivingly" than indirect regulation (Bardach and Kagan 1982:294). Since the tax would be based on the amount of emissions, accurate and continuous monitoring of emissions presents a substantial problem; it might be just as cumbersome, and not any more effective than enforcement of standards under directives regulation.

In analytic terms, the problems are considerable; in particular the calculation of the exact level of taxation that would reduce pollution to the level defined by a quality standard. To the economic-analytic problem, we must add political problems. In our system, taxes and governmental fees are not administered with great flexibility and are not changed easily. Congress does not often delegate its constitutional power to tax, and few legislators are anxious to vote for tax or fee increases, even if the initial tax level is too low to accomplish the job, or if the growth of industrial activity requires a stronger incentive to keep the pollution level down. When the Clean Air Act amendments of 1970 were being discussed, the use of market incentives was considered, but abandoned for a variety of reasons: the Treasury Department and some congressmen balked at the use of taxes for regulatory rather than revenue purposes; environmentalists did not trust government to set the price for pollution high enough, while industry thought the price might be too high, and that they would be paying taxes plus the cost of pollution-reducing equipment (Marcus 1980:300).

Turning to tradeable permits, there would be a substantial problem of equity in the initial distribution of the rights. For the government to sell the rights (say, by auction) would be considered unfair to existing firms, which would now have to pay for what had been an implicit property right. If the agency gave up the rights to the existing polluters, then they would have a windfall profit when they sold them later to new firms coming into the area. After initial issuance, later changes by issuing additional permits or making them de facto scarcer by not increasing them as new firms came in, could severely affect the property values of permit holders (Bardach and Kagan 1982:295–96). Looking at the problems mentioned and others, Willey, an economist, asserts that implementation of tradeable permits would "create a new regulatory bureaucracy in which a substitution of economists for lawyers and engineers will occur on a broad scale" (Willey 1982:166). Except to new graduate economists, that is hardly the objective of environmental policy.

For emission fees and tradeable permits, there would still have to be a governmental system of punishments for violation—failure to pay the appropriate fees, or emitting more than the permit called for. Given the political strength of industry, it is unlikely that the penalties would ever be legislated at a sufficiently high level to be a certain deterrent against offending action. For example, in 1985, when the California Department of Food and Agriculture found several batches of watermelons contaminated with the illicit pesticide, albicarb, it threatened severe penalties. However, it then found that the criminal penalty was set so low that only civil action provided a possible deterrent to future pesticide misuse.

Perhaps an even greater problem of the emissions fees system is that it leaves the decision of how much pollution to emit to the judgment of the private party. Even if the fee is set at a level that works most of the time, the control machinery can break down, and may not be repaired for some time. It may be more profitable to pay additional emission fees, and continue to produce (Elkins and Cook, 1985). Also, note that in the case of acute toxic chemicals, such as the methyl isocyanate that killed two thousand people in the Bhopal disaster, an emission fee system that accepts payments without correcting the problems could not be permitted.

In addition to the economic and political problems, there are also ethical-philosophical criticisms, which have best been enunciated by Kelman, who expresses three ethical concerns about economic incentives in environmental policy: that use of economic incentives (1) "makes a social statement of indifference toward the motives of polluters," (2) fails to stigmatize polluting behavior, and (3) brings environmental quality "into a system of markets and prices of which it previously has not been a part" (1981d:27–8). If environmental protection is more important than normal market calculations, one may be dubious about applying economic incentives. When the environmental laws were passed, air and water pollution were widely perceived as wrongs rather than as economic costs—and to a considerable degree today. The tradeable permit is seen in this context as a license to pollute, and an emission fee similarly leaves the quality of our environment to the profit-oriented decision of private industry. Further, tradeable permits place a dollar value on the quality of the environment. While the moralistic approach to economic incentives inhibits the least-cost pursuit of our environmental objectives, that may be a price that society is willing to pay—and such willingness is not a matter that can be decided by the criteria of the discipline of economics.

On the basis of these considerations, it is certainly not clear that market incentives would be a net advantage on all criteria over the existing system of directive regulation. On the other hand, the potential advantages do suggest that it can sometimes be worthwhile to utilize quasi-market techniques of regulation.

Financial Incentives Within Directives

Although much of the literature, and our own discussion, have been written as though directives regulation and market incentives were mutually exclusive, there is in fact a substantial overlap. As De Muth has written, "a standard affects incentives and a fee is a command made in order to control, and both require administration and enforcement at some level of government" (1983:267). Specifically, despite the meaningful distinction between economic and social regulation, it is still business regulation in the sense that the direct impact falls on regulated firms, and inevitably affects their economic incentives. Because directives place additional costs on firms, they necessarily affect a firm's decisional calculations. Therefore, we can purposefully structure financial incentives that will operate within the existing pattern of directives, without actually creating a market. A good example is the provision in the 1977 Clean Air Act amendments, modelled on experimentation in the state of Connecticut, which instituted a noncompliance penalty equal to the estimated present value of failing to comply, thereby increasing the financial incentive to comply (Crandall 1983:99).

Other current examples include the tax expenditure subsidies, which provide tax credits to encourage investment in pollution control by industrial firms; industrial development bonds; and rapid amortization. The Superfund has been largely financed by an excise tax on chemical feed stocks. By setting a higher excise tax on acutely toxic and hazardous chemicals, rather than on safe chemicals, an incentive is provided to stimulate more ways of meeting industrial needs with safe chemicals, as Pope has suggested (1985:46). Given the strong public reaction to news of toxic problems, another suggestion of Pope's offers a substantial potential: prominent labeling of product packages containing toxic chemicals. Since such labeling would lead many consumers to choose a product without the toxic label, manufacturers would have a substantial incentive to spend research funds on developing safer chemicals.

On the other hand, some monetary incentive proposals have seen negative results; for example, a waste-end tax, which was in use in 23 states by 1984. A tax of this type, which is imposed at the time that hazardous wastes are sent to a dump, may create an economic incentive to dispose of such waste illegally. The problem may be overcome through the hazardous waste manifest system, which tracks wastes from "cradle to grave," but the paperwork problems of the system may be too great a burden for effective administration.

While environmental groups have often objected to such economic approaches as cost-benefit analysis and the use of market incentives, some are now finding that they can use the approaches to their advantage. The Environmental Defense Fund (EDF), for example, has persuaded the California Public Utilities Commission, and some of the private utilities, to encourage customers to conserve energy—a better route to profits than expensive power plants (Roe 1984). Generalizing this approach, Thomas J. Graff of the EDF is cited by Peirce as stating that the real challenge for environmentalists now is to "change the way that the huge systems that have an impact on the environment (utilities, water systems, agriculture) plan and operate" (1985:1,808). Pope (1985) also argues that we should structure the incentives of industry through regulatory steps that would be taken into account in estimating production costs, market prices, volume of sales, and overall risks.

These are the steps that can be taken within the existing system. They capitalize on the fact that direct regulations have to be taken into account by industrial decision makers in their cost calculations, and thus can be used to affect environmentally-related products and markets indirectly—even though such devices may not satisfy the aesthetic pleasure that economists would derive from movement toward a true environmental pollution market.

The quasi-market approach, one that is in limited use with some success, is that of bubbles, offsets, and banks (something like "baubles, bangles, and beads"!).

The Bubble Concept: A Workable Reform?

One of the more reasonable objections to the existing system of direct regulation, especially regarding air pollution efforts, is that a uniform emissions requirement may impose much greater costs than necessary to achieve a desired pollution level. If, for example, a manufacturing firm or an electric power plant has seven smoke stacks of varying age and technology, it might cost from two to ten times as much to bring one of them to the required level as it does another. If, on the other hand, the firm were allowed to trade a reduction considerably below the required limit on the least costly smoke stack, for permission not to change another—while reaching the target for the plant as a whole—then the firm would save money and the air would be as clean as if each emissions source had been modified to the same level.

This is what the bubble concept is designed to accomplish (Levin 1985; Tietenberg 1985). Operating within the standard framework established by the Clean Air Act, the bubble treats a plant as if it were enclosed by a superdome or bubble, and the regulation applies to the emissions escaping through an imaginary hole at the top of the bubble. By allowing the complying entity to make trades between the least and most cost-efficient sources under the dome, substantial savings can be achieved.

In one instance, at a DuPont plant in New Jersey, an emissions reduction greater than that required for the totality of 119 stacks, vents, and valves was achieved by reducing the emissions of only 7 large stacks by over 99 percent, achieving an overall 90 percent reduction for the plant. This exceeded by 5 percent what the state of New Jersey required, and saved DuPont $12 million in capital and $3 million a year in operating costs (Levin 1985). We can see that a plant-wide permit system of this type offers a considerable incentive for business firm compliance, and for better relations between the firms and state and federal regulators.

The bubble concept has now been extended from a single plant to entire airshed areas, through a system of offset trading. Under regulation promulgated in 1982, and upheld in a 1984 Supreme Court case (*Chevron U.S.A.* v. *Natural Resources Defense Council*), a firm seeking to build a new plant, or a new firm seeking to build a plant, may produce new pollution emissions in that area if it accomplishes a trade that reduces emissions from existing sources enough to compensate for the emissions from the new source. This can be accomplished by an existing firm by closing part of an old plant in order to get the emissions credit for building a new plant. Or, a new firm in the area can buy out an older emission source and close it down.

Obviously, offset trading would benefit a great deal if an institutionalized trading system existed. In the form of emissions "banking," which gives firms a legally protected credit for reductions achieved beyond those required, there are credits that can be used in the future by the firm achieving them, or sold or leased to other firms. For example, in Louisville in 1981, General Electric wanted to install a new plastic-parts line at its appliance plant. However, it could not meet Kentucky's emissions control deadline with the cleaner new plant, and was threatened with having to close the existing line, or spend $1.5 million for an incinerator that would be of no use once the old line was replaced. Offset trading permitted G.E. to lease from International Harvester several hundred tons of emissions at a cost of only $60,000, which placed the earlier reductions in the Louisville emissions bank (Levin 1985).

The bubble concept (offset trading is really a bubble over a larger area) has achieved some notable successes from the viewpoints of both the EPA and the regulated firms, but it is not without problems. When offset trading is just beginning in a given area, it is not difficult to find trading partners, and the "bank" has a good supply of emission credits. Once the easier reductions have been accomplished, however, the supply of available credits decreases. As an area's industry grows, and particularly if it is an area that has not yet attained the desired overall standards, it becomes difficult to find the reductions needed to permit new pollution sources, while still achieving gradual reduction toward attainment, as required by law.

Another problem with offset trading is that it is open to abuse. Firms claim credits for reductions that took place a long time ago, or that do not achieve a particular source reduction needed for health-related reasons. It has been alleged that regulators did not look closely enough at some of the trades made in the early 1980s, although by 1985 the EPA was reported to be scrutinizing trades more carefully. An example of inappropriate trading is one in which National Steel had a furnance spewing out particulates just a few hundred yards from a schoolhouse in Detroit. When a federal court ordered the company to control emissions on the furnance by the end of 1982, the company offered to cash in a clean air credit, which was achieved by paving dirt roads for dust control in another area. The court-imposed deadline passed without action being taken, and the Natural Resources Defense Council (NRDC) filed suit and won a case in which National Steel was required to install the pollution controls, and was fined $2.5 million. No possible trade of a savings from elsewhere could have achieved the reduction of particulates near the school children.

Yet another criticism of offset trading is that the total reduction of emissions can be greater if every smoke stack has to meet the mandated emissions levels, rather than exempting some by achieving a larger reduction elsewhere. While theoretically true, this argument ignores the practical realities of the Clean Air Act in operation. Levin describes the gulf between statutory ideal and actual practice as follows:

> In the ideal world of the statute books, the states have complete inventories of pollution sources. SIP [State Implementation Plans] requirements are based on these inventories; firms' prompt compliance with these requirements will produce clean air by fixed national deadlines; and SIP's contain clear guidelines that citizens' groups can enforce. But in the real world, inventories are grossly inadequate; firms have reason to conceal emission sources or better ways of controlling them, so as to avoid becoming regulatory targets; and a "SIP limit" is only the starting point for lengthy negotiation. Agencies do not know feasible ways to control many emission points; states merely impose requirements on industries thought able to bear the cost—or on future plans whose owners are not present to object. Compliance is routinely

determined through self-certification by regulated businesses, and the air quality effects of genuine compliance are often uncertain. Moreover, a SIP can occupy ten file cabinets that no one has fully reviewed (1985:35).

As a consequence, Levin points out that "where prescriptive controls are costly enough to prompt bubble proposals, the likely alternative to the bubble is years of litigation and pollution as usual" (1981:36).

While regulatory inadequacies, and profit-oriented efforts to avoid compliance justify a "show me" attitude on the part of environmental protection advocates; and while the bubble concept may not in practice reduce pollution as rapidly as the ideal enforcement of the straight standard system can, the quasi-market approach is still worth pursuing vigorously. Otherwise, single-minded pursuit of unattainable perfection is likely to produce less pollution reduction in the aggregate than will a system that attains actual reductions more quickly, more cooperatively, and with less litigation. Because of technical problems—defining appropriate airshed trading areas, and the thinness of offset trading markets in less populous areas—this system cannot substitute for directives regulation. The greatest danger, perhaps, is that it will be oversold because of the enthusiasm of economists for something that approaches their market ideal.

As this is written, the bubble's operational future—no matter how intriguing in concept—remains in doubt. It was reported (Stanfield 1986) that because of problems such as those described above, and the extreme difficulties involved in reaching an accommodation between industrial and environmental demands, the EPA had suspended the issuance of new bubble authorizations. Lee M. Thomas, EPA administrator, faced industry complaints that the bubble did not offer enough flexibility, and internal criticism from the agency's own clean air office that the bubble had "been used only as an escape from compliance."

One other market-like alternative to conventional regulation should be mentioned: the extension of liability law. Where the harm that one person's activities may impose on another is not irreversible, and not of serious consequence to health or safety, we often use liability law rather than regulation. Liability law does not require a bureaucratic structure—it operates through the individual, who claims to have been harmed and sues for damages. Some commentators, in their desire to avoid using government, would extend the liability concept into areas of health and safety. One anecdote will suffice to illustrate how the concept can conceivably be used. In 1981, the FTC faced the question of whether some survival suits intended for ocean accident use should be recalled because it was found they were not waterproof. Instead of a recall order, the FTC decided that the relatives of drowning victims could sue the manufacturer for damages if the suit failed to do the job (Meier 1985:111). (For further discussion of liability's possibilities and limits, see Bardach and Kagan 1982:271–87).

THE ESSENCE OF REGULATION: BARGAINING

"Politics is haggling," Daniel Bell has written, adding "or else it is force" (Bell 1973:365). Our concern here is with the haggling, or bargaining. In a political system often analyzed through the conceptual lens of incrementalism (Wildavsky 1984), and described as a system in which policies are made through "partisan mutual adjustment" (Lindblom 1965), bargaining is an endemic element of government operations. This is true of both directives and market incentives types of regulation; thus bargaining is the common element of how we regulate.

From the view of bureaucratic rigidity that advocates of market incentives often use when describing the system of regulatory standards, one cannot expect much bargaining in the system, since bargaining presumes the flexibility of discretion. However, it is clear that bargaining is crucial to the implementation of directives regulation. It is also likely, as we shall see, that utilization of a price system approach to regulation does not de-personalize and de-governmentalize the regulatory process as much as market incentive proponents expect.

With regard to pollution control, Downing argues that the regulatory agency "is inhibited from being tough on emitters by its political vulnerability and by the cost of enforcement actions through the courts," while "pro-control political forces constrain the agency from being lenient with emitters. Faced with these constraints, the agency finds it advantageous to bargain with the sources" (1983:584). This bargaining extends from the beginning to the end of the administrative process. Before the installation of controls, the pollution source and the agency bargain about the "level and timing of controls, the type of technology to be used, monitoring requirements, and certification test conditions" (Downing 1983:579). In this way, the effective standard is operationally defined as it is applied to the source. Compliance follows, during which one of the typical practices is to grant delays rather freely. When violations are detected, informal contacts between the agency and the polluting entity are used to seek a solution, which may range from ignoring violations (such as equipment breakdowns that can be quickly repaired), to the negotiation of a consent decree for the more serious cases. "Sources are given repeated opportunities to comply without penalty for failure" (1983:581). Downing (see also Downing 1984) writes that studies of England and Germany show that this pattern goes beyond the United States and its particular institutional setting.

Although the OSHA has some unusual statutory barriers to negotiations, such as the requirement of first-offense citations, discussion with field-level personnel suggests that the OSHA inspectorate also exercises discretion through bargaining in an effort to maximize net gains to safety and health in the workplace. Furthermore, in affirmative action, negotiated agreements regarding remedies for discrimination, with compromise somewhere between the initial positions taken by the agency and the charged entity, are almost universally accepted as the operational mode of regulatory implementation. Courts have approved bargains struck between the Office for Civil Rights (OCR) and citizen groups unhappy with some of the agency's priorities. In 1976, the OCR was sued by the Mexican-American Legal Defense Fund, and by the Women's Equity Action League on the basis that it had been giving excessive priority to racial complaints, compared with ethnicity and gender complaints. A federal judge eventually ratified an enforcement priority plan created through extended negotiation between the OCR and the complainant groups.

The term "regulatory negotiation" is used increasingly to refer to alternatives—mediation, negotiation, policy "dialogues"—to confrontational litigation as a way of resolving regulatory disputes, most often in environmental matters. Note, however, that this type of bargaining is unlike agency-violator bargaining, and occurs between private parties, typically environmentalists and business firms.

A decade ago, Wessel pointed out that in environmental and consumer affairs disputes, "the absentee public is an important and often key party in interest," because the impacts of decisions between two parties are felt by others. Thus, "society as a whole, rather than any of the traditional litigants, must be considered the main party in interest" (Wessel 1976:7, 4). An early effort to take cognizance of societal externalities in this way was made by the National Coal Policy Project (NCPP), through which 30 corporate executives and 30 environmental group representatives engaged in an experiment to produce agreements on coal mining issues (Fox 1982:ch. 30). Surprising success was achieved (Murray 1978), although the organizations represented failed to accept much of the consensus. Nevertheless, the NCPP publicized the concept of alternative dispute resolution, and stimulated further efforts (McFarland 1984). An attorney-advocate published an extended essay providing rationale, history, and detailed procedural recommendations (Harter

1982); a policy analysis of negotiated development disputes was recently published (Sullivan 1984); and The Conservation Foundation publishes an occasional newsletter, *Resolve*, focusing on information about environmental dispute resolution approaches and events. In 1986 the Foundation published a book (Bingham) that analyzes 150 instances of alternative dispute resolution efforts, and notes lessons for the future about factors associated with successful mediation (e.g., that the mediator conduct a preliminary dispute assessment; whether the parties have clear incentives to negotiate an agreement; and whether those with authority to act on agreements reached participate directly in the negotiations).

Additional signs of such around-the-table approaches to bargaining among parties who might otherwise pursue narrower, more litigious modes of settling disputes include these developments:

> Formation in 1984 of Clean Sites, Inc., a nonprofit company initiated by leaders from chemical firms and major environmental organizations, to accelerate efforts at private clean up of toxic waste sites.

> A negotiated agreement in 1985 by the National Agricultural Chemical Manufacturers Association, and environmentalists led by the Natural Resources Defense Council on pending revisions in federal pesticide regulations, revisions that would enhance public safety while providing industry with desired patent extension.

> A National Groundwater Policy Forum composed of environmentalists, business leaders, and state government officials, which has worked out a set of recommendations for protection of groundwater from contamination.

In its early years of use, regulatory negotiation has achieved less costly, less time-consuming, and better resolutions in a number of instances.

Turning to market incentive regulation (and again stressing the environmental arena, to which most of the price system advocacy has been addressed), enhanced flexibility in suiting the regulatory impact to the situation of particular emitting sources is second only to economic efficiency in the hierarchy of good things claimed. Does this mean that bargaining would no longer be necessary? That the visible hands of agency representatives and business officials meeting across the table to seal a bargain would no longer be necessary? Again, drawing on Downing (1983), the answer is: probably not.

In the quasi-market situation of emissions offsets, Downing envisions the new firm seeking to build a plant bargaining over the technical parameters that might make its emissions seem lower than they are, in order to save control costs, and to minimize the need to lease and buy emissions credits from existing sources. Conversely, the latter also have an incentive to bargain over technical details to make their proposed controls look more effective, thus increasing the amount of emission offsets that they would be able to sell or lease. If an actual effluent charge were placed on water pollution emissions, bargaining would take place over the level of the charge (unless that was fixed at law, in which case the vaunted flexibility of market incentives would be largely lost), or the technology essential for monitoring whether a firm was emitting more than its permit allowed (Downing 1983:583).

At a macro level of analysis, a significant difference between bargaining under directive or incentives regulation is that the primary bargaining takes place at the legislative level in the latter case, and at the implementation level in the former situation. An air emission fees system has a core problem of setting an effective monetary level for the fee. We can be absolutely certain that whatever economic analysis may be done to propose an objective monetary level for the fee, the political process in the legislature will modify it through bargaining between the representatives of industrial firms and environmental protection citizens groups. While it is possible that Congress would enact a statute with hundreds of specific subcategories with specific monetary values, it is hard to envision it operating at that level of disaggregation.

Under the regulatory standards or directives system, although the law is written in absolutist terms, the need to determine the best available control technology, or the technically appropriate number of parts per billion of a pollutant to permit, is subject to such great technical uncertainties that supposedly specific regulatory standards are actually rather flexible. If the fundamental goal is maximum protection against risk, confronting the polluting sources with a strong, explicit prohibition against polluting has psychological enforcement advantages that may be substantial over confronting them with a psychologically and morally neutral controlled price environment.

While the price system is not concerned with whether the regulated entities gain an advantage, the law presumably is: it has been written to protect the public against health and safety dangers arising from environmental pollution. From this viewpoint, regulatory standards have an advantage over the price system by the way in which they influence the bargaining and negotiation of implementation. Standards set symbolic limits to agency discretion, and thus provide focal points for citizen suits to discourage agencies against bargaining with polluting sources. By defining the "rules of the game," what Yaffee calls prohibitive policy has "a heavy influence on the initial distribution of power in the arena" (1982:153). In the case of the Endangered Species Act, according to Yaffee, the existence of absolutist protection clauses "gave the proponents of preservation an extremely strong position from which to start" (1982:149–53).

From the viewpoint of the values embedded in protective social legislation, there is much to be said for a method of regulation that reminds those managing the regulated entities of the human purposes of the concededly irksome regulations. Kelman puts it well:

> Both "saving health" and "saving money" are values that are widely regarded as positive. Environmentalists and industry representatives know this, and, seeking laws and regulations reflecting different levels of environmental protection as they do, they realize that they want to get people to think about the aspect of environmental regulation that best promotes the choice that they would hope to see people make. What some environmentalists were worried about is that, if environmental policy were set using charges, debates would be over the monetary amount of charge levels, and that this would inevitably make people think more about costs than otherwise. Debates on standards can be phrased—and are phrased by environmentalists—as a question of what is required to protect public health; this presents a face more favorable to environmentalism. (Kelman 1983:326–27)

Schelling makes a reverse argument in favor of pricing systems on the basis that they use fees instead of fines, and "no moral or legal prejudice attaches to the fee" (1983:6–7). The connotations of such a fee system are not as conducive to enlisting the moral sentiments of conscientious businessmen and businesswomen in the cause of minimizing pollution. As suggested in the section above on cost-benefit analysis, public policy may want not only to minimize pollution, but also to label it as a social "bad"; and doing so may help in gaining voluntary compliance.

In summary, this chapter has discussed a variety of dimensions of the existing techniques of regulation, and has given major attention to the much-argued-for alternative of a market incentive system. In fact, the two are not mutually exclusive, and a leading economist has concluded that directive regulation can be as efficient as a pricing system (Schelling 1983:xviii–xiv). Each has or would have some elements of the other. Conceding both that there are situations for which a system of charges seems to have great advantages and few drawbacks (e.g., bottle deposits), and that more use can and should be made of monetary incentives within the regulatory standards system, the concluding judgment is that moral, policy, and practical considerations indicate that we should use the regulatory directives system as our primary technique—it embodies a clear preference for the protections we have legislated. The bubble concept, cautiously applied, seems worth pursuing further as a work-simplifying and money-saving supplementary modification to the standards system, but one that does not raise all of the questions that a more completely market-oriented system does.

Techniques have consequences; and the fundamental point on which to end this chapter is that the choices of how we regulate are not simply matters of neutral efficiency, but embody competing values. Policy analyses of competing proposals for modes of regulation must place great weight on the compatibility of each proposal with the values that are to be served.

chapter seven

REGULATING THE REGULATORS: THE PRESIDENT AND CONGRESS AS OVERSEERS

The regulators, whether in IRCs or executive agencies, are appointed officials, and are not directly subject to the discipline of the polling booth. Some regulators are appointed by the president with Senate confirmation, others are appointed by agency heads outside of civil service competitive examination procedures, and some are civil servants. Therefore, regulatory policy makers and top staff are part of the question of administrative accountability.

All regulatory agencies, not just IRCs, are "creatures" of president and Congress together, through their statutory origins. Constitutionally and politically, both president and Congress have the authority and obligation to watch what and how the agencies regulate. The accountability of administrators, whether in regulatory agencies or elsewhere, is through the elected officials. One major function of the elected layer of government is, therefore, "oversight," which is the customary term denoting the executive and legislative activities aimed at reviewing and controlling the operations of agencies in implementing statutes.

The most basic goal of such oversight, from the viewpoint of democratic theory, is to achieve political accountability. At a less abstract level, another major goal of oversight is improved governance: coordination, efficiency, and effectiveness in the implementation of the laws. Since the mid-1970s, economic efficiency has been an increasingly emphasized criterion in oversight evaluation, particularly from the White House perspective. While congressional oversight (performed almost entirely by particular committees over particular agencies, rather than by the institution as a whole) continues to focus primarily on whether the regulatory agencies are vigorously pursuing congressional intent, presidential concern has increasingly come to reflect government economists' focus on the costs borne by private business as a result of regulatory standards, and the impact that such costs may have on productivity as a macroeconomic goal. The economists (more particularly, members of the Council of Economic Advisers and their staffs) have provided a valuable corrective to the traditional congressional and public administration perspective on costs, which focuses on federal budget dollars used for the people and processes of the regulatory agencies. As we have seen, these costs are a small portion of the federal budget. Much greater are the costs of compliance with federal regulations—costs that fall on the business firms, and other nonfederal entities subject to regulatory requirements. Whether it be "scrubbers" on smoke stacks, or costly equipment to remove hazardous wastes from water effluents, such compliance costs have justifiably been called a major externality of government regulations; that is, a cost that falls outside the usual boundaries of governmental budgetary discussions.

Because of the universal concern over the decline of industrial productivity in the United States in recent years, any contribution made to that loss by regulation should be minimized. Although, as we saw earlier, that contribution is sometimes overstated, the concern is a real one, and has dominated presidential oversight of regulation in recent years, culminating in certain steps taken by President Reagan that have generated controversy in Congress, and on the part of external critics expressing varying perspectives.

In this chapter, we will first review the general levers of oversight available to presidents and Congress, and then the specific institutional developments of the past decade, especially those involving the presidency. We will examine more closely the executive orders issued by President Reagan for the purpose of centralizing White House control over regulatory developments, and briefly evaluate the present oversight situation with suggestions for the future. Presidential oversight will receive more attention than congressional oversight, because it has been most active in recent years (judicial oversight—mentioned in chapter 5—is omitted because our focus is on electoral accountability). Finally, some of the chapter will not apply to IRCs, because of their special structure, and the protections given them from direct presidential accountability (these matters were covered in detail in chapter 3).

BASIC LEVERS OF CONTROL

Although the term oversight applies to both presidential and congressional review of administrative behavior, the points of control, the modes of control, and the purposes differ between the two branches. Although one can speak of a common goal of "holding the bureaucrats accountable," it is often the case at a less abstract level that the goals of legislators are highly particularistic in terms of the constituency profiles of individual congressmen, while White House oversight is more often focused at the macro level of regulation's place in the presidential program. These are tendencies (sometimes exaggerated), not absolutes, as suggested by the broad-gauged perspective on environmental protection taken by Senator Edmund Muskie in the 1970s, and by representative Henry Waxman in the 1980s, as well as by the special attention that the Reagan White House sometimes gave to particular business sectors (e.g., the automobile industry) in shaping its regulatory priorities.

Another major difference between Congress and the presidency: in recent years there have been specific White House units whose primary function is regulatory oversight, while Congress most often delegates this process to the entrepreneurial inclinations of subcommittee chairpersons.

This does not necessarily mean that the White House can easily watch or control the actions of the regulatory and other executive agencies at a given moment. Nathan (1983) has argued vigorously, from the perspective of one who worked within the presidential orbit, that it takes a great deal of effort for any president to get hold of the government; but it is even harder, of course, for the legislators, who are further removed from day-to-day action.

Congress' most fundamental mode of controlling administration is legislation itself. An agency's organic statute (i.e., the law bringing the agency into existence) establishes goals and objectives, and often prescribes a basic strategy of means, plus a budgetary authorization ceiling. If Congress becomes displeased with agency operations, it can return to the legislative process, and pass amendments prescribing or proscribing certain agency activities—as when Congress more than twenty years ago overrode the Federal Trade Commission's (FTC) very stringent proposed cigarette health warnings, and legislated the language that then appeared on cigarette packages and advertising, until twenty years later Congress again intervened to authorize rotating use of four different messages. Michael Pertschuk, chair of the FTC in the late 1970s, zealously battled against advertising of sugared cereals on children's television programs, and began to investigate the insurance industry, along with other activities perceived in Congress as constituting an over-zealous consumer "crusade." Congress responded with the Federal Trade Commission Improvements Act of 1980, which effectively killed the "kid-vid" studies, and limited insurance investigation to work done at the request of the majority of an appropriate congressional committee. It also established a veto system, whereby commission rules can be overturned by the majority of both houses in Congress (Pertschuk 1982).

Legislation can be used for congressional oversight control, and specifically to stop an agency action before it takes effect. However, the legislative calendar is crowded, and the attention that authorizing committees can give to the particularities of regulation is limited (and that of the full Congress more so). The legislative route can be used only when the legislators are hearing high-decibel protests from powerful constituencies.

The second classic tool is that of appropriations. The budget level constitutes a basic control over an agency's ability to implement a statute, but for oversight purposes it is less the funding than the suggestions and directives—given with increasing frequency in reports accompanying appropriations bills—that make the appropriations process "the most potent form of congressional oversight," as it was called in a 1977 Senate study (Senate Study, vol. II 1977:33). Mark S. Fowler, FCC chairperson, discovered oversight in 1984, when the FCC voted to remove limits on the number of TV stations that a single owner could hold. Only a few days elapsed before the Senate passed an amendment to an appropriations bill ordering the action postponed, after which Fowler went up to the Hill to negotiate a compromise. Through this incident and others, Fowler "found he needed more than three votes [out of five members of the FCC] and a philosophy in tune with the President" to gain his strong deregulatory objectives. "What he needed, and often didn't have, was the support of Congress" (Cooper 1985a:732).

A third form of congressional control, one that became increasingly popular in the 1970s and early 1980s until declared unconstitutional by the Supreme Court in 1983, is the legislative veto. It is a device by which specified types of decisions by particular agencies are subject to reversal if so voted by Congress, or sometimes one House of the Congress, through a variety of specific arrangements. Unlike a law, the congressional veto does not require presidential signature. It was an attempt by the Congress to reverse the constitutional veto system, and enable the legislators to counterbalance executive authority more frequently than could be done by passing actual laws requiring presidential approval. Since the Supreme Court struck down the legislative veto in the case of *Immigration and Naturalization Service* v. *Chadha* in June 1973, advocates of the veto have tried to find a judicial-proof substitute—perhaps a provision that if Congress passed a resolution to block a proposed agency rule within 90 days and the President signed the resolution, the rule would be vetoed—but passage seemed unlikely (Cooper 1985b).

Legislation, funding levels, and vetoes can be called forms of "hard" oversight: actual control of what an agency has done, is doing, or might do. It seems that oversight in this sense has been increasing in recent years, perhaps as a function of the ratcheting up of congressional-presidential competition that has developed since the Nixon years. The more traditional form of oversight has been "softer," one might say, comprising "continuous watchfulness" of the execution of the laws through "study, review, and investigations" (as congressional reform statutes and reports have stated), through hearings that are not tied to specific new legislation or to appropriations, and held by substantive legislative committees or by broad-jurisdiction committees on government operations in both Houses. Such hearings may lead to amendatory legislation, but often accomplish their objectives short of legislative action. By the law of anticipated reactions, a regulator who is obligated to explain his or her actions on some particular matter to a skeptical subcommittee, will reconsider whatever may be offending the overseeing legislators. A major political incentive to hold such hearings exists when one or both Houses of Congress are controlled by the party not in the White House. Hearings can be used to embarrass the administration, as well as to pursue the more institutionally acceptable role of insuring that agency operations are in accord with the legislative intent of Congress, or that they are effectively achieving the legislated objectives. The outstanding recent example of congressional hearings that performed all of these functions consists of investigations by no less than six congressional committees in 1982–83 of the running of the EPA by Anne Gorsuch Burford.

As examples used from the FCC and the FTC illustrate, the fact that a regulatory agency is an IRC does not significantly limit interventions by Congress under the guise of oversight. Congress periodically makes clear that it will resent very strongly any presidential intervention into the affairs of IRCs. Yet, it justifies its own interventions on the basis that these bodies are "arms of the Congress"; their rules should be perceived as the equivalent of laws that Congress would have passed if it had the time and knowledge available to the specialized personnel of the regulatory commissions. When congressional interventions are aimed at general policy, that justification may suffice. However, when legislative interventions are made by individual congressmen or senators on behalf of specific constituent groups wanting particular decisions (and when the legislator is not routinely asking for information about the status of a given situation), then the legitimacy of the intervention has to be questioned. A major part of the problem, as has often been noted, is that oversight by Congress often means oversight by a committee, subcommittee, or individual lawmaker—not by the entire legislature or House. Because of such fragmentation, Congress often produces "mixed mandates" (Tolchin and Tolchin 1985:270), directing an agency to do one thing through the full legislative process, and then countermanding that when political pressures build up on a particular subcommittee.

Before moving on to White House oversight, attention should be called to the supplementary staff arms that Congress has developed to strengthen its hand in the oversight function, as well as for other purposes. These are the Congressional Research Service (CRS), Congressional Budget Office (CBO), Office of Technology Assessment (OTA), and General Accounting Office (GAO). While each of these has been used for oversight purposes, the GAO has been the most important. Since the Congressional Budget Act of 1974 specified that the GAO should increase its program evaluation capacity, it has developed an extensive program for reviewing the effectiveness and efficiency of a wide range of executive branch activities, including regulatory activities. Despite its name, the modern GAO does more than audit dollars spent; it audits (i.e., evaluates) program implementation as well (Study on Regulation, vol. II 1977:68–76; Mosher 1984).

BASIS FOR PRESIDENTIAL OVERSIGHT

The constitutional clause calling for the president to faithfully execute the laws plausibly gives each president authority and responsibility for oversight, and for much more. The elected head of the executive branch is ultimately responsible for implementation of line agency activities, and also has important if limited responsibilities for the membership and budget recommendations for IRCs (as discussed in chapter 3). Because of the president's responsibility for directing, as well as for reviewing the implementation of statutes, there is an implicit tendency to emphasize the review of actions already taken when discussing congressional oversight, but control over what is to be done when discussing the presidency. As we shall see, emphasis on current, active control accurately characterizes the development over the last 15 years of institutional innovations usually described under the heading of presidential oversight.

A second noteworthy dimension of presidential oversight is the special claim of a mandate to steer the ship of state in the directions enunciated during a presidential election campaign. Presidents Carter and Reagan both made more consistent use of regulatory agency appointments than had their predecessors in attempting to institutionalize their self-styled mandates.

Quite apart from recent White House staff developments aimed at stronger centralized control of regulation, every president has a number of leverage points available for oversight control. The appointment of department and agency heads, and related top non-civil service personnel is the most basic. The president's authority to determine who will chair the regulatory commissions was extended in the 1950s, and with some apparent effect. Carter took care to appoint protection-oriented persons to head such agencies as the EPA and OSHA, and also in such IRC appointments as Pertschuk at the FTC. President Reagan's thrust toward deregulation, and minimal regulatory intrusion on business was accomplished to a very considerable degree despite little legislative change because of a careful selection of agency appointees whose regulatory philosophies were clearly in agreement with his own.

Presidential authority to take funding requests from all executive branch (and independent commission) agencies, and to combine them (with such revisions as the president wishes to make) into a single executive budget for submission to the Congress, was legislated in 1921 and reinforced by the transfer of the Bureau of the Budget (now OMB) from the Treasury to the Executive Office of the President in 1939. Before concerning themselves with how Congress may treat a budget request, agency heads must first negotiate approval of the funding levels they want from the OMB as the institutionalized representative of the president. So strong is the OMB's clout that few appeals are taken to the president from its judgments, even by cabinet secretaries. In 1986, for example, cabinet officers had less than four days in which to appeal OMB budget cut proposals for fiscal 1987.

Less tangible than appointments or budgets, but hardly less important as a lever of presidential control, is the unique standing of the president in terms of the expectations of the national electorate that puts him or her into office. Using the claim of electoral mandate, and speaking from the "bully pulpit" of the presidency, as Theodore Roosevelt put it, presidents exercise both direct authority of position and the indirect authority of popular support (in varying degrees on various topics) to help persuade agency heads to see their responsibilities in the same way the president does.

It would seem, then, that the president is in a position to use the executive chain of command to insure that the heads of the EPA, OSHA, OSM, NHTSA, and other social regulation agencies (excluding the CPSC, EEOC, and NRC) move in accord with White House requests. In fact, it is not that simple. Just as IRCs sometimes closely follow a presidential lead despite the absence of such an obligation (e.g., the FTC under Miller, III, during 1981–84, or the FCC under

Fowler), line agencies sometimes successfully resist White House desires in regulatory matters despite the fact that agency heads serve the president, and are clearly subordinate.

How can this be? Much of the answer lies in the fact that White House oversight (which is usually what the agencies face), and personal oversight by the president are not the same thing, despite the work-a-day fiction that most often permits the presidency to substitute for the president. Second, Congress often delegates authority directly to an agency. Finally, agency heads have constituencies of their own—those with vested interests, financial or programmatic, in the operations of an agency—and can sometimes draw on these to persuade the White House that political protection of the president and his administration may require that the agency position be upheld.

Recent regulatory history is replete with illustrations of such de facto independence. In an inside story of the EPA's early years, John Quarles (1976:122–42) relates in detail a confrontation between the EPA and the OMB in 1973 over the promulgation of health-based lead-in-gasoline regulations. Representatives of the OMB and the White House Domestic Council (who had no legal authority to act in the matter) pressed for minimal regulations, while Quarles and the EPA thought that the inconclusive evidence regarding health damage from airborne lead was sufficient to justify the regulations. In the end, the EPA made a relatively small concession on the timing for phasing in the regulations, and on that basis won, over the OMB's objections, the right to issue health-based regulations. The lead-in-gasoline saga continued in the Reagan administration. In 1981, the EPA proposed easing the regulations, but had second thoughts after objections from environmentalists and public health officials. It then informed the OMB that it was moving in the other direction: preparing a proposal to tighten the existing standard. The OMB objected, and the dispute was eventually resolved "with EPA the apparent winner" (Eads and Fix 1984:133). In 1985, on the basis of research showing that more than 170,000 cases of lead poisoning could be avoided each year, saving thereby some $600 million in medical and special education costs for afflicted children, the EPA promulgated new rules calling for the elimination of 90 percent of the lead currently in automobile fuel by the end of the year. Potential OMB opposition was presumably muted by a cost-benefit analysis showing that there would also be savings of more than $900 million a year for automobile owners in reduced maintenance and repair expenses through the use of gasoline with lower lead levels.

In March of 1985, the EPA issued regulations to reduce emissions from trucks and buses over OMB opposition. A newspaper editorial reported that then-OMB director David A. Stockman had visited the EPA administrator Lee M. Thomas to express the view that the proposed rules were too tough. After Stockman returned to his office, Thomas issued the order as planned. Said the *Los Angeles Times* (March 13, 1985), the "logical conclusion seems to be that Thomas stared Stockman in the eye and told him there would be no compromising the nation's health and environment."

What these examples add up to is the unstartling fact that the formal governmental chain of command is no more rigid in regulatory agencies than it has been in all other sectors of government. Agency heads and bureau chiefs have their own sources of political power—internal skills and expertise, and external constituency relationships (for the classic statement, see Rourke 1984)—and the strongest of presidents have sometimes had to bend the organizational chart lines. Subordinate-superordinate relationships are, in general, much less firm in public sector organizations than in private corporations. On the other hand, major specific efforts have been made to rein in the marauding regulators, as perceived in recent years by economists in the CEA and other presidential staff agencies. These efforts have reduced the pace of regulatory initiatives and enforcement, particularly in the Reagan years. More significantly, concerns have been expressed by scholarly observers, as well as by political opponents, that the particular decisional rules adopted by the Reagan administration appear to authorize the OMB to scuttle the legislative intent of particular regulatory statutes in the name of economic efficiency.

THE WHITE HOUSE TAKES ON THE REGULATORY AGENCIES

Presidents Nixon, Ford, Carter, and Reagan have all worried over the costs of regulation—costs to regulated industry even more than those reflected in agency budgets—and their successive creations of institutional mechanisms for reviewing such costs have culminated in a system that gives the OMB extraordinary authority to second-guess the EPA, OSHA, and other agencies in deciding what to regulate and how stringently. One author terms this the process of "controlling regulatory sprawl" (Ball 1984). (Here we will summarize pre-1981 developments, and then concentrate on the current system, especially designed to suit the "regulatory relief" theme of the Reagan administration. For more detail on these developments, see Eads and Fix 1984, on which the following summary is largely based.)

The EPA was hardly in business when complaints from industry about environmental regulation reached the sympathetic Nixon administration. Then-OMB director George Schultz, and senior White House staffer John Ehrlichman created a Quality of Life review process to balance environmental and safety interests with industrial requirements. Schultz had found that the OMB's usual budget review authority could be undermined by the EPA's regulations, which would compel budgetary increases for implementation. If the OMB could take a hand in reviewing the regulations, however, it might be able to minimize budgetary implications. Although the Quality of Life program was written as applicable to many agencies, it was in practice used only on the EPA. An unintended but valuable byproduct was that the EPA was stimulated to initiate its own office for economic analysis of regulatory proposals. Under President Ford, the primary motivation for review of regulations changed from controlling the government's budget to fighting inflation. Ford initiated a Council on Wage and Price Stability (COWPS), whose economic staff was told to monitor the cost of governmental actions in terms of their contribution to inflation in the private sector. Inflation impact analyses became the hallmark of the Ford approach, and took the form of COWPS filings. These were analyses and recommendations—125 of them during the Ford years—regarding rule-making proposals from various social regulation agencies, focused on least-cost ways of regulating, and often questioning the value of proposed rules in terms of a trade-off with anti-inflationary values. Note that these filings were placed on the public record that the regulatory agency concerned used to explain its ultimate decision when promulgating the rule by publication in the *Federal Register.*

At least from an after-the-fact perspective, President Carter's approach can be described as ambivalent. He made strongly protectionist appointments of senior regulators, and paid more attention to the policy views of those he placed in charge of regulation than had his predecessors. However, he also followed the advice of his senior economists, especially CEA chairman Charles L. Schultze, in pushing the application of economic analysis to regulation by an executive order creating a Regulatory Analysis Review Group (RARG). It is unclear whether he realized that in so doing he was imposing the normative criteria (i.e., the implicit values) of economists, as well as what we can call a technical analysis. Noting that Schultze had a double role in the process of developing regulatory policy through the fact that he chaired the RARG as well as the CEA, Tolchin and Tolchin called this a "turning point in presidential management and regulation: the ascendancy of economists over lawyers." According to these authors, White House economists expressed "disdain for what they considered rigid, legalistic approaches" in the regulatory agencies (1983:49).

In the spring of 1978, soon after Carter had established his oversight system, a strong dispute arose between the OSHA and its boss, Secretary of Labor Ray Marshall, and Schultze concerning cotton dust standards. The issue was taken to President Carter personally, with Schultze appearing to have won a softening of the rule initially, but with Marshall then persuading the president to allow the rule to go forward largely unchanged (Eads and Fix 1984:58–59). After newspaper stories publicized the dispute and the presidential intervention, Schultze was reported to be disinclined to take such issues to the president, and Carter apparently decided that such interventions were not worth the political costs involved. However, Schultze's group did continue to push its views of appropriate regulatory limits on the agencies strongly enough to produce both legal and congressional charges that White House staff went too far in intervening after the comment period had been closed on particular regulations. By establishing rules that such postcomment involvement would be summarized on the record, the Carter administration turned back the legal challenge (*Sierra Club* v. *Castle* 1981).

A separate innovation of the Carter years was the introduction of a regulatory calendar, a compilation twice a year of forthcoming federal regulations under consideration in the agencies—a step widely approved by observers of all political stripes as a way of getting beyond a simple case-by-case review in order to develop some sense of priorities among competing regulatory proposals.

As should be clear from earlier sections of this book, President Ronald Reagan brought a strong, new perspective to the regulatory game, one dimension of which altered sharply the focus and litmus tests of presidential oversight. We have earlier discussed Executive Order (EO) 12291, issued in February 1981, as the institutionalization of cost-benefit analysis; here we will review the changes in institutional relationships that this order engendered.

President Reagan disbanded the COWPS and the RARG, and instead made the Office of Information and Regulatory Affairs (OIRA) in the OMB (created in 1980) the centralized focus for White House oversight. In contrast to the modus operandi of the Carter administration, cost-benefit analysis was not only permitted but required, and no major regulation was to be proposed until the proposing agency had assured itself through analysis that the "potential benefits to society for the regulation outweigh the potential costs to society" (even though admitted intangibles might often make it impossible to perform a meaningful quantitative net benefit analysis). The OMB was given authority to decide which proposed rules were "major," and thus requiring detailed review, whereas this judgment had been left earlier to the agencies. (Less than 2 percent of the proposed rules have required full cost-benefit analysis.) Finally, not content that agencies should set their priorities for regulations on the basis of explicit statutory requirements or administrative discretion left by a broader statute, the Reagan order superimposed a new litmus test for establishing agency regulatory priorities: the taking into account of "the condition of the particular industries affected by regulations, the condition of the national economy, and other regulatory actions contemplated for the future."

With regard to "filings" on the public record, none were now to be required of OMB interventions, because these would take place before the public comment period through the early submission requirements of the executive order. It could be presumed that OMB views would be reflected in the rules actually proposed, but that is quite different from having available to the public the original agency views and the recommendations of the OMB. A reported example of such OMB intervention asserts that in November 1983 the head of the OIRA, Christopher C. DeMuth, wrote to EPA administrator Ruckelshaus that his agency was being too cautious in its approach to toxic risks, and suggested more tolerance on the part of officials assessing the hazards of new chemicals before they could be marketed. After the EPA had suffered a credibility loss during the time that Burford and her colleagues were widely perceived as letting industrial consultation amount to industrial rewriting of tentative regulations, and Ruckelshaus had picked up the pieces, his successor, Lee M. Thomas, achieved a major concession from the OMB in the spring of 1985: a "treaty" specifying that the OMB would add to the public record its involvements in environmental issues. Asked how he got such an agreement, Thomas was quoted as replying, "it took a lot of negotiation, believe me" (*New York Times,* June 20, 1985).

In January 1985, Reagan attempted a further strengthening of centralized control over regulation, this time for the purpose of reviewing the total pattern of regulatory development in a given year, rather than individual rule-making proposals. Specifically, EO 12498 established a regulatory planning process, to begin with submission by each agency of an annual "overview of the agency's regulatory policies, goals, and objectives for the program year and such information concerning all significant regulatory actions of the agency, planned or under way . . . as the Director deems necessary to develop the Administration's Regulatory Program." These draft regulatory programs are reviewed by the OMB director's office for "consistency . . . with the Administration's policies and priorities," with disagreement between the agency and the director to be raised for further review by the president, or in such "other forum" as the president may designate. Once the Administration Regulatory Program has been issued, the order provides that any rules submitted during that year, but which had not been included in the agency program, may be returned "for reconsideration" (i.e., scuttling) in the absence of certain specified "unusual circumstances," such as a judicial order. To the extent that this carries further the concept of a regulatory calendar begun in the Carter administration, it is a step that most regulatory reformers would agree with. To the extent, however, that consistency of agency programs with "the Administration's policies and priorities" might twist out of shape the apparent intent of the agency's own statutorily imposed requirements, or that the system might overly inhibit agency initiatives in pursuing the regulatory goals of their statutes, the order stimulated negative reactions, particularly in Congress. Since such reactions were of a piece with earlier complaints about the thrust of EO 12291 four years earlier, we can treat the challenges together.

HAS PRESIDENTIAL OVERSIGHT BEEN CARRIED TOO FAR?

Criticism of the Reagan administration's vigorous extension of presidential oversight follows several lines of attack. Most basic is a constitutional challenge asserting that EO 12291 exceeds presidential authority by substituting the substantive principle of a positive ratio of benefit to cost, for the variety of substantive decisional principles that Congress laid down in establishing regulatory agencies and their basic programmatic responsibilities. The most often cited legal analysis to this effect is that of Morton Rosenberg, written for the Congressional Research Service (Rosenberg 1981a, 1981b). Although recognizing that "the practical realities of administrative rule making . . . demand Executive coordination and supervision," Rosenberg sees such supervision as something different from substituting White House for agency decisions on the issuance and content of regulations. His basic point is that issuing rules "remains law making even when it is performed by an administrative agency; and law making remains a task committed by the Constitution to the Congress." The cost-benefit system, and the institutional authority given the OMB for its exercise are seen as taking "out of the hands of the individual agencies not only the method and means of informal rule-making but, effectively, the statutorily reserved prerogative of an agency to decide whether to make a rule or not" (1981a:38, 46).

Because Rosenberg wrote in 1981, he was for obvious reasons unable to comment on the 1985 changes that added procedures for the administration's Regulatory Program. In my view, that order may more seriously interfere with the delegations of authority given to the agencies by Congress. It would seem that the OMB director, without any requirement of justifying his actions on the record (as agencies must do in promulgating specific regulations through the *Federal Register*), may reject a proposed rule made by, say, the OSHA or EPA because he thinks it would be too costly, without leaving the final judgment to the agency head regarding whether, despite costs, such rule may be an essential means for carrying forward the job that Congress has assigned.

Although the OMB role is officially termed "advisory," a potentially recalcitrant agency head would be subject to dismissal; in bureaucratic reality, the agencies are not truly autonomous. Furthermore, since EO 12498 requires that each agency explain in its annual proposed regulatory program how its proposals "are consistent with the Administration's regulatory principles," and since it is abundantly clear that the most basic of current principles is to minimize regulation and its costs, it is arguable that centralization "presents a greater shift in power from the Congress to the President than did the consolidation of oversight power within OMB in 1981" (Fix and Eads 1985:314). In Rosenberg's terms, it would seem also unconstitutional.

A quite different approach to the separation of powers issue is taken by Sunstein, who has argued that EO 12291 embraces a normative conception in which economic efficiency (through cost-benefit analysis requirements) becomes the sole decisive factor in making regulatory decisions—he terms it a "trump"—whereas, "no plausible theory of legislation treats congressional enactments as intended to promote efficiency, save in unusual circumstances" (1981:1,270–73). If, suggests Sunstein, "regulatory statutes are generally not animated by a desire to promote efficiency," then is it legitimate for the executive branch to "implement them only when implementation will maximize wealth?" (1981:1,274).

Sunstein's view is supported by the great variety of circumstances and motivations described in chapter 2 as contributing to the origins of various regulatory programs. The legislative role of Congress is usurped if the executive imposes "a unitary conception of regulation" on a very diverse set of statutory intentions (1981:1,280). Accordingly, Sunstein concludes his analysis by suggesting that administration of the EO must be severely restricted to those few statutes that have exclusively efficiency-oriented purposes. Regulations dealing with Medicaid, civil rights provisions, the Endangered Species Act, and protection of the handicapped are suggested by

Sunstein as examples of areas in which the requirement of a positive benefit-cost ratio would be improper because none "is plausibly regarded as intended to promote efficiency" (1981:1,280). Across-the-board application of the administration's centralized substantive standard would raise serious questions of the separation of powers. (Note that the constitutional challenge here would be much diminished if the EOs required only that each agency not forbidden by statute from doing so, perform a cost-benefit analysis on its proposed rules, without requiring that a favorable ratio be found as the only basis on which to proceed with regulation.)

Congressional reaction to both of Reagan's executive orders was antagonistic, as one would expect. Note that Rosenberg's analysis was made for a congressional committee that held hearings to protest against EO 12291. Although Congress did not fight for very long, selected members erupted with protest again when the Supreme Court overturned the legislative veto, and then the Reagan administration issued EO 12498. In response to the latter development, Representative John D. Dingell, who chairs the House Committee on Energy and Commerce—which oversees the FDA, FCC, FERC, and others—mounted a small counter-attack by requiring that the regulatory agencies under his jurisdiction submit periodic reports on all regulatory delays or modifications made at the insistence of the OMB. In their frustrations over executive administrative powers, congressional committees were in the habit of requesting original agency budget submissions as made to the OMB, so that they could compare these with the "sanitized" budget requests made on behalf of the agencies when the president's consolidated budget was sent to Capitol Hill. Similarly, now Dingell's committee wants agency submissions for the Regulatory Program to be given to the committee as well.

Besides objecting that the OMB system keeps needed information from Congress, Representative Dingell has also been concerned that due process principles are violated, and a number of commentators otherwise sympathetic to White House oversight are inclined to agree. It is a basic principle of the Administrative Procedure Act that the material on which a regulatory decision is made be on public record. Two charges are made against the OMB system in this regard. The first focuses on the fact that the OMB's role is not made evident by filings on the record, as had been done with the COWPS filings in the Carter years. By reviewing regulations before they are published in the *Federal Register* for comment and again after the comment period closes, the super-regulators act without public scrutiny, especially in terms of failing to provide justifications for the positions they take. Viscusi, an economist who has contributed significantly to the critical literature on present modes of regulation, nevertheless expresses great concern about the lack of public accountability for the OMB's actions, and has argued that the OMB "should be required to make public the reasons for its regulatory decisions and to document these decisions" (1984b:130). Portney makes the point that "much of the educational function of a regulatory analysis is lost if citizens are unable to examine both an agency's supporting analysis and a constructive criticism of that analysis by the relevant oversight group" (Portney 1984:238).

When the OMB role was more strictly budgetary and less directly programmatic, with the latter activity simply one advisory input to a total White House process, the tradition of secrecy that went with an intimate staff relationship to the president was justifiable. Many feel that an enlarged policy-deciding role calls for the OMB to operate as much in the public eye as do the line departments. Most of the critics (at least economics and political science observers) would not like to dismantle presidential staff oversight, however, but to subject it to the public airing that has become a basic part of our system of democratic accountability. The present concern is that while accountability of agencies to the president has been increased (something for which political scientists have sought for years), it has paradoxically been accompanied by a decline in public information regarding the activities of the OMB as the president's regulatory arena.

A 1981 decision, by Judge Patricia Wald of the District of Columbia Circuit Court of Appeals, has been widely interpreted as sustaining the general concept of a strong White House oversight role, although not written specifically about the Reagan executive orders. In Judge Wald's opinion (*Sierra Club* v. *Costle*), our government "simply could not function effectively or rationally if key executive policy makers were isolated from each other and from the Chief Executive. Single mission agencies do not always have the answers to complex regulatory problems." It is hard to disagree with that position, which fits the older political science view favoring presidential coordination, and the newer concerns for economic efficiency through institutional centralization that tend to be favored by economist observers (e.g., Littan and Nordhaus 1983:51–53, 67–81). However, there is a difference between presidential policy guidance, and central staff intervention in particular regulatory cases, the latter having substantial due process implications.

Another dimension of the due process concern, however, was not addressed in the *Sierra* case. That is the question (important throughout administrative law) of ex parte communications, in which private parties make contact with White House officials without the fact of such contact or its content being placed on the public record. The problem is not entirely new: Henry Ford II and Lee A. Iacocca met with President Nixon privately in 1971 in a successful effort to squash federal regulations that would have put airbags into new cars 15 years ago (*Los Angeles Times*, November 29, 1982). This is known as the "conduit" problem, in which the OMB is perceived as a possible conduit for expressing off-the-record views of business objectors to pending regulations. The requirement that all contacts with the OMB or other White House officials concerning proposed regulations be placed on the record, with regard to both factual material and policy views, would go a long way toward legitimizing a strong White House oversight role. As a GAO study put it, "without publicity provisions regarding such matters, the public cannot determine either who made the regulatory decision or on what basis it was made" (quoted in Eads and Fix 1984:124; see also Sohn and Litan 1981). (We should note here that in 1955 Bernstein saw presidential intervention in regulatory matters as "essential in order to safeguard the public interest from . . . surrender to private pressures" [1955:153], whereas now the reformist concern is that such private pressures may be privately exerted at the more central point of the OMB.)

One final, rather different criticism of the system imposed since 1981 is that the task given to the OMB is beyond its capacities because the executive order arrangements ignore bureaucratic realities. Nager argues that although the OMB is given "unprecedented access to and control over the development of regulations by the executive agencies," this does not necessarily make it certain that social benefits will outweigh social costs, for the OMB may turn down a proposed regulation because of conflict with its own bureaucratic goals, rather than because of an analysis. Secondly, since the OMB cannot duplicate the technical staffs of the EPA, OSHA, and other agencies, it cannot "match wits" with those agencies on subjects such as acid rain or benzene. According to Nager, because cost-benefit analysis is strikingly sensitive to assumptions about the discount rate, methods of valuing life, and so forth, it is easy to make "slight alterations in a series of assumptions and thus to make the analyses prove just about anything" (Nager 1982:41). From Nager's analysis, it would appear that the OMB role may be duplicative of the agencies, or an arbitrary way of expressing presidential preferences without due process for the parties concern.

A related organizational side effect of the publicity that putting the OMB system into place has had, appeared in the fall of 1985 when the administration was seeking a new head for the OSHA. Several prominent persons mentioned declined to be considered on the reported basis of their concerns that the OMB would interfere with agency decisions (*New York Times,* October 22, 1985). Presumably, the better a candidate for the head of an agency is, the less that person will want to take on a position in which the administrator's decisions are effectively countermanded by a White House agency, lacking both statutory responsibility and staff expertise.

ASSESSING THE COSTS AND BENEFITS OF WHITE HOUSE OVERSIGHT

One's assessment of congressional and presidential oversight depends on one's expectations. Is oversight intended primarily to produce textbook economic efficiency in the allocation of resources, or is the primary objective political accountability in a democratic republic? Should one expect detailed decison-making by the oversight authorities, pre-empting the delegated roles of the agencies, or should Congress and the White House limit themselves to trying to "set the tone" (Eads and Fix 1984a:67)? Whatever the answers, it is important that they are not narrowly bound by the particular situation that is being assessed. That is, although economic efficiency has been the priority goal of most recent reform suggestions, it would be equally possible for the primary orientation of oversight "to promote the openness of visibility or regulatory schemes, to guarantee public participation during regulatory decision making, or to ensure protection of statutory 'rights' by federal agencies rather than courts" (Sunstein 1981:1,270).

The choices we make will be functions of both professional norms and personal philosophy. Those who have read this far will not be surprised that I posit as my own basic criterion a proposition that, as Don K. Price has put it, "we must pay at least as much attention to ensuring the accountability of our Executive [and legislative] institutions as to improving their efficiency and economy" (Price 1982:79; see also Price 1983, 1985: 129–52). When Congress and the president disagree substantively it is difficult, of course, to hold both accountable simultaneously, especially when one recalls that we can only hold accountable those to whom we have given sufficient authority to obtain results. When an asserted presidential electoral mandate does not operate in the same direction as received congressional statutes, the question of whose authority is to be held accountable to whom is difficult to answer. In the context of regulation, the response would be to accept presidential leadership as an essential ingredient for effective political coordination in our fragmented political system, but to insist that such leadership be exercised in full public view, and clearly within the limits of existing statutory provisions (see Reagan 1985). Further (and some will see this as a manifestation of populist ideology, perhaps accurately), Congress should play as strong and detailed a role in regulatory matters as its ability to form effective legislative majorities may permit.

We will now apply these basic positions of values and institutional mechanism choices to make a more particular assessment of the existing oversight pattern.

The dominant doctrine of reform has always called for Congress to stay out of details and to focus on the larger picture. Lave and Ommen adopt this view when commenting on the role of Congress in air pollution:

> Congress should focus its attention on settling conflicts and values and on designing the goals and framework of the air pollution statute within which the federal and state agencies implement environmental policy. Congress should not continue to set detailed regulations such as standards and deadlines for motor vehicle emissions. Instead, all standard setting should be delegated, while Congress retains its oversight role. (1981:49)

Similarly, Fix and Eads state that "regulators need more, not less, discretion," and they therefore argue that Congress should "focus on promoting the responsible use of discretion and not second-guess day-to-day decisions of regulators who seek to fashion coherent regulatory programs" (1985:315–16). (They do, however, give Congress an important role by suggesting that it take "a comprehensive look" at regulatory priorities.)

A very different position has, of course, been taken by Congress itself in recent years. Recall our discussion in chapter 5 of the trend toward more specific legislative mandates in social regulation. Support by a political science observer for this level of intrusiveness by the Congress was provided in a classic text of a generation ago. Charles S. Hyneman argued in the name of democratic accountability:

> Congress should specify in the statute every guide, every condition, every statement of principle, that it knows in advance it wants to have applied in the situations that are expected to arise. This rule . . . is based on the conviction that Congress, being the nation's representative assembly, ought to have authority to provide in law for anything that it wants any part of the government to do, so long as it does not violate a prohibition of the Constitution. (1950:81)

For some years, Hyneman was arguing against the mainstream of his own discipline; after Vietnam and Watergate, his view may again have more supporters.

While there are problems if either view is carried to extreme, in the present political context of the United States, Congress should be reasonably assertive, particularly in the area of social regulation where almost all of the major stimuli have come from Capitol Hill, rather than from 1600 Pennsylvania Avenue.

Although oversight itself refers to review and control of the implementation of statutes, its potential effectiveness is in considerable part determined by the clarity with which Congress has legislated in the first place—so that there is an unambiguous standard against which to measure implementation activities. In this regard, aspirational legislation (i.e., that which sets goals and deadlines that force technology, and, therefore, may have to be modified later, whether in administration or by informal amendment) makes sense. There will always be trade-offs, and sometimes only 10 percent of what Congress mandates may be possible. EPA regulations, for example, require cities to apply for the same kinds of permits for their municipal storm drains as they must obtain for their sewage systems in an effort to tackle the problems of urban run-off (670 pounds of lead and 380 pounds of zinc wash off streets into Chesapeake Bay every day). These regulations, which the EPA is only beginning to implement, are tentatively written into law by their incorporation into the 1984 extension of the Clean Water Act.

Fundamentally, the nature of our political process suggests that the superficial appeal of the doctrine that Congress should settle value conflicts in its legislation, provide great programmatic discretion to the administrative implementors, and limit itself to reviewing the efficiency and effectiveness of the administrators who will make most of the decisions, is not in tune with reality. No matter how explicit Congress is at the legislative stage, all value conflicts cannot be shown or resolved at that time. The extent of necessary delegation to agencies is sufficiently great that many value conflicts will only emerge as decisions are approached regarding particular trade-offs embedded in the rules that implement the legislation. If Congress is to have a major role in settling value conflicts, it must play a major role throughout the various stages of the regulatory process (Fisher 1981).

Since the legislative veto has now been "vetoed" by the Supreme Court, how else can Congress best provide itself any major role beyond the legislative stage? One way, already in considerable use, is to put sunset provisions on regulatory program statutes: authorize a program for a limited time period, so that the legislative reauthorization process provides a predictable, formal opportunity for major review, reconsideration and fine-tuning. The 1982–86 period of temporary extensions and eventual amended reauthorizations of some environmental and health protection statutes suggest that sunset provisions should now be considered of proven value in compelling periodic rethinking of objectives and means.

A number of approaches are under consideration in Congress, one of which is for Congress to adopt the OMB system of EO 12498, and use it for its own purposes (see Litan 1985:26–7). This can be done by creating a Joint Committee on Regulation (JCR), modeled on the Joint Economic Committee that receives the president's annual economic report. The JCR would receive the Administration Regulatory Program, hold hearings to provide an opportunity for a broad spectrum of viewpoints to be heard, and issue reports recommending to the separate program committees the changes in priority that it might prefer to those provided in the president's program. Such hearings could also be an opportunity to explore with particular agencies legislative initiatives that the OMB had turned down.

While we should not expect too much of it, this approach does hold some promise, both as a way of throwing a publicity spotlight on the OMB's enlarged regulatory policy role, and providing some informal political accountability of the presidency to the legislature in terms of how faithfully its laws are being executed. Such a process would be less vigorous than the legislated regulatory calendar recommended by Litan and Nordhaus (1983:159–82), but politically much more feasible, since it would not require an official reaction of a formal legislated majority. (The more ambitious regulatory budget concept that enjoyed a bit of a fad a few years ago can be dismissed as impractical; Litan and Nordhaus 1983:133–58.) The JCR (which, like the JEC, would not have legislation writing authority) might be composed of representatives from the standing legislative committees, which include the major regulatory agencies in their respective jurisdictions.

The first job of Congress is to specify its priorities where it can, and as much as it can. To the extent that it cannot, it will then turn to the president and the agencies. Or, when it wants to insulate a particular regulatory function, while not being able to specify in detail its own expectations, it may introduce an IRC, although that option is now rarely used.

Specification by Congress of its regulatory objectives, criteria, and programmatic expectations constitutes an appropriate legislative role. It is not likely to get overly detailed in what is statutorily specified, given the perennial difficulties of forming majority coalitions. The legislative and oversight roles here prescribed for Congress are also fully compatible with the concept of presidential leadership.

No successor to Reagan is likely to voluntarily abandon the potential for centralized policy control provided by the OMB system developed over the past decade and a half. The choice is not whether to retain or abandon a central role, but how to reshape it to fit our expectations for political accountability, and the multiplicity of goals toward which regulatory statutes have been addressed. One of the essential steps would be to place the OMB on the record with regard to its interventions, and their justifications. To emphasize the importance of our government operating as publicly as possible, this change should be made by legislation,* giving the OMB the same kind of statutory basis for "filings" in the *Federal Register* as was the case with the COWPS, and should clarify that the OMB's role is advisory only, with regard to specific cases.

If encouragement of the agencies to engage in analysis of costs and benefits, and review of their efforts, are to be part of an even-handed analytic process, and not a screen behind which to reject rules that will cost industry money, then it is essential that the president's budget include funds for strengthening the research and analysis staffs, both in the agencies and in the OMB. This does not only mean adding more economists, although clearly that would be part of the strengthened financial analysis capability. Much stronger physical science research staffs are also needed in agencies such as the OSHA, EPA, and FDA if regulations are to be maximally sound in scientific terms. The acid rain problem, toxics, and pesticides all show the need. Since regulatory choices involve the impact of alternative institutional arrangements on effectiveness and accountability, the analytic staff needs professional attention to the institutional dimension as well. That might mean the addition of expertise from the fields of public and business administration, and political science to supplement the prescriptions derived from the more abstract view of economic modeling.

To correct for the imposition by EO 12291 of a single economic efficiency standard, the order should be modified to eliminate the requirement of a positive benefit-cost ratio as a prelude to regulation. Cost-benefit analysis might still be mandated as a way of insuring that the financial dimensions of regulatory proposals are looked at closely, but the results should be used as informational data points for agency decision-making. The less stringent decisional framework of cost effectiveness analysis could be substituted with the soft requirement that a rule-making agency make a cost-effectiveness comparison of various options, and that it would

---

*In June 1986, the OMB and a group of senators agreed that the agency would henceforth make public—upon request—lists of meetings, phone calls, and correspondence concerning pending rules; but this is only informal. (*National Journal*, June 21, 1986, p. 1565)

"normally" be expected to choose the most cost effective, unless other values involved had higher priority. Such changes would engender a sufficient degree of flexibility in agency rule-making and OMB review to permit better articulation of executive regulatory steps with the diverse goals and criteria trade-offs embedded in the various statutes.

If the proper tasks of the institutionalized presidency are to set a tone in policy development, and to encourage agency actions that accommodate that tone (which may be largely a matter of pace or budgetary priority), then the OMB might profitably be redirected from review of particular regulations, for which it may well lack competitive expertise vis-a-vis the line agencies, and toward a focus on the forest instead of the trees (cf. Salamon 1981). Let the OMB work on developing common assumptions and criteria, both within what existing statutes permit, and toward the eventual objective of proposing statutory changes that Congress might enact to its own benefit as well as that of the executive, to provide a more unified regulatory framework for all of the social regulation programs. The OMB could examine overall problems of approach and technique, those of coordination among agencies handling related regulatory problems, and criteria for maximizing the overall effectiveness (not necessarily the least expensive) of the total federal regulatory effort.

To the extent that economic regulation remains a matter of interest—in transportation, consumer protection, and financial institutions matters—the OMB's regulatory overseers might fruitfully expend some effort on informational group discussions with the chairs of IRCs, to encourage voluntary coordination of their efforts with other parts of the administration's overall economic policies. That this could be done without violating either the statutory or the political independence of IRCs, is suggested by the long-standing tradition of frequent meetings of the heads of the FRB, Treasury, and CEA.

The conventional wisdom knows that fragmentation is the leading characteristic of American government, and that the consequent task of both the president and Congress is to take control of the vast bureaucratic establishment that they have created together. Attempts to devise effective means for regulatory oversight are but one small part of the total picture, although understandably discussed disproportionately because of the political controversy surrounding regulation in recent years. Academic political scientists and economists have, by in large, been in basic agreement that the rapid growth of social regulation, and attempts to redraw the limits of economic regulation warrant a vigorous effort to make regulation more effective in reaching its goals, financially efficient, and politically accountable.

Congress, on the other hand, tends to focus on effectiveness and accountability, and less on economic efficiency. Recent presidents have tended to focus not on regulatory goals as such, but on the costs that regulation imposes—broader macroeconomic objectives, in terms of inflation (Nixon, Ford, Carter); possible contributions of regulation to declining productivity (Carter, Reagan); and costs to and complaints by business, regardless of the regulatory rationale (Reagan). While there is a considerable pause in the development of major new regulatory programs or agencies, it is time to perform the tasks of consolidation that alternate with periods of innovation in American Government. However, while consolidation in efficiency terms is needed, the greater need is to take control of the regulatory oversight itself, to make it more accountable, and a stronger force for regulatory effectiveness.

chapter eight

THE MARBLE CAKE DIMENSION: INTERGOVERNMENTAL RELATIONS

We will begin this chapter with a multiple-choice question:

Regulation is a function of which level of government?
   A. Direct federal action;
   B. Autonomous state action without federal involvement;
   C. Federal-state joint action that is compulsory on the part of the states;
   D. Federal-state joint action that is voluntary on the part of the states;
   E. All of the above.

If you chose "all of the above," you are correct.

Airport control tower personnel of the Federal Aviation Administration (FAA) directly impose on private airlines safety regulations, or landing and take-off procedures at airports, and regulate safety features in the design and construction of commercial aircraft. Under the Clean Air Act, each state is required by federal law to develop what is known as a State Implementation Plan (SIP), comprised of an analysis of the specific air pollution sources and problems within a given state, and a strategy for meeting a set of emissions targets established in federal EPA standards.

Under the Occupational Safety and Health Act, state actions are permitted in areas where the secretary of labor has not chosen to promulgate national regulations and, more importantly, each state may run its own OSHA program. It submits details of such a program that the federal OSHA evaluates as "at least as effective" as the national standards promulgated under the 1970 statute. However, no state has to run an OSHA program; the national agency will run it directly in states that do not exercise the option. Finally, regulation of the traditional professional fields of medicine and law is largely a matter for the states alone, as is the regulation through licensing of hundreds of occupations seeking professional status, ranging from cosmetologist to frozen dessert handler.

What do these examples show? They illustrate the fact that regulatory objectives are pursued at both state and national levels, separately and jointly. Direct federal regulation tended to be the pattern in the older agencies of economic regulation, such as the FCC, SEC, NLRB, FRB, and ICC (which, you will recall, came into being exactly because of the inadequacy of state regulation under Supreme Court interpretations). States might have parallel agencies to cover the same functions with regard to intrastate activities, but these (even when cooperating with federal agencies) acted autonomously, and were in no sense administrative dependents of the corresponding federal regulatory agencies. Simultaneous joint operation of regulatory programs is more characteristic of the newer risk management programs, such as the OSHA, air and water pollution, and surface mining reclamation. Through the "togetherness" programs, the societal authority of both the national and state governments has been enhanced, in the sense that public sector activities have been enlarged. Of greater constitutional significance is the fact that the newer regulatory programs have created a far more intimate day-by-day working relationship between Washington and the state capitals than ever existed before. Paradoxically, this development has meant not only the strengthening of state governments by enlarging their roles vis-a-vis the private sector, but also broader scope for national determination of the responsibilities and activities of the states in selected areas of regulation—to the extent that the Advisory Commission on Intergovernmental Relations recently published a lengthy study called *Regulatory Federalism* (ACIR 1984) that refers to regulation of the states, which are in turn mandated or encouraged to regulate private sector entities.

In short, regulation today is a strongly intergovernmental activity, after having been mostly at the state level prior to the Civil War, and most noticeably at the national level from 1887 through the 1950s. For present purposes, however, our interest lies not in the impact of regulation on the concept of federalism, but in the ways in which the policy development and program implementation of regulations are affected by the fact that all levels of government are involved in pursuing regulatory objectives, and that we are a federal system. Before discussing the specifics of intergovernmental regulatory implementation, therefore, we need to establish our context by a review of the concepts of federalism and intergovernmental relations, and the major landmarks in their historical development.

FROM FEDERALISM TO INTERGOVERNMENTAL
RELATIONS

To encapsulate a larger discussion of American federalism today (Reagan and Sanzone 1981), let us state the matter in fairly bold
(and therefore necessarily simplified) propositions. In classic terms,
federalism is a legal concept, and its primary elements are:

> a division of governmental functions on a constitutional ba-
> sis between the national government and some sort of regional
> governments (states, in our case);
> each of these levels is autonomous, and makes the final
> decisions in some sphere or spheres of action; and
> both levels act directly on the citizenry (by contrast with a
> *con*federation, in which the central government acts only on
> the regional governments rather than directly on the citizens).

Despite the fact that the Constitution was explicitly designed to
avoid the weaknesses of the confederation that existed during the
Revolutionary War, by establishing a unified nation with a strong
central core symbolized by a clause asserting the supremacy of national over state law, rhetorical debate continued regarding state
"sovereignty" until the Civil War. As rapid industrialization came
into the picture in the 1870s and 1880s, there were political struggles
and Supreme Court decisions bearing on the scope of the now
firmly established central government. The commerce clause of the
Constitution provided a legal basis for the national government to
regulate interstate commerce, and that continues to be a primary
constitutional "peg" on which to hang federal statutes today. However, many court decisions were made, and political battles fought
before it was established that the word "commerce" included both
manufacturing and trading. It was an equally long time before it was
established that the power to regulate interstate commerce included
the power to regulate what is de facto intrastate commerce, on the
basis that manufacturing and commercial activities within a single
state should be treated as interstate commerce, because they could
have indirect impacts on commerce among the states.

For a substantial period of time, roughly from the Wabash decision (1886) until the late 1930s, the relationship of governments to
the economy fell under what the late constitutional scholar, Edward
S. Corwin, called "dual federalism," and which today we would call
a "catch-22" situation. This meant the combination of Supreme
Court doctrines that said the states could not enact social legislation
(e.g., child labor laws) to ameliorate the appalling conditions of human labor under early industrialization because it would interfere

with interstate commerce, and that the national government could not act because it would interfere with "freedom of contract" under the Fifth Amendment. In the late 1930s, a judicial revolution took place. A Supreme Court that had voided much economic and social legislation by 5–4 votes, turned around through the change of one justice's votes and began to uphold the activist, interventionist legislation of Roosevelt's New Deal.

Since that time, the predominant stance of the Supreme Court has been to defer to the "political branches" (i.e., the president and Congress) in social and economic matters, reserving most of its own judicial activism for the areas of civil rights and civil liberties. In legal terms, then, federalism stopped being an obstacle to national and state government activism regarding economic life. The courts made it possible for the positive state to burgeon forth, and the politics of a now highly industrialized and urbanized society has since emerged. In the process, federalism has changed from a formal legal concept, to the operational reality that we now call intergovernmental relations. In the expressive metaphor popularized by the late Morton Grodzins (1960:265), the national-state-local government relationship changed from one that could be called a "layer cake," to the more complex swirl labeled "marble cake" federalism. In short, new-style federalism refers less to a matter of legal status than to a multifaceted positive relationship of shared action, in which interdependence describes the national-state relationship better than the traditionally presumed independence of old-style federalism.

Ever since the constitutional revolution in 1937, the term "cooperative federalism" has been widely used to indicate that the two primary levels of government often act together. It was suggested earlier (Reagan 1972:175–79) that the term "permissive federalism" is also a useful label to suggest that the states' share of the powers exercised at both levels of government rests on the permission and permissiveness of the national government. The national government has often entered into new areas of activity formerly handled at the state level, but has done so without excluding the states. In fact, both in subsidy and regulatory program areas, the national government not only permits the states to act, it sometimes insists that they share in the burdens of positive government.

The best summary of the characteristics that differentiate intergovernmental relations (IGR) from traditional federalism is that of Deil S. Wright, who suggests the following points:

1. IGR included federal-local, state-local, and inter-local relations, whereas federalism focuses only on the national-state relationship.

2. IGR stresses the interactions of people, rather than a constitutional relationship.
3. IGR has a continuous, day-to-day focus, rather than being a one time statement of a static relationship.
4. All public officials are potential participants in IGR.
5. IGR always has a definite policy component and is administratively focused.
6. IGR does not per se specify a hierarchic structure (Wright 1982, 1985).

These features of the current federal-state system are byproducts of an extraordinary legislative output during the 1960s and early 1970s, mostly of grant-in-aid programs that subsidize (and supervise, through purse string conditions) existing state and local functions—airport construction, police force equipment and systems, local mass transportation—and what amounted to state administrative assistance in helping the national government to reach its own goals (e.g., urban renewal, child development, and compensatory education for disadvantaged children). Although subsidy and regulatory programs were often mixed (as in water pollution regulation, accompanied by grants for the building of sewage treatment plants), all but a small percentage of the domestic enactments of the 1960s and early 1970s, which called for joint intergovernmental implementation, were grants. The programs that were primarily regulatory were smaller in number, and came mostly toward the end of the active legislative period, through the mid-1970s. Two measures of grant-in-aid programs will adequately summarize the extent of such intergovernmental growth:

1. As of 1962, there were 160 programs, and by 1980 there were 492.
2. As of 1962, federal funding of grants was less than $8 billion, and in 1980 reached $83 billion, after which growth slowed substantially.

Focusing now only on that numerically small, but politically and socially very significant subset of the intergovernmental regulatory statutes of the 1960s and 1970s, the major laws are:

1965	Water Quality Act
	Highway Beautification Act
1967	Wholesome Meat Act
1968	Wholesome Poultry Products Act
1969	National Environmental Policy Act
1970	Occupational Safety and Health Act
	Clean Air Act Amendments

1972	Federal Water Pollution Control Act Amendments
	Coastal Zone Management Act
	Federal Insecticide, Fungicide, and Rodenticide Act
1973	Endangered Species Act
1974	Safe Drinking Water Act
1976	Resource Conservation and Recovery Act
	Toxic Substances Control Act
1977	Surface Mining Control and Reclamation Act
1978	Public Utility Regulatory Policy Act
1980	"Superfund" (Comprehensive Environmental Response, Compensation and Liability Act)

By calling these measures intergovernmental acts, we mean that they require or permit implementation by the states in cooperation with, and under the supervision of, the national government. That implementation ultimately falls on private sector organizations—business firms, educational institutions, nonprofit organizations—and yet there is a curious fact about the system: the immediate object of the regulation becomes the state government, which is itself rather closely supervised by the national government regarding how it will impose nationally mandated regulations on the private sector. The phrase "regulatory federalism" is used by the Advisory Commission on Intergovernmental Relations (ACIR 1984) as a label for the mandates (i.e., requirements) that Washington lays on the state capitals. However, since that term works as well for discussions of the overall system of regulation, we will speak of regulatory federalism when we mean the entire system, with emphasis on its ultimate impacts in the private sector, and use the term intergovernmental mandates when referring to programs whose regulatory actor targets are the states. Examples of this are Title VI of the Civil Rights Act of 1964, bilingual classroom instruction, and a 55 mph speed limit. Our concern here is almost entirely with the former type—regulation that the national government imposes through the states on nongovernmental parties.

Most intergovernmental regulatory programs developed slowly as bit-by-bit responses to the proven inadequacies of regulation at state and local levels. Given the historically strong element of localism in American political ideology, including the "states rights" strain specifically, the relative lateness on the scene of the federal government is not at all surprising. We will illustrate the movement from local through state to national regulation in the area of environmental protection responsibility, specifically regarding water and air pollution. (This account is drawn from ACIR 1981.)

By 1900, the relationship between water pollution and disease was known, and some states were enacting water pollution laws. However, when an immediate spell of disease had been ameliorated, the issue was forgotten; prevention was not a major concern. Air pollution was seen as a strictly local matter for a longer time than was water pollution, perhaps because it was harder to disregard the movement of water through a series of communities. There were inherent problems with local regulation of water and air pollution. The polluter and the pollutee were not always in the same community. Also, a single dominant industry could stop action in a particular city, but not as easily in an entire state. Some of the support for national action came from cities and city associations wanting to prevent harmful intercity competition.

There were national water controls on the books from 1899 onward. In that year, the Refuse Act required permits to dump in navigable waters—a requirement not enforced for more than half a century. An Oil Pollution Act of 1924, prohibited oil discharge into coastal waters. Substantial federal involvement came with the Water Pollution Control Act of 1948, which provided for nationally funded research (economies of scale and the problem of "reinventing the wheel" make it highly inefficient for each state to undertake its own basic research in such matters), and technical assistance to the states. In doing so, the statute also stated explicitly that it was the policy of Congress that the states held the "primary responsibilities and rights" in controlling water pollution. Nevertheless, that act did identify water pollution as a national problem.

Similarly, the Air Pollution Control Act of 1955 established federal research, training, and demonstration grants, although an accompanying Senate report again stated that it is "primarily the responsibility of state and local governments to prevent air pollution." A large sewage disposal plant grant program was enacted in 1956 over President Eisenhower's objections, and in 1965, then-Senator Edmund S. Muskie entered the picture as a major policy entrepreneur with the Water Quality Act of that year, in which for the first time it was established as a national policy to keep waters "as clean as possible." In a typical intergovernmental compromise, each state was to set standards of quality that it wanted in its waters and the federal government was to act only if the state did not do so within a specific period of time. The 1963 Clean Air Act let federal authorities set nonmandatory air quality criteria, and moved the recipients of its grants from the local to the state level. Emission standards for automobiles were enacted in 1965, modeled on a 1961 California law. (A generalization: the states often do make fine experimental laboratories, but it takes national action to achieve uniform spread of the results of the experiment.) By 1967, the Air Quality Act required the Department of Health, Education and Welfare (now Health and Human Services) to establish air quality control regions and clean air criteria, and also required the states to prepare state implementation plans (SIPs). Finally, clean air amendments and water pollution control act amendments in 1970 and 1972 brought the strongest mandates yet, as a result of political competition between Muskie and Nixon (as described in chapter 2). Given the absence of environmental protection activity in most states in earlier years, "massive federal intervention into the field of environmental protection has had the effect, in many instances, of creating an environmental role for the states rather than undermining a previously viable role" (ACIR 1981:41).

While air and water pollution control programs are only a small fraction of the total number, they are also among the earlier and more substantial ones, and have to some extent been viewed as prototypes by friends and enemies. In terms of the gradual growth of a federal role, the picture presented is one that fits most of the federal social regulatory programs. In all such programs, we should note that additional complexities arise from the triadic relationships legislated. Although regulation is usually discussed as a bilateral, government-business matter, what actually exists is triadic, government (national), government (state/local), and business—a structural fact that considerably complicates the carrying out of the congressional mandates.

Why are so many regulatory programs intergovernmental? Why doesn't the national government implement its own policies in the field? The answer is partly a matter of political acceptability, and partly of programmatic effectiveness and efficiency. Politically, to have the national government emphasize the defining of nationally uniform goals, and insure nationally uniform minimum standards, while calling on the states to develop specific programs to achieve these goals, has two advantages. First, it is consistent with the element of localism that is still strong in American politics. Second, when state government employees inspect factories for health and safety violations and monitor air and water pollution emissions at manufacturing plants, even if half of their salaries are reimbursed by the federal government, the size of the government is not obviously increased. The budget may be slightly larger (actually, regulatory programs constitute a minute segment of the total national budget), but the size of the federal civil service is not enlarged by the program implementors who work for state governments.

Before proceeding to the implementation of IGR regulatory programs in greater detail, this is a logical point at which to ask, why does the national government get into these areas of health and safety regulation at all? Granting the justifications for government regulation presented in chapter 2, why not leave it to the states? The basic political answer is simple: because the states aren't doing the job, or doing it very well. In more abstract terms, C. Boyden Gray (Counsel to Vice President Bush in the regulatory relief effort of 1981–83) has suggested that there are four situations that can sometimes justify a federal role in regulation, even when one's starting point is a presumption that it should be left to the states (Gray 1983:96–110). The first is when the diversity of state laws comprises a burden on interstate commerce. A national standard to require labeling of chemicals to inform workers of their dangers has been endorsed even by the Chemical Manufacturers Association, in order to avoid the variety (and sometimes greater strictness) that regulation by each of the 50 states seemed likely to produce.

The second reason is what Gray calls "federal accommodation," which means that the federal government can take the political heat and the states cannot. Automobile safety legislation is an example. A third condition justifying national as opposed to state level regulation is one requiring extensive and highly specialized scientific and technical expertise. It would be most inefficient to establish as many different centers of expertise as there are states. The technological problems of environmental statutes are a good example.

Finally, one of the most significant arguments for not leaving social regulation to the states is the problem of interstate competition. Rowland and Marz put it well when they likened interstate regulatory competition to Gresham's Law: just as bad money drives out good, they say, "lax regulation drives out stringent regulation" (1982:572). In their opinion, the governmental regulation role of the federal government is necessitated by the competition in regulatory laxity among the states. The argument is that any state whose industry can gain competitive advantage through lax regulation will be motivated to reduce the stringency of its regulation, and that other states will be motivated to move to the lowest common denominator of their region. Where regulation is shared with the national government, they expect the minimum allowed by federal statute to be the least common denominator among the states. This won't happen in all cases, they claim, but it is particularly likely when regulated substances and firms are concentrated in states where they make a significant contribution to the economic well-being of that state, and when the regulated activities are concentrated in a small number of regulated firms (1982:573).

To test their hypothesis informally, Rowland and Marz examined pesticide regulation in six midwestern states, and found that the evidence supported the Gresham's Law analogy. For example, federal regulations (which were themselves somewhat weakened by 1978 changes) require safety training for those who will apply restricted-use pesticides, and delegate discretion to the states regarding whether such applicators will be tested to determine the extent of their understanding of the dangers, and precautions regarding such pesticides. Given that delegated choice, in the states covered they found legislation that expressly forbids the requirement of a written test for those who have attended a training session. In Minnesota, in fact, the certification can be done through the mails, and a private applicator is deemed competent when he swears that he has read and understands the registered labels (1982:576). The Rowland and Marz thesis also has a long line of related historical precedent behind it, stretching back to the 1840s when some states, such as Delaware, began to offer easy terms for business incorporation, so to obtain the incorporation fee business. (For an interesting argument favoring federal pre-emption on the basis of ethics more than economics, see Kelman 1982.)

INTERGOVERNMENTAL IMPLEMENTATION

Looking at regulation through a chronological lens, let us assume that we have had the prelegislative development of public opinion, interest group bargaining, entrepreneurial initiatives, and so forth, and that a law has now been passed. Further assume that this statute sets forth certain national goals and standards, and contemplates that the administrative agency to which the law is turned over, will develop a set of cooperative programs with the states for carrying out the law's intent. The point of implementation has been reached, which is the focus of this section. Two concepts need to be explored in order to illustrate the problems of carrying out regulatory policies through the intergovernmental system. One is that of implementation, which has been defined in both managerial and political terms, as we will see. The other, which we will discuss first, is the concept of partial pre-emption.

Partial Pre-emption

Partial pre-emption is a way of characterizing the triadic relationship suggested above. First the national government assumes jurisdiction over an area of public policy activity, thus potentially displacing any acts of the states in such areas that are inconsistent with federal regulations, or simply filling a void where the states have not acted. However, unlike older instances of pre-emption, in which the national government enacted and implemented its own program, totally displacing the states in the area covered (e.g., licensing and allocation of routes, and setting fares for interstate transportation carriers through the ICC and CAB), under the partial pre-emption statutes the Feds turn around and give some of their newly assumed authority back to the states.

Partial pre-emption has both compulsory and voluntary forms. Leading examples of the compulsory form are the requirements of the Clean Air Act that the states must submit SIPs, and the energy conservation mandate of the 1978 National Energy Conservation Policy Act requiring that state public utility commissions develop residential energy conservation plans with their private utility companies. Dubnick and Gitelson call this "legal conscription" (1981:57). Voluntary partial pre-emption (the more common variety) is exemplified by the OSHA statute, and the Surface Mining Control and Reclamation Act. In these instances the states are given the option of running their own programs, with the carrot of a substantial (often 50 percent) federal subvention of administrative program costs. If a state chooses not to participate in this way, however, the statute calls for full pre-emption and the running of a directly federal program by national personnel operating out of a regional office. The degree of discretion granted to the states was not contemplated as being very substantial in most of the statutes. Rather, the option is available only when the state submits to the relevant federal agency a set of proposed state regulations that are at least as effective or as stringent as those of the national government, and that meet specific requirements established by the overseeing national agency. The flavor of this relationship is best indicated by a substantial quotation from the Occupational and Safety Health Act of 1970:

> Sec. 18. (a) Nothing in this Act shall prevent any State agency or court from asserting jurisdiction under State law over any occupational safety or health issue with respect to which no standard is in effect under section 6.
>
> (b) Any State which, at any time, desires to assume responsibility for development and enforcement therein of occupational safety and health standards relating to any occupational safety or health issue with respect to which a Federal standard has been promulgated under section 6 shall submit a state plan for the development of such standards and their enforcement.

(c) The Secretary shall approve the plan submitted by a State under subsection (b), or any modification thereof, if such plan in his judgment:

(1) designates a State agency or agencies as the agency or agencies responsible for administering the plan throughout the State,

(2) provides for the development and enforcement of safety and health standards relating to one or more safety or health issues, which standards (and the enforcement of which standards) are or will be at least as effective in providing safe and healthful employment and places of employment as the standards promulgated under section 6 which relate to the same issues, and which standards, when applicable to products which are distributed or used in interstate commerce, are required by compelling local conditions and do not unduly burden interstate commerce,

(3) provides for a right of entry and inspection of all workplaces subject to the Act which is at least as effective as that provided in section 8, and includes a prohibition on advance notice of inspections,

(4) contains satisfactory assurances that such agency or agencies have or will have the legal authority and qualified personnel necessary for the enforcement of such standards,

(5) gives satisfactory assurances that such State will devote adequate funds to the administration and enforcement of such standards,

(6) contains satisfactory assurances that such State will, to the extent permitted by its law, establish and maintain an effective and comprehensive occupational safety and health program applicable to all employees of public agencies of the State and its political subdivisions, which program is as effective as the standards contained in an approved plan,

(7) requires employers in the State to make reports to the Secretary in the same manner and to the same extent as if the plan were not in effect, and

(8) provides that the State agency will make such reports to the Secretary in such form and containing such information, as the Secretary shall from time to time require.

(d) If the Secretary rejects a plan submitted under subsection (b), he shall afford the State submitting the plan due notice and opportunity for a hearing before so doing.

We might call attention to Section 18a above, which does limit the extent of federal pre-emption by permitting the states to act on safety and health matters with respect to which no national regulations have yet been developed (which is the meaning of "no standard is in effect under section 6"). Apart from that, however, it is clear that the major thrust is one that strongly constrains the extent of state discretion, in as much as the federal government is statutorily mandated to develop a very extensive set of programs whose purpose is "to assure so far as possible every working man and woman in the Nations safe and healthful working conditions." To make the medicine easier to swallow, the act provides for 90 percent federal funding of the cost for each state for developing its plans and its federal application, and 50 percent federal funding for the annual operating costs for administering and enforcing the state programs. Thus, a partial pre-emption program of this kind combines the grant-in-aid and regulatory approaches to intergovernmental cooperation.

The Surface Mining Control and Reclamation Act of 1977 provides a similar example of partial pre-emption, but with interesting variations. In this case, Congress made a specific finding in the act—that the primary responsibility for surface mining regulations should rest with the states because of the diversity of terrains and other physical conditions involved—while recognizing a need for national standards in order to eliminate competitive advantages or disadvantages in interstate commerce among the producers of coal from the various states. The act is also quite specific with regard to the elements that a state program must contain if it seeks federal approval, among these are sufficient administrative and technical personnel, sufficient funding to provide for effective regulation, and specified civil and criminal sanctions against violators. In an unusual bit of horizontal (i.e., at the same level of government) intergovernmental relations, the act also requires that the Secretary of the Interior (in whose department the Office of Surface Mining was established) solicit the views of the EPA and the Department of Agriculture before approving any state program. The law provides for direct federal programs in the case of states that fail to submit an acceptable program within a given period of time, and in circumstances where a state program has been approved, but has to be recalled because the state is not realizing its obligations.

That such provisions are indeed real, even in an administration that tried to make the federal surface mining requirements easier on the states, is demonstrated by the federal takeover of strip mining enforcement in Tennessee in April 1984. Tennessee had only 6 inspectors instead of the required 25, and had performed only 39 percent of the mine inspections required, according to reports at that time. (On the other hand, the Office of Surface Mining was so tardy in enforcing legal provisions requiring that states be ordered to suspend or revoke mining permits of strip mining scofflaws and in collecting penalties overdue from violators that a congressional committee held special hearings in 1984 and early 1985 to put the agency on the spot and stimulate intergovernmental enforcement.)

Reverse-Twist Programs

Although partial pre-emption has become the most frequent single type of intergovernmental regulation, it is not the exclusive approach. One of the more intriguing alternatives found in a few statutes is to establish a national program that permits states to delay or veto plans made by the national government. This reverses the normal supremacy of federal law, but does so constitutionally because it is accomplished as an application of permissive federalism, rather than a state right.

One example is provided by the Coastal Zone Management Act (CZMA) of 1972, which gives states an opportunity to veto federal plans for permitting oil drilling in outer-continental shelf areas. Actually, some of the provisions of the CZMA are sufficiently ambiguous so that the courts are still settling the extent to which, and the circumstances under which the states may veto, and the national government may override state objections. At the least, the states are given a substantial delaying power under the Act.

Another example—one that is making headlines as we approach the end of the 1980s—is provided by the Nuclear Waste Policy Act of 1982. The intent is to develop repositories for the permanent disposal of high-level radioactive waste, and spent nuclear fuel. The Act provides research assistance on the physical science technicalities of radioactive waste disposal, but the provisions of interest here are those concerning site selection, and the participation of the states in that process. The Act provides that the Secretary of Energy will nominate five sites that he deems suitable for consideration with three of these as preferred locations. (Washington, Nevada, and Texas held the three sites initially recommended.) The nominated sites are undergoing environmental assessments, and consultations are required with the affected states and Indian tribes.

By 1991, the president is to submit to Congress a recommendation of one site, but "the Governor or legislature of the State in which such site is located may disapprove the site designation and submit to the Congress a notice of disapproval" within 60 days of the date of presidential recommendation. Then, such site is to be considered disapproved unless the Congress passes a resolution of repository siting approval, under very detailed procedures. This point has not yet been reached. One can hazard a guess that the politicking, especially in the Senate, necessary to override disapproval by a selected state would be horrendous. (See Downey 1985, for a view that the DOE and the states constitute adversarial representatives of conflicting interests, to be resolved by Congress.)

Having now seen something of the intergovernmental program structures through which regulations are "delivered" to the ultimate private sector targets, we will look at some general characteristics of how the government moves from a regulatory statute to a regulated result—the processes of implementation.

Implementation: Managerial, Political, and Problematic

As enacted by Congress, a regulatory policy states a goal (e.g., assuring a safe and healthy workplace, less polluted air or water), and establishes some strategy (meaning, the choice of an approach, such as licensing, the use of standards, market incentives, or compulsory or voluntary partial pre-emption), and assigns (or creates) an agency to turn the basic policy into a detailed set of programs. This task, called implementation, can best be conceptualized as the operationalization of broad-stroke guidelines by promulgating rules that translate them into program details.

A considerable body of recent literature has developed under the heading of policy implementation, which is generally given as one of the four or five major stages in the chronological model of policy development from agenda building to ultimate impact. While writings on implementation vary greatly in scope, approach, and propositions, one generalization on which all agree is that the path from legislative policy program results is difficult, winding, and never more than partially reaches the target. Furthermore, these characteristics are even more pronounced when the path is intergovernmental. Let us, therefore, sketch here the general outlines of the implementation problem, and provide some conceptual lenses; then we will apply this material to the intergovernmental implementation of partial pre-emption social regulation programs, as the most prominent type.

Although political scientists have recognized—even insisted—since the 1930s that policy and administration overlap considerably, the most widely used conception of implementation remains one in which the post-legislative stages are depicted as "all the further steps necessary for the provisions of the policy to be put into effect" (MacRae and Wilde 1981:223), or as "the carrying out of a basic policy decision" (Mazmanian and Sabatier 1983:20). One of the best recent books in this genre (Mazmanian and Sabatier 1983) synthesizes a set of six conditions for effective implementation. These range from clear and consistent policy objectives to the skills and commitment of agency leadership, and the negative condition that the relative priority of statutory objectives is not undermined by conflicting policies or changes in socioeconomic conditions. In their schema, the conditions most closely related to intergovernmental program implementation call for:

1. a "sound theory identifying the principal factor and causal linkages affecting policy objectives";
2. "sufficient jurisdiction over target groups and other points of leverage";
3. a legislative structuring of the implementation process that involves "assignment to sympathetic agencies with adequate hierarchical integration, supportive decision rules, sufficient financial resources, and adequate access to supporters";
4. and the active support of "organized constituency groups" (Mazmanian and Sabatier 1983:41–43).

Although this listing does include some explicitly political factors, it is fair to say that the overall thrust fits (following Barrett and Fudge 1981) what we can call the managerial model of implementation, as distinguished from the political or bargaining model. All of these factors are by implication concerned with obtaining compliance at the bottom with edicts from the top, and they contain an explicit hierarchic assumption for effective implementation. Emphasis is on the achievement of the objectives set forth in the legislative policy enactment, and no explicit recognition is given to the notion that the strategy, and even to some extent the objectives themselves, may have to undergo some unanticipated adjustment as they are defined further along the path of operationalization. Certainly, this is the way that national officials, both legislative and executive, like to define implementation. After all, they are trying to establish some national standard, and the best implementation is that which comes closest to achieving the statutory objective as they have defined it. While such officials would assent to the proposition that program applications should take local circumstances into account, the managerial conceptualizations rarely connect this with its implied corollary: taking local circumstances into account will mean at least partial redefinition of the objectives, at least as a matter of emphasis among the multiple elements that most policy objectives contain.

The political bargaining model espoused articulately by Barrett and Fudge, on the other hand, sees implementation as "getting something done" rather than "carrying something out" (1981:21). In their conception, things must be made to happen; implementation is in no way an automatic consequence of a policy decision. Those who implement are not neutral bureaucrats or passive agents, but semiautonomous individuals and groups actively pursuing their own goals and objectives, which will sometimes be in more and sometimes in less accord with those of the policy makers (1981:23). To get something done, in this view, those charged with achieving results must negotiate and compromise with those from whom compliance is sought. In turn, the top policy group will have to accept some compromises that are "sold to them" by the implementors as necessary to achieve target-group compliance—which after all, means the consent of the governed. In other terms there will always be an "implementation deficit," a gap between policy intent and implemented reality (Downing 1984:219). Political skills can affect the size of this "deficit." Akin to this bargaining view is the perception of MacIntyre (1983:11) that a focus on the attainment of statutory goals can be a misleading approach to implementation when the goals are vague or ambiguous. MacIntyre's example was the Federal Insecticide, Fungicide, and Rodenticide Act. Its ambivalent goals include enhancement of food production through the use of pesticides, and regulation to protect both farm workers and consumers from the ill-effects of the same pesticides. (See also Bower's book, *The Two Faces of Power*, 1984, for the delineation of technocratic and political dimensions of management, a conception that closely parallels that of Barrett and Fudge, but written in the context of private sector management.)

A full and realistic picture of implementation is best developed by using the managerial and political approaches together. They can be united, we may suggest, through the proposition that the degree of workability of the managerial approach depends on the prior success of the political bargaining dimension, which is best seen as setting the context within which and the extent to which the managerial process can go forward. In fact, these mutually complementary conceptions can be economically reduced to two essential propositions:

1. Getting something done or carrying something out can only be accomplished in a free and democratic polity if adequate political support can be generated and maintained.
2. Within a supportive political environment, the hierarchic and technical dimensions of implementation can only be effective if the actions taken embody the "sound theory identifying the principal factors in causal linkages" that Mazmanian and Sabatier specify. On the latter point,

policies imply theories. Whether stated explicitly or not, policies point to a chain of causation between initial conditions and future consequences. . . . programs make the theories operational by forging the first link in the causal chain connecting actions to objectives. . . . implementation, then, is the ability to forge subsequent links in the causal chain so as to obtain the desired results. (Pressman and Wildavsky 1973:xv)

The intellectual and administrative tasks are to analyze and operationalize those causal factors and linkages; the political task is to forge the conditions of acceptance in which the causal linkages can be applied.

One additional element, closely related to the political side of implementation, is needed to examine intergovernmental regulatory implementation. This is the concept of value integration. The primary source of successful cooperation or policy undermining, at any level, will lie in the degree of harmony existing in the values held among the diverse participants. As Brewer and de Leon put it, "programs and policies that accord with the needs and values of those asked to execute them stand a better chance than those in which conflicts are created" (1982:287). It may be that value integration or divergence, more than structural fragmentation, separation of powers, or federalism constitutes the largest impediment to effective implementation. While we all have a "zone of indifference," in which we may accept actions with which we do not fully agree, acceptance on the basis of hierarchy alone is more limited and less effective as an incentive than voluntary agreement with the values of those asking one to do something. As we shall see shortly, intergovernmental program implementation has some built-in obstacles to hierarchic compliance and value integration, as compared to operationalizing a policy within a single governmental jurisdiction.

Delivering Implementation Under Partial Pre-emption

At first glance, it would seem that the federal government should have no difficulty attaining the full cooperation of the states in handling their part of regulatory implementation and enforcement. Article VI, Section 2 of the Constitution—the supremacy clause—seems to create a hierarchic structure that puts the Feds in command. Some partial pre-emption statutes, as we have seen, have been equated with "legal conscription" of the states. And an environmentalist attorney, Jonathan Lash of the Natural Resources Defense Council, is quoted as describing EPA statutes as having created "a relationship in which the states are in reality serving as contractors to carry out a federal program" (Stanfield 1984:1035). Some of the structural conditions for effective implementation, as suggested by Mazmanian and Sabatier, would appear to be satisfied. However, not enough.

Despite these hierarchic elements, the formal constitutional system of federalism continues to set some basic constraints on national authority. First, although the national government can attach conditions to its grant programs, such as requiring a merit system for state personnel whose salary funding comes from Washington, what the national government cannot do is hire and fire state personnel. Since the employer-employee relationship provides the most basic of all leverages for exercizing authority over program personnel, the absence of that relationship constitutes a strong limitation on federal authority.

In some partial pre-emption programs, there is very little oversight authority left for the Feds after a state's program has been approved and given jurisdiction, such as in the surface mining control program. In some EPA programs, residual authority for supplementary enforcement exists, but the national agency lacks the personnel, time, and funds to make that authority effective—not to mention that the White House would get indignant phone calls from the governors, senators, and representatives of any state in which the overseeing federal agency tried to intervene in any substantial way. As the Advisory Commission on Intergovernmental Relations (ACIR) states in its discussion of implementation problems,

> Even when their own personal commitment is strong, however, federal officials may be reluctant to adopt a stance as tough enforcers, and there are good programmatic and political reasons for not doing so. Because they depend upon the state and local governments to achieve their own agency's mission, federal regulators need to maintain some kind of a working partnership. Harsh sanctions undermine the bonds needed to make programs work, and if they result in grant withdrawal, it can totally frustrate the attainment of national objectives. (ACIR 1984:143)

Thus, although these limits on federal authority over state personnel are classically managerial, they are also intensely political.

A parallel situation arises with regard to rule-making. As Martha Derthick has written, "Given the nature of a federal system, federal rules can be effected within the state only after being reincarnated as state rules" (1970:206). If the balance of political forces within a state is such that certain important industries that would be subjected to substantial financial burdens by certain regulatory programs also are dominant in that state's political economy, then it may be very difficult politically for that state to write a set of regulations that will be seen by the pertinent federal officials as being at least as effective as federal rules. Since these programs anticipate that the states will handle the implementation, and the federal agencies will find it very difficult to obtain the funding necessary to run them on a direct national basis, it is clear that bargaining will be the order of the day before a compromise set of state regulations can be put in place as a basis for managerial implementation.

A state in which any single industry dominates the industrial base will be much more subject to this kind of pressure than states that are more diverse in their economic composition. Broadly speaking, the greater the dominance of particular industries in a state, the greater the value differential that will exist between what the state finds it politically feasible to offer, and what the national legislation and regulations envisage as the appropriate standard. David and Kantor (1983) argue, for example, that there is a systemic bias in the political economy of the different levels of government, such that developmental priorities dominate in the cities while national politics is more open to social reform and income redistribution. We can safely say that a parallel difference exists between local development priorities, and national protective regulation policies.

Assignment of regulatory tasks to a sympathetic agency is another of the Mazmanian and Sabatier conditions for implementation. In the case of insecticide regulation, there is a notable intergovernmental divergence on this dimension. Since 1972, the federal insecticide program has been in the EPA, which is presumably more health protection oriented than the Department of Agriculture. It previously had responsibility for insecticides, and because of its clientele interest had emphasized food production utilization rather than health protection. However, it is the decision of each state to determine for itself which agency it will assign its level of responsibility under the FIFRA, and in a substantial number of states it remains the department of agriculture that handles the program. While the state program may occasionally, despite this locus, be stronger than the federal level on a particular pesticide, as has been the case occasionally in California, most of the time the agribusiness orientation of such state departments means greater hesitancy in writing and enforcing strong regulations, whenever any uncertainty about risks makes such hesitancy plausible. Thus, the triadic structure adds government-to-government value disputes to those that generally exist between government and business.

While the pesticide case may pose sharper national-state value differences arising from institutional structure than most other areas, one would expect some differences of focus to be commonly created from differences in the political party orientation of the president and the governors who appoint state-level officials, and between the president and Congress, and the party composition and difference in degrees of professionalism among state governors and legislatures.

Another important factor is personnel. In arguing that the quality of public policy was diminished by the fact that the number of problems being addressed was increasing faster than the supply of able executives, James Q. Wilson made the point that "good people are in very short supply, even assuming we know how to recognize them. Some things literally cannot be done—or cannot be done well—because there is no one available to do them who knows how" (Wilson 1967:7). While this problem exists in single-level programs, it becomes a greater problem in intergovernmental regulatory relationships, because state salaries are often lower than national salaries. For example, the ACIR estimates that the states "cannot compete successfully in the marketplace for professional engineers" to staff environmental protection agencies. A survey in Indiana showed that its toxic waste employees were leaving to receive an average of 36 percent higher salaries in private employment, with the starting salary for engineers $10,000 behind the market (*Los Angeles Times,* June 22, 1985). The ACIR reports occasional competition between federal and state agencies for the scarce supply of expert personnel, and cites an instance in which the Office of Surface Mining solved a staffing problem by hiring away inspectors from states' strip mining control agencies. Some of the states protested on the basis that they could not match higher federal salaries, and that they had borne the cost of training the inspectors (ACIR 1984:142). Such situations can only exacerbate the inevitable tensions between levels of government.

The personnel question also relates closely to the matter of values integration. In a study of the extent to which the kinds of environmental deregulation that the Reagan administration sought in the early 1980s were being carried out in the field, Hedge and Menzel found that "site level decisions frequently reflect the attitudes and values of inspectors as much as they do statutory requirements or directives issued by superiors" (Hedge and Menzel 1985:600). From the general literature on personnel management, and such special studies as Kaufmann's on forest rangers (Kaufmann 1960), we have the proposition that the stronger the tradition of professional training specific to a given field, the greater the likelihood that inculcated norms will produce substantial similarity in attitude and orientation of personnel. In many of the newer regulatory areas, however, there is no long tradition of specific professional schooling, which may help to explain the substantial variations that studies find.

On the other hand, problems exist across regions even when they are part of the federal agency. For example, in a careful study of surface mining enforcement (Shover et al. 1984), regional personnel responded to what they saw as different industrial "cultures" between the eastern and western regions, differences that permitted more flexible enforcement in Region West than in Region East, where it was felt to be necessary to prove that the OSM was not playing favorites as was suspected of earlier state mining regulation programs. The Region West director was quoted as saying, "It isn't a regionalization of the objectives. It's a regionalization of the implementation" (Shover et al. 1984:136).

A final factor in relating the difficulties faced by the intergovernmental approach to regulation is the question of state government capabilities. There are two questions: What is the general level of such capabilities? Does the extent of unevenness in state capabilities seriously undermine intergovernmental delegation?

Writing 25 years ago, one would have assessed the situation as bad overall, and the degree of unevenness as worse. Today, while even sympathetic observers still find a lot of room for continuing improvement in state constitutions, the organization and operations of legislatures and governors' offices, and openness to participation by their citizens, the situation is clearly much improved. In a recent report written for ACIR, Mavis Mann Reeves provides this summary assessment of the situation:

> Since the mid-1950's states across the country have been reexamining and remodeling their institutions and processes. One by one, and little by little, particularly in the decades of the 1960's and 1970's, they changed them to conform more closely to the model reformers had advocated for years. Sometimes this reformation was accomplished at the behest of national actions but more frequently it was the result of the indigenous initiatives. Changes were so piecemeal and intermittent, so disconnected in geography and so largely unrelated in media notice, however, that few people realized the profound restructuring of the state governmental landscape. Today, states, in formal representational, policymaking and implementation terms at least, are more representative, more responsive, more activist, and more professional in their operations than they ever have been. They face their expanded roles better equipped to assume and fulfill them. (Reeves 1985:363)

After pointing out that state government structures have been modernized in the last 25 years in a substantial number of ways—such as "one person, one vote" reapportionment, an increase from 0 to 38 in the number of states having professional staffing of legislative committees, and lengthening of the gubernatorial term of office beyond 2 years in 11 more states so that only 4 two-year term states remain—Stenberg concisely summarizes by saying that "a revolution—albeit a quiet one—has transformed the states over the past quarter century" (Stenberg 1985:320). The problems remaining are exemplified by such facts as these: as of 1981, 35 states (compared with 39 in 1970) still paid their legislators less than the salary recommended to attract professional-level talent by the Citizens Conference on State Legislatures (Reeves 1985:87); the gap of tax effort among the states has widened since 1975; and although at least 35 states now have overall merit systems for administrative personnel, such systems are "systematically abused in some states so that they exist in name only." Furthermore, administrative salaries "frequently lag behind those of the federal bureaucracy and often are too low to attract the desired competence in specialized fields" (ACIR 1985:168), a factor of considerable relevance to the increasingly technical character of many regulatory programs in the health and environmental areas. The complexity of the new regulatory program may also mean a lesser state capacity in these areas than for less technical programs. For example, a state air program administrator has asserted that only 10 to 15 states had a good capacity for handling the "prevention of significant deterioration" air quality program—though 25 had it delegated (Hambright 1984:180).

Perhaps it is fair to suggest that the overall capacity of state governments to govern effectively has been increased in surprising degree, but that there also remains a number of weaknesses. However, the partial pre-emption system seems to provide an ameliorating factor: the weakest of the states may not be able to submit acceptable plans for assumption of IGR regulatory responsibilities, in which case the national government will be obligated to run direct programs, which one hopes would not suffer as great debilities as might accompany management by the weakest states.

Intergovernmental regulatory implementation, in summary, represents a very major development in American federalism, as well as in the arena of regulation. Looking at both the conditions for effective IGR regulation, and the special obstacles presented by the IGR process, the importance of political and managerial factors is very clear. Political strength at both levels of government is a necessary condition for effective managerial administration, and effective program implementation on a decentralized basis requires a strong, clear central policy as a focal point. One then has to accept some policy dilution in order to achieve field-level "compliance." In this system, regulatory policy can sometimes be jointly delivered effectively; it can rarely, if ever, be successfully imposed.

Delegation as Deregulation: Reagan's New Federalism

In chapter 5, we covered 1981–83 attempts at social deregulation as such. Here we want to review briefly the way in which devolution to the states constitutes or reinforces deregulation at the national level.

In his 1980 presidential campaign, Ronald Reagan made it clear that he wanted to get the federal government "off the back" of the states, as well as of business firms. In 1982, he proposed a sweeping reallocation of functions between the national and state governments under the same heading (New Federalism) that President Nixon had used when pushing revenue sharing a decade earlier (Reagan 1972). A subsidiary part of the Reagan New Federalism called for speeding up and maximizing the extent to which potential state assumptions of jurisdiction under the partial pre-emption programs would be realized. For example, the stringency of rules (Interior Secretary James G. Watt called them "unnecessary and burdensome") that the states would have to agree to for assumption of regulation under the Surface Mining and Reclamation Act was substantially diminished, and the number of assuming states consequently increased greatly between 1980 and 1983. The OSHA closed a number of its state compliance offices in 1981, and cut back sharply on its monitoring and issuance of directives to state programs (Thompson and Scicchitano 1985:594).

Since the Reagan administration's desire to give the states a larger role in intergovernmental programs was accompanied by a substantial relative cutback in the level of federal grants-and-aid to help the states perform their functions, the enthusiasm of the states for assuming additional responsibilities was somewhat diminished. Further, it seems logical to suppose that increased responsibility and tighter budgets would combine to produce (whether purposely or inadvertently) de facto partial deregulation. Definitive research is not yet available, so firm judgments cannot be made. However, some of the early evidence is surprisingly counter-intuitive. For example, one study covering the OSHA during the period of 1977–83, found that state enforcement was not deregulated as much as enforcement under national OSHA, where it ran direct programs. Furthermore, most state agencies conduct more inspections, and cite more violations than do national government inspectors, although they are less inclined to issue citations "that have a bigger financial bite" (Thompson and Scicchitano 1985:594, 592). Perhaps the most significant fact is the diversity in state responses that the same study identified, with one third of the states reflecting changes in national policy, and seven "stradling" (strengthening enforcement on some indicators but lessening it on others), while six resisted the trend (Thompson and Scicchitano 1985:596). One might speculate that a substantial time lag is necessary for changes initiated at one level to permeate through the other levels in the labyrinthine maze that constitutes our regulatory apparatus.

By early 1986, contradictory trends were apparent with regard to environmental regulation. In Congress, the swing of the pendulum was clearly back toward a stronger federal role, as the Safe Drinking Water reauthorization and pending changes to strengthen Superfund, and the Clean Water Act evidenced. President Reagan's administration, on the other hand, was considering relaxing federal rules attached to grants. It had promulgated new air toxics (Stanfield 1985), and water cleanup strategies that would limit the national government's role to providing information and technical advice to the states, but leaving actual regulation to them—for which many are not prepared. Continuing weak regulatory budgets, and diminished national monitoring, set against increasing public concerns over problems such as toxicity in water supplies and chemical spills, augur for a crisis in environmental protection policies before much longer.

As executive branch monitoring slows down, we may expect federal level review of the effectiveness of state-run regulatory programs to come only sporadically, through media reports of scandals and damage caused by weak or absent enforcement. Congressional investigative hearings will follow. Thus, monitoring of intergovernmental regulation will predictably produce a higher level of congressional-executive tension.

THE STATES AS AUTONOMOUS REGULATORS

The focus of this book is regulation initiated at the national level. In a chapter on intergovernmental dimensions of regulation, however, we want to provide a brief sketch of what the states do as regulators, apart from their role as middlemen in carrying federal programs to local and private levels. Reeves provides a good starting point with a listing of state responsibilities for the regulation of business, which encompass almost every phase of business activity, and include the enactment of commercial codes governing business relations; entrance into business; laws on contracts; legal provisions for property ownership, use and disposal; taxation; sale of securities; and unfair business practices, among other things. They regulate closely certain businesses such as utilities, banks, common carriers and insurance companies; license professions and occupations; and institute certain provisions relating to labor and employment. . . . States now do more in environmental protection both on their own and at the instigation of the federal government. They also have moved to prescribe standards for both mobile and modular home construction, nuclear waste disposal, and nursing homes, for example, and prohibit such actions as the use of children for pornographic pictures. (Reeves 1985:23)

Clearly, the states are actively engaged in regulation, quite apart from what is mandated by Washington. Included in their areas of autonomous regulation are those that fall within the general scope of federally pre-empted activity, but embrace particular activities that the Feds have not yet chosen to regulate. For example, by 1984, 19 states had more extensive programs than the EPA's regarding air toxics. As we noted earlier, OSHA legislation explicitly permits the states to act on health and safety matters that the federal government has not touched. Other partial pre-emption statutes have similar provisions, and a number of states have not been hesitant to make use of the opportunity. Sometimes state autonomy also takes the form of rules that are more stringent than the corresponding federal regulations. California's restrictions on automobile emissions, for example, are of this character, but are an explicit statutory exception. More generally, the federal statutes say that a state's regulations must be at least as effective or as stringent as federal regulations; they do not forbid being more stringent. California rules on restricting certain pesticides used in agriculture, for example, have made use of this opportunity.

State regulation has two notable characteristics that differentiate it from regulation at the national level. The first concerns the activities regulated: the states engage very heavily in occupational licensing, while the national government largely restricts itself to regulating products rather than services. The second concerns the political source of regulation: state regulations are frequently adopted by direct action of the electorate.

Some 800 different occupations are regulated in one or another of the states, with about 20 being regulated in every state. This group includes accountants and attorneys, medical doctors and real estate agents, and even cosmetologists (Meier 1985:175). New York State licenses about 360 occupations, including outdoor guides, second-hand bedding wholesalers, frozen dessert handlers, and wrestling match tickettakers.

Although there is a clear public interest rationale for occupational licensing in such cases as physicians and attorneys, where the public requires some assurance of minimum quality, it is also true that professional regulation has been used to artificially restrict the supply of practitioners, and to restrict the modes of competition, as by forbidding advertising of fees. It is difficult to find much public interest rationale in the regulation of barbers, chauffers, and dry cleaners (Kirp and Soffer 1985). The explanation lies in the self-protective aspects of regulation, rather than the public interest dimension. This is indicated, for example, by the frequency with which occupational regulation statutes include a "grandfather clause," one that permits all existing practitioners to be licensed without an examination. If the primary purpose was to protect the public, presumably such clauses would not be found. Furthermore, if there ever was an area in which regulatory bodies were designed to be captured by the regulated interest, it is that of occupational licensing. Typically, the regulatory board is established from among members of the licensed group, and in only some states is there a requirement that there be any public members. Professional regulatory boards are often financed by a licensing fee, rather than by state appropriations. In such cases, there is a tendency to feel that they should be exempt from close state monitoring.

Although public health and safety are sometimes part of the purported justifications, occupational licensing is almost entirely a matter of economic rather than social regulation. As such, it has recently begun to receive some of the critical governmental attention that other areas of economic regulation have undergone, where there is good reason to believe the competition would be an adequate protector of the public, if not of the economic interest of the practitioners. Thus, we have seen that the FTC is giving some attention to services, representing one of the few instances of federal attention to this area. Scholarly attention is also showing some increase. (See, for example, Meier 1985:ch. 7; Blair and Rubin 1980; and Rottenberg 1980.)

Regulations instigated through the initiative and referendum processes include gun controls, bottle deposits, hospital pricing, nuclear power plant siting, and the creation in California of a coastal zone commmission to regulate coastland use patterns. Since 23 states have the initiative and 26 the referendum, there is a substantial potential for popular initiation of regulatory measures. One suspects a trend toward increased use as a concommitant of the general pattern of increased direct participation in governmental decision-making that has developed in the past 20 years.

By whatever means, state regulation is an important if little known part of the total regulatory picture. Given the deregulation and devolution efforts made at the national level in recent years, the proportionate role of the state level is probably increasing. Even back in 1980, a New York State legislative committee produced an estimate that business in the state spent $2.5 billion a year to comply with state regulations, and another $8 billion to comply with federal regulation. While these estimates are probably biased, they provide at least one empirical indicator of the financial significance of state regulation. And in our day-to-day lives, much of traditional state and local regulation is very basic to us: weights and measures in the grocery store and at the gasoline pump, hygienic cleanliness of restaurants, and the pricing and information policies of funeral establishments (which are now regulated by the national government).

ISSUES OF REGULATORY FEDERALISM

We have seen that present-day regulation, especially in the health-safety-environmental areas, is a matter of intergovernmental relations and is affected by the federal nature of our political system. We have also seen that substantial problems arise from adopting this halfway house between leaving regulated matters to the choices of individual states, or having them pre-empted by national programs that are nationally operated. The major questions for the future can be quickly summarized as those of a pragmatic, efficiency-oriented nature; those relating to the political system as a whole; and those concerning state versus national specification of value preferences.

First, the basic pragmatic question is: can the states be effective conduits for the achievement of regulatory goals established through national legislation? Our hopeful answer is: yes, to the extent that there is a goal consensus, which will provide a basis for voluntary, positive implementation at the state level, and that strong federal leadership and effective federal monitoring exist. These conditions are rarely fully achieved, but the very strong continuing support given to health-safety-environmental protection in public opinion polls suggest that the basic constituency for goal consensus is there for exploitation on behalf of the public interest.

Because regulation is operated intergovernmentally, and has created a large role for the states as implementors of national programs, a question naturally arises of the impact on the federal system as a whole: does this use of the states violate our basic sense of federalism? Or does it strengthen our federal system as we understand it today? From the viewpoint of those who hanker for the return of traditional federalism (many of whom probably would also like to see a diminished federal role in domestic affairs generally), the new national-state relationship created by partial pre-emption regulatory programs (as well as by nonregulatory grant programs) is looked on with great disfavor. A more hopeful view is that the states as significant political entities have been strengthened by their growing middleman role in the intergovernmental system. Since the realistic alternative is not an absence of regulation, but total federal pre-emption, the balance of the federal system may be better maintained by present arrangements.

Assuming a continuance of intergovernmental regulation, there remains a question of the extent to which the value preferences of the regulations will be those established through the national political system, or those of individual states or local communities. In such areas as civil rights, income maintenance, and publicly provided health care, a very great political effort has been mounted and maintained during the past few decades to achieve uniform national minimum standards. These efforts are based on (1) the moral principle that we are all citizens of the same national community, in which the assurance of personal rights and conditions of human dignity is a proper matter of national concern, and (2) the practical facts of great interstate differences in financial capacity for providing services and interstate competition to enhance economic development. Increasingly, even national industries are expressing a preference for uniform national regulation. In a national market, regulatory uniformity is a substantial advantage.

Despite this basic thrust toward a national definition of the values to be served in domestic programs, the microeconomics-oriented "public choice" school of thinking about policy argues that public provision of goods and services should come as close as possible to operating on the basis of individual preferences, as does the private market (for a discussion and critique, see Rhoads 1985). Proponents of this ideology argue that regulatory and other programs should be delegated more strongly to the state level, permitting the politically effective value preferences of each state to determine the level of health-safety-environmental protection to be provided in competition with value preferences for economic development. While it is clear that there are diverse political cultures among the states (for the classic study, see Elazar 1972), those who believe strongly in the value of developing national community standards would respond that the inherent discretion of field-level administrators provides sufficient room for legitimate accommodations to state-by-state differences without vitiating the argument for uniform minimum standards and protections.

National regulation is here to stay. States are here to stay. Our perennial political tension between localizing and nationalizing forces and values is also here to stay. The result of all of these? Regulation will continue to be strongly intergovernmental. Our need, therefore, is not to waste time trying to sort out what topics with which each level of government will concern itself, but to place maximum effort on improving the bases for effective intergovernmental cooperation in the achievement of partially common objectives.

chapter nine

THE REGULATORY FUTURE

As this exploration of regulatory institutions, processes, and values approaches a close, we want to suggest the likely directions of regulation during the next few years. Before looking forward, however, we will provide a brief summary of the themes discussed in the first eight chapters.

MAJOR THEMES SUMMARIZED

First is the theme that institutional arrangements—multi-headed commissions or subcabinet bureaus, directives or incentives, detailed legislative directions or broad administrative discretion—do matter. They matter partly because they sometimes affect efficiency, but more because they affect and symbolize the political system values of accountability and legitimacy.

A closely related point is that regulation, as a governmental activity, always depends on political circumstances for its inception and operation; it is not legislated as a deduction from microeconomic analysis of markets (although such analysis has been a significant factor in deregulation of transportation); and its purposes are as diverse as its political origins. While the functions that regulation may serve sometimes include the strengthening of resource allocation on market principles, alliances forged to create a regulatory program are more likely to be unified by a perception of consumer protection, or abuse of corporate power, than by economic principles.

Therefore, the role of economic principles in our regulatory system does not lie primarily in stimulating new regulations. What economic analysis contributes to the big picture of regulation is instead an intellectual structure by which to justify regulatory thrusts that arise from nontechnical motivations. In economic regulation, the concept of market failures attributable to natural monopoly, or to inadequate consumer information, rationalizes some regulations (e.g., of retail distribution of natural gas and electricity), and criticizes other programs as unnecessary because of competition, actual or potential, as an alternative form of social control (e.g., motor freight and airline deregulation). (At a detailed level, economic analysis is the essential tool for working through specific regulatory questions, such as elasticity of demand for a price-regulated product, or for establishing a rate structure that will provide a public utility with a return adequate to attract capital for expansion.)

In social regulation, the economic concept of externalities has played a dual role. It provides the major economic justification for regulation of health, safety, and the environment, and it serves to differentiate social from economic regulation in the context of deregulation. That is, by showing that competition cannot solve (and instead may exacerbate) some problems requiring intervention by government, the externalities concept serves to protect the programs of agencies such as the EPA, OSHA, and CPSC from the demise that the more extreme free market ideologies had anticipated.

From these summary propositions flow two other basic themes. One is that regulation cannot be adequately described, analyzed, or evaluated by any single academic discipline. The three that have each had periods of explanatory supremacy—law, political science, and economics—are all necessary tools of the regulatory observer's trade. (For that matter, disciplines ranging from psychology to biochemistry to anthropology also have contributions to make in looking at particular regulatory questions—see Noll 1985—but the first three are the most universally relevant.)

The other theme is that regulatory policy issues turn at least as much on questions of values imbedded in competing criteria for action as on any "scientific" analysis, whether by the social or physical or biological sciences. All policy formation, it has been argued, arrays values and facts against posited goals. While values can be analyzed for internal consistency (conflicts with the value assumptions of other programs, and so forth), they are peculiarly the public's province in a democracy, not the expert's. And the public's realm is the realm of politics.

Because of the central salience of values in shaping regulation (and regulatory policy disputes), another theme is that quantitative analytic techniques (risk analysis; cost-benefit analysis) should not be determinative of policy choices in themselves. Executive Order 12291 therefore goes too far in establishing a requirement that every major new regulation is to show a net social benefit, both because we can rarely measure the relevant factors (especially the benefits) with sufficient precision to ensure accuracy in such calculations, and because benefits—particularly clear cases of life-saving relevance—we want even if the costs clearly outweigh any measureable benefit.

Two more themes bear summarization at this point, both suggesting what we might call "golden mean" propositions. One concerns the mixed economy, the other the mix of levels of government involved in regulation.

Neither laissez-faire capitalism nor socialism, the American system of regulation constitutes a halfway house on the spectrum of political economy. Our study points toward continuance of that position. Public attitudes and assumptions of a supportive relationship between a market economy and political freedoms are too solid to warrant any belief (for good or evil, as different observers might see it) that the United States might move very far toward socialism. Equally, public attitudes—supported by daily reporting of harms resulting from inadequately regulated market transactions—militate against any strong move in the direction of a capitalism held unaccountable for negative impacts (even when inadvertent) upon health, safety, individual dignity, or the natural environment.

So also with respect to the roles of national and state-local governments; we will not (despite current budgetary pressures) tear down the structure of national regulatory goals and strategies in favor of a political laissez-faire regime, although we may weaken it for a time. We will not permit each state to choose whether or not to regulate in matters where we have established a sense of national community standards. The states will likely develop stronger roles in implementing regulatory programs, but it is also likely that the benefiting clienteles—and their supporting interest groups—will retain sufficient political strength to fend off extreme turn-it-back-to-the-states proposals, as we saw in the early 1980s. The intergovernmental mix is a major and stable feature of our regulatory system. Partial preemption with state operations under federal guidelines may not be a tidy form of federalism, but it is pragmatically successful and suits our basic nonideological governmental behavior pattern.

PREDICTION: MORE? LESS? DIFFERENT?

In summarizing the major themes of this book, we have already ventured to some extent into the realm of prediction. Because the themes concern the most basic characteristics of the system, our predictions are probably not risky. At greater risk, a few comments are ventured now in operational areas of greater potential change, in both substance and process.

Taking the latter first, our starting point is a proposition about regulatory legislation well-stated by James L. Regens: "Laws inevitably reflect the times in which they were written, expressing the social objectives, scientific knowledge, and technical capabilities of that era" (Regens 1982). We can extend that observation to rule-making, modes of procedure, and litigation patterns: none are static and unchanging if one's time span is more than a couple of years.

Within this context, the greatest force for change in regulation is the change in the nation's economy from seemingly unbounded growth to seemingly long-term reduction of national resource afflu-ence. At least as currently perceived, this means a sharp reduction in resources likely to be made available for societal needs that have to be publicly met—even if a national administration should come after 1988 that gives greater weight to social regulation needs. The constraints lie in economic resources, as well as in political will.

The primary implication, therefore, is that more hard choices will have to be made in setting regulatory priorities, especially in such high-cost areas as long-term health and environmental protection. It is not suggested that we should let our guard down, or reduce our protective objectives. We mean to say that we will make more effec-tive use of the limited resources available in the next few years if we concentrate our efforts on those risks that we know to be the great-est, while simultaneously pushing research on suspected dangers. More concretely, we suggest that it will become necessary—proba-bly over strong objections from some of the major health and envi-ronmental advocacy groups—to employ comparative risk analysis to help set priorities, rather than claiming to give equal regulatory attention to every risk, and to weigh known high frequency expo-sures (by types of populations and geographic areas), more heavily than lesser or problematic ones.

The executive director of the American Council on Science and Health has pointed out that detection techniques "are now so sensi-tive that we are approaching the time when we can find trace amounts of anything in everything" (Whelan 1985). Given that sit-uation, and limited public health dollars, Whelan argues that we should concentrate on known strong risks while "accepting expo-sures to innocuous trace levels of manufactured chemicals known to be animal carcinogens" I think we are more likely to follow this advice as budgets tighten, and as we become more aware that a risk-free world cannot exist.

Furthermore, it appears to be inevitable that greater delegation to state governments will occur, probably on the basis of the controver-sial EPA strategy that emerged in 1985 of providing data and techni-cal assistance to the states regarding air and water pollution, but largely confining its own regulatory enforcement to those pollutants identified as having major interstate dimensions (e.g., acid rain), and severe potential impact. It is important that change accomplishes useful concentration of effort in cost-effective ways without scuttling or unnecessarily delaying further extensions of protection as knowledge and finances permit. Legislative mandates—which industry and regulatory opponents will object to—that set timetables within which the EPA (or the OSHA, as appropriate) must evaluate the risks in a congressionally supplied list of potential problem products or processes are necessary companion elements in a revised regulatory strategy. Such mandates were included in the 1984 amendments to the Resource Conservation and Recovery Act (RCRA), and, as of 1986, a reauthorization bill for the Superfund contained a similar timetable for starting cleanup of abandoned hazardous waste sites. The bill also contained provisions for citizen suits if the agency did not comply with legislated mandates—but recent history suggests that such a provision is also an essential counterbalance if the impossible dream of simultaneous high priority attack on every conceivable problem is to be abandoned in favor of a more selective approach.

Despite a general tendency toward state delegation, in circumstances of perceived crisis or dramatic evidence of state failure to act effectively, national regulation will be increased. A recent example is in the field of health care. With long-term care for chronic illness, especially of the increasing elderly population, bringing nursing homes to greater public attention, the ability of the states to insure the quality of care in such institutions is being watched closely. A recent National Institute of Medicine study (1986) takes a dim view of the nursing home situation, and vigorously argues the case for an enhanced national government role in this area.

We cannot expect market incentives, as a replacement for direct regulation, to achieve more than the bubble concept. However, there may be greater use of financial incentives within the existing regulatory system (e.g., waste-end fees to discourage the use of toxic chemicals in manufacturing processes, or toxic labelling requirements that might make unsafe products less profitable than safer alternatives, the search for which would thus be stimulated).

As suggested in our discussion of cost-benefit analysis, this mode of weighing regulatory options is more likely to be widely accepted when the physical costs and benefits are clearly identifiable, and when pro-regulation advocates are able to turn this technique against parties accustomed to using it against regulation. However, it is not likely that costs and benefits will be easier to measure when used by environmentalists and health advocates than when used by industry. Furthermore, citizen interest groups that adopt dollar-valuing analytic strategies for some cases are likely to find their objections in other cases less credible. This is, however, the current direction of events.

One more point regarding future regulatory style: legislation is not likely to revert to the New Deal pattern of very broad, vague mandates. In the major areas of social regulation, Congress is capable, with strengthened committee staffs and the research advice of the CBO, OTA, GAO, and the Congressional Research Service, of defining its objectives and expectations in reasonably specific terms. Even too specific for those critics wedded to a conception of executive discretion. Given a choice of being specific regarding scope, objectives, and deadlines for administrative actions, but occasionally having to amend a deadline, versus stating a general topic, and asking an agency to use its own expertise and value judgments to determine how much of what regulation to push, Congress will opt for the former.

Switching from the processes of regulation to its substance, what are likely to be the areas of decline and growth? The answer is necessarily speculative, yet some lines of development are clearly more probable than others.

On the basis of economic theory, one would suppose that so long as the dominant perception is of a strongly competitive system, business (i.e., wallet-protecting) regulation would remain in decline, while social (i.e., person-protecting) regulation would increase in accord with the discovery of new risks. While there is some validity to this argument, the exceptions on the business regulation side are likely to be substantial. As discussed in chapter 2, the actual political causes of regulation lie more in abuses of power and perceived crises, than in the theory of market failure. Also, in deregulation (as generally in public policy development) major policy changes never anticipate all consequences, and a need for additional steps of a course-correcting or fine-tuning variety arises.

A brief discussion of regulatory proposals initiated in 1985 will illustrate the point. Aside from an occasional call for re-regulation of the airlines, the most notable grouping has been in the financial services field, some directly related to consumer protection, and others designed to safeguard the integrity of the financial services and markets system. Proposals in the latter category include the following:

> The Commodity Futures Trading Commission reacted to failure of a member firm by proposing larger capitalization requirements.
>
> Reacting to the failure of two major unregulated secondary

dealers in government securities (i.e., a firm that buys securities from one of the 36 primary dealers that the Treasury deals with, and that are regulated by the Federal Reserve Bank of New York), in which Maryland and Ohio savings institutions had invested, the House of Representatives passed a bill that would bring the secondary firms (about 100) under the regulatory eye of the Fed and the SEC.

Wall Street guru Henry Kaufman told a congressional committee that the deregulated banking environment, in which the demarcations between banks, brokerages, savings and loans, and underwriters had largely been erased, would come to resemble "a zoo with the bars let down." He also asserted that deregulation of the interest rates paid to depositors, in combination with continued government guarantee of deposits, was creating incentives that would lead even the most conservative institutions to "compromise standards and engage in practices that they would not have dared to pursue" earlier. He proposed several new regulatory steps (a National Board of Overseers, expanded financial disclosures by financial institutions, and an official, published credit-rating system for such firms) in order to balance "entrepreneurial drive" with public responsibilities.

Proposals more directly related to protecting consumers in the new atmosphere of unregulated finance included a bill to reduce sharply the time that banks would be allowed to take in clearing checks deposited by customers; a call for state disclosure requirements by self-styled financial planners and counselors; and mandated "lifeline" checking accounts for low income persons.

The most discussed area of financial regulation proposals in 1985 was that of controls on corporate takeovers. Demands for action were made by congressmen, financial columnists, corporate attorneys, and even the Federal Reserve Board, which approved rules—effective at the beginning of 1986—limiting to 50 percent the purchase of a corporation's stock that could be financed by loans secured by the stock. Such debt—called "junk bonds"—had become something of a scandal, both as a matter of financial ethics, and as a danger to the economic system because of the perceived danger to investors.

Regulatory responses to newly surfaced problems also continued outside of the financial services field. One was a model law proposed by the National Association of Insurance Commissioners to regulate collision-damage waivers on car rentals as an insurance-equivalent that may duplicate renter coverage, alleged to be outrageously priced. Another was a variety of proposals to regulate the esoteric business of art auctions in New York, stimulated by two instances of alleged improper behavior by officials of the two major auction houses, Sotheby's and Christie's. As always, problems and scandals produce calls for protective regulation—despite rhetorical obeisance to the free market ideal.

In the area of social regulation, a clear prediction of regulatory expansion is warranted by ever-changing social ideals for the protection of human dignity, the incredible ability of our laboratories to devise new chemical products whose benefits carry a toxicity price tag, and the ever-increasing ability to detect existing but previously unrealized or unattended risks. Perhaps some older regulations will be eliminated as a trade-off that makes room (in budget and staff) for new regulations of higher priority.

Consider that existing statutory mandates of the clean air and water acts, the OSHA, and the 1984 amendments to RCRA, mandate the testing for toxicity and other health hazards of hundreds of substances. The EPA and OSHA are behind schedule (the latter promulgated standards for benzene and cotton dust at the end of 1985, to avoid a contempt of court citation for failing to regulate in accord with its legislated mandate), but Congress seems to be increasing the pressure, so a number of new rules are to be anticipated over the next several years as the studies are completed. Scheduled phasing out of landfill disposal of hazardous wastes means new regulations to channel the replacement modes.

Next, note again that early drafts of reauthorizations of several environmental protection statutes under consideration in 1986 are strengthening the scope, timetables, and enforcement processes. For example, the Superfund renewal bills that await final action in 1986 raise the budget authorization from $1.6 billion to $7.5 or $10 billion (against $5.3 billion requested by the Reagan administration); require the EPA to start cleanup on 600 abandoned dumps in the next five years; and permit citizens suits to compel action—the clearest result of the 1982–83 EPA scandals. The most likely future is, therefore, not one of pulling back on earlier regulation, but of creating new regulation that will move environmental regulation away from the aspirational to an operational part of industrial life.

Is environmental regulation unique in the continuing strong public support that legislators perceive? It seems not. When Attorney General Edwin Meese initiated discussion with some other cabinet members in the hope of encouraging President Reagan to diminish the force of implementing regulations under Executive Order 11246—the order initiated by President Johnson that set Affirmative Action in motion—Secretary of Labor William Brock objected strongly, and business magazines reported that many larger corporations preferred to keep existing regulations, having found that the efforts to achieve a more diversified workforce produced a better workforce. To the possible response that they could continue such efforts without the prod of regulations, the practical rejoinder is made by labor law attorney Judith Vladeck that "Without the Labor Department involvement, employees with grievances would have fewer options, and they'd be a lot more confrontational" (Fisher 1985:30). Two Supreme Court decisions of July 2, 1986, supported affirmative action in terms that made most unlikely the changes desired by Meese.

Among problems yet to be addressed with specific regulations, but likely to reach that point within the next few years, are urban runoff pollution (twice as much heavy metal washes into San Francisco bay from rain runoff through storm drains as from industrial and sewer sources); acid rain (scientists say that a reduction of 12 million tons annually of sulfur and nitrogen oxides is needed to protect lakes and forests); and the greenhouse effect (possibly changing the earth's climate disastrously through the accumulation of carbon dioxide). Genetic engineering regulations, recently issued, are controversial among scientists, and agencies such as the National Institutes of Health, the EPA, the FDA, the Center for Disease Control, and the Department of Agriculture. (One of the early field tests of an altered gene involves a bacterium that will protect certain crops from freezing until the temperature drops a few degrees beyond the normal freezing point.) The novelty and complexity of the issues raised by genetic engineering technologies challenge the capacity of scientists and policy makers alike. The only certainties at this time are that the potential for social good is so great that genetic engineering will be done, and the potential for harm is so great that some kind of explicit controls are inevitable; the self-accountability of scientists and biotech firms will not be accepted as sufficient.

HEALTH CARE: PROTOTYPE OF THE MIXED ECONOMY?

Finally, the complex reality of regulation as a blend of private provision of goods and services with public supervision for reasons of equitable distribution, as well as for health and safety, is best illustrated in the field of health care, where a new "competitive" atmosphere is being regulated into existence. It is an example of complexity, and of the fact that the regulatory frontier moves on, with new agenda items replacing the old.

In 1983, Congress legislated (with strong administration backing) a new system for paying hospitals under Medicare. Until then, the government had been a third-party payer, like Blue Shield or an insurance company. (The other two parties are, of course, the hospital, as provider of services, and the patient.) The third-party system, which paid hospitals in accord with their usual and customary billed charges, provided the wrong financial incentives, for neither the patient nor the hospital had any strong stake in holding down costs that the government would reimburse. Since the medical care component was rising much faster than the overall Consumer Price Index (CPI) at the beginning of the 1980s (e.g., 11 percent for health care versus 3.9 percent in the CPI in 1982), and hospital charges were the most rapidly increasing elements within health care, cost containment became the major theme of the Medicare program. Actually, an earlier attempt at comprehensive cost containment had been made in the Carter administration, but it was defeated by medical lobbying.

The system inaugurated by the new legislation set up 470 Diagnostic Related Groups (DRGs), with a flat fee (i.e., price control) for hospital care associated with each group, whether an appendectomy, hysterectomy, or whatever. Because the hospital would receive the same payment if the patient stayed three days or five, or if one nurse was on duty or three, the DRG system created strong incentives for the hospital to monitor its own costs closely, so that its aggregate income would cover its costs. Hospitals that were most successful in pursuing cost controls would reap a surplus; those least successful would be in a financial crisis.

The prospect of a surplus that might become a lucrative profit for the best cost-cutters encouraged profit-seeking private hospital chains to develop and grow, creating competition with the more customary nonprofit community hospitals and public institutions— county general hospitals. Since hospital admissions were beginning to fall as a result of a form of private regulation—group insurance requirements for second opinions, advance clearance for hospital admissions, and encouragement to utilize the burgeoning "free standing" surgery facilities—competition to fill hospital beds became stronger.

Note that although the competition is for the patient, the situation is far from one of normal "consumer choice," since it is the doctor and insurance company that typically decide whether and where the patient is to go, not the "consumer" directly. It is primarily a competition among the hospitals for the business of other providers and payers, of whom the patient-consumer is largely captive.

The DRG system provides an incentive for hospitals to maximize the number of admissions, and minimize the length of stay. If an average stay for a given procedure is three days, a two-day stay may mean a profit, but a four-day stay may mean a loss. Stories have arisen of hospitals keeping two charts on a patient: the health chart, and the number of days remaining in average treatment for the ailment. Charges arose of patients being discharged "quicker and sicker." Dumping of patients without insurance coverage or private funds—transfer from profit-seeking to public facilities against the will of the patient, and sometimes before an emergency patient has been stabilized—had become a large enough problem after only two years of the DRG system that the Texas Department of Health adopted a stringent rule in 1985 forbidding the transfer of patients for economic reasons, while legislation then pending in the House of Representatives would require that patients be given "necessary stabilizing treatment" before transfers for financial reasons.

In short, the competition that new regulations had created was showing substantial unintended side effects. When the financial changes have bad effects on patient care, the next step is to expand regulations designed to protect patients from having hospital finance control medical practice. This is not an area in which we are willing, in terms of national values, to let the market have whatever results it may, so regulations intended to create a competitive "market structure" for economic reasons will inevitably produce new regulations to alleviate undesirable market effects.

Another dimension of the mixed private-public health care system is the fact that public provision of medical care is limited to those over 65, the disabled (Medicare covers both), and the poor (through federal-state programs known as Medicaid). The DRG system, therefore, applies only to the Medicare group (many states are going to equivalents, or capitation fees, in their Medicaid programs). Since this provides an incentive for hospitals to "cost-shift" (i.e., charge more to insurance and private patients to make up the lost income from Medicare) on cases that exceed the DRG norms, insurance companies and employers paying for health insurance benefits, object that they and their clients are subsidizing the DRG system. Government-induced competition in one sector of the health system, produces a third-party effect on another sector. The result, of course, is more regulation: New Jersey and some other states have now extended their own price regulation to all hospital charges, regardless of who the payer is for a particular patient (Morone and Dunham 1985). Equity among providers is an issue, as well as equity for patients of varying financial circumstances.

The one certainty of health care policy at this time is that further significant changes—in the financing and organization of health care services, and in the mix of business-government responsibilities—will develop over the next few years (Califano 1986; Lewin 1985).

Therefore, financial regulation (what we have termed business regulation throughout this book), and health quality (i.e., social) regulation go hand in hand, as they do with private enterprise and some kinds of competition, in our increasingly hybrid national system of medical care.

This is the regulatory pattern of the future: continued ad hoc adjustments between private market provisions of goods and services, and governmental intervention (continuing participation is a better term today) to safeguard the citizen's person and pocketbook. Whatever the particularities of the mix, the essential role of government is clear: to act as our agent in accomplishing tasks of social control that we cannot, as individuals, perform effectively, and with equitable distribution, or through the unaided efforts of the price system. Such is the vital function of regulation in the American political economy.

REFERENCES

The following references cited in the text are intended to provide a bibliography that will be useful to readers seeking more information about particular topics.

Ackerman, Bruce A., and Hassler, William T. 1981. *Clean Coal/Dirty Air.* New Haven, Conn.: Yale University Press.

Advisory Commission on Intergovernmental Relations (ACIR). 1984. *Regulatory Federalism: Policy, Process, Impact and Reform.* Washington, D.C.: ACIR, February.

Aharani, Yair. 1981. *The No-Risk Society.* Chatham, N.J.: Chatham House Publishers.

Anderson, Douglas D. 1981. *Regulatory Politics and Electric Utilities.* Boston: Auburn House.

Anderson, Frederick, Kneese, Allen V., et al. 1977. *Environmental Improvement Through Economic Incentives.* Baltimore, Md.: Johns Hopkins University Press.

Anderson, James E. 1970. *Politics and Economic Policy-Making.* Reading, Mass.: Addison-Wesley Publishing.

Andrain, Charles F. 1980. *Politics and Economic Policy in Western Democracies.* North Scituate, Mass.: Duxbury Press.

Argyris, Chris, ed. 1978. *Regulating Business.* San Francisco: Institute for Contemporary Studies.

Ashford, Nicholas A., and Hill, Christopher T. 1980. *Benefits of Environmental Health, and Safety Regulations.* Washington, D.C.: U.S. Senate, Committee on Governmental Affairs. Center for Policy Alternatives, Massachusetts Institute of Technology. Committee Print, 96th Congress, 2d Session.

Baig, Edward C. 1985. "Low-Budget Banking." *Fortune* 25 (November): 83–84.

Ball, Howard. 1984. *Controlling Regulatory Sprawl: Presidential Strategies from Nixon to Reagan.* Westport, Conn.: Greenwood Press.

Bardach, Eugene, and Kagan, Robert A. 1982. *Going by the Book: The Problem of Regulatory Unreasonableness.* Philadelphia: Temple University Press.

Barrett, Susan, and Fudge, Colin, eds. 1981. *Policy and Auction: Essays on the Implementation of Public Policy.* London and New York: Methuen.

Bator, Francis M. 1958. "The Anatomy of Market Failure." *Quarterly Journal of Economics* 72 (August): 351–79.

Behrman, Bradley. 1980. "Civil Aeronautics Board," James Q. Wilson, eds., *The Politics of Regulation.* New York: Basic Books, pp. 75–120.

Bell, Daniel. 1973. *The Coming of Post-Industrial Society: A Venture in Social Planning.* New York: Basic Books.

Berle, Adolf A., and Maans, Gardiner C. 1932. *The Modern Corporation and Private Property.* New York: Macmillan.

Bernstein, Marver H. 1955. *Regulating Business by Independent Commission.* Princeton: Princeton University Press.

Bernstein, Marver H. 1972. "Independent Regulatory Agencies: A Perspective on their Reform," in Marver H. Bernstein, ed., *Government as Regulator.* Annals of the American Academy of Political and Social Science, vol. 400, pp. 14–26.

Berry, Jeffrey M. 1984. *The Interest Group Society.* Boston: Little, Brown.

Berry, Jeffrey M. 1977. *Lobbying for the People: The Political Behavior of Public Interest Groups.* Princeton: Princeton University Press.

Berry, William D. 1984. "An Alternative to the Capture Theory of Regulation: The

Case of State Public Utility Commissions." *American Journal of Political Science* 28 (August): 524–58.

Bingham, Gail. 1986. *Resolving Environmental Disputes: A Decade of Experience.* Washington, D.C.: The Conservation Foundation.

Blair, Roger D., and Rubin, Stephen. 1980. *Regulating the Professions: A Public-Policy Symposium.* Lexington, Mass.: Lexington Books-D.C. Heath.

Bollier, David, and Claybrook, Joan. 1986. *Freedom from Harm: The Civilizing Influence of Health, Safety and Environmental Regulation.* Washington and New York: Public Citizen and Democracy Project.

Bower, Joseph L. 1983. *The Two Faces of Management.* Boston: Houghton Mifflin.

Brewer, Garry D., and deLeon, Peter. 1983. *The Foundations of Policy Analysis.* Homewood, Ill.: Dorsey Press.

Breyer, Stephen. 1982. *Regulation and Its Reform.* Cambridge, Mass.: Harvard University Press.

Breyer, Stephen G., and Stewart, Richard B. 1979. *Administrative Law and Regulatory Policy.* Boston: Little, Brown.

Brownstein, Ronald. 1983. "Above Politics?" *National Journal,* June 18, p. 1291.

Burford, Anne. 1986. *Are You Tough Enough?* New York: McGraw-Hill.

Califano, Joseph A., Jr. 1986. *America's Health Care Revolution: Who Lives? Who Dies? Who Pays?* New York: Random House.

Califano, Joseph A., Jr. 1981. *Governing America.* New York: Simon and Schuster.

Carson, Rachel. 1962. *Silent Spring.* Boston: Houghton Mifflin.

Clark, John Maurice. 1957. *Economic Institutions and Human Welfare.* New York: Knopf.

Clark, John Maurice. 1939. *Social Control of Business,* 2nd ed. New York: McGraw-Hill.

Claybrook, Joan. 1984. *Retreat from Safety: Reagan's Attack on America's Health.* New York: Pantheon.

Cohen, Steven. 1984. "Defining the Toxic Time Bomb: Federal Hazardous Waste Programs," in Norman J. Vig, and Michael E. Kraft, eds., *Environmental Policy in the 1980s.* Washington, D.C.: CQ Press, pp. 273–291.

Congressional Budget Office (CBO). 1985a. *Hazardous Waste Management: Recent Changes and Policy Alternatives.* Washington, D.C.: Congressional Budget Office, May.

Congressional Budget Office (CBO). 1985b. *Environmental Regulation and Economic Efficiency.* Washington, D.C.: Congressional Budget Office, March.

Conservation Foundation. 1984. *State of the Environment: A Mid-Decade Assessment.* Washington, D.C.: The Conservation Foundation.

Cooper, Ann. 1985a. "Fowler's FCC Learns Some Hard Lessons About What It Means to be 'Independent,' " *National Journal,* 6 (April): 732–36.

Cooper, Ann. 1985b. "Without Regulatory Villains, Who Needs Veto?" *National Journal,* May 25, pp. 1,211, 1,232.

Cotter, Cornelius P. 1960. *Government and Private Enterprise.* New York: Holt.

Crandall, Robert W. 1983. *Controlling Industrial Pollution: The Economics and Politics of Clean Air.* Washington, D.C.: The Brookings Institution.

Crandall, Robert W. 1982. "Twilight of Regulation." *Brookings Bulletin* (Winter-Spring): 1–5.

Cushman, Robert E. 1941. *The Independent Regulatory Commissions.* New York: Oxford University Press.

Dahl, Robert A., and Lindblom, Charles E. 1953. *Politics, Economics, and Welfare.* New York: Harper and Brothers.

David, Stephen, and Kantor, Paul. 1983. "Urban Policy in the Federal System: A Reconceptualization of Federalism." *Polity* 16 (Winter): 284–303.

DeMuth, Christopher C. 1983. "What Is Regulation?" in Richard J. Zeckhauser, and Derek Leebaert, eds., *What Role for Government? Lessons from Policy Research.* Durham, N.C.: Duke University Press, pp. 262–78.

Derthick, Martha. 1970. *The Influence of Federal Grants: Public Assistance in Massachusetts.* Cambridge, Mass.: Harvard University Press.

Derthick, Martha, and Quirk, Paul J. 1985. *The Politics of Deregulation.* Washington, D.C.: The Brookings Institution.

Dimock, Marshall. 1961. *Business and Government: Issues of Public Policy,* 4th ed. New York: Holt.

Dolbeare, Kenneth C. 1982. *American Public Policy.* New York: McGraw-Hill.

Douglas, Mary, and Wildavsky, Aaron. 1982. *Risk and Culture.* Berkeley: University of California Press.

Downey, Gary L. 1985. "Federalism and Nuclear Waste Disposal," *Journal of Policy Analysis and Management* 5 (No. 1): 73–99.

Downing, Paul B. 1984. *Environmental Economics and Policy.* Boston: Little, Brown.

Downing, Paul B. 1983. "Bargaining in Pollution Control," *Policy Studies Journal* 11 (June): 577–586.

Dubnick, Mel, and Gitelson, Alan. 1981. "Nationalizing State Policies," in Jerome J. Hanus, ed., *The Nationalization of State Government.* Lexington, Mass.: Lexington Books-D.C. Heath, pp. 39–74.

Dubnick, Mel, and Gitelson, Alan R. 1980. "Regulatory Policy Analysis: Working in a Quagmire." *Policy Studies Review* 1 (February): 423–35.

Eads, George C., and Fix, Michael. 1984a. *Relief or Reform: Reagan's Regulatory Dilemma.* Washington, D.C.: Urban Institute Press.

Eads, George C., and Fix, Michael, eds. 1984b. *The Reagan Regulatory Strategy.* Washington, D.C.: Urban Institute Press.

Easton, David. 1953. *The Political System.* New York: Knopf.

Edelman, Murray. 1964. *The Symbolic Uses of Politics.* Urbana, Ill.: University of Illinois Press.

Edwards, George C., III, et al., eds. 1985. *The Presidency and Public Policy Making.* Pittsburgh: University of Pittsburgh Press.

Elazar, Daniel J. 1972. *American Federalism: A View from the States,* 2nd ed. New York: Thomas Y. Crowell.

Elkin, Stephen L., and Cook, Brian J. 1985. "The Public Life of Economic Incentives." *Policy Studies Journal* 13 (June): 797–814.

Fainsod, Merle, Gordon, Lincoln, and Palamountain, Joseph C., Jr. 1959. *Government and the American Economy,* 3rd ed. New York: W. W. Norton.

Fiorina, Morris P. 1984. "Legislative Uncertainty, Legislative Control and the Delegation of Legislative Power." Occasional Paper No. 84–4. Cambridge, Mass.: Center for American Political Studies, Harvard University.

Fisher, Anne B. 1985. "Businessmen Like to Hire by the Numbers." *Fortune* (September 16): 26–30.

Fisher, Louis. 1981. "Congress and the President in the Administrative Process: The Uneasy Alliance," in Hugh Heclo and Lester M. Salamon, eds. *The Illusion of Presidential Government.* Boulder, Colo.: Westview Press, pp. 21–43.

Fix, Michael, and Eads, George C. 1985. "The Prospects for Regulatory Reform: The Legacy of Reagan's First Term." *Yale Journal on Regulation* 2: 293–318.

Flanigan, James. 1984. "Interest Rate Ceilings—Time for a Comeback?" *Los Angeles Times* (August 1).

Ford, Daniel F. 1982. *Three Mile Island.* New York: Viking Press.

Fowler, Mark S., and Brenner, Daniel L. 1982. "A Marketplace Approach to Broadcast Regulation." *Texas Law Review* 60 (February): 207–57.

Fox, J. Ronald. 1982. *Managing Business-Government Relations: Cases and Notes on Business-Government Problems.* Homewood, Ill.: Richard D. Irwin.

Freedman, James O. 1978. *Crisis and Legitimacy: The Administrative Process and American Government.* New York: Cambridge University Press.

Friendly, Henry J. 1962. *The Federal Administrative Agencies: The Need for Better Definition of Standards.* Cambridge, Mass.: Harvard University Press.

Galbraith, John Kenneth. 1952. *American Capitalism—The Concept of Countervailing Power.* Boston: Houghton Mifflin.

Gormley, William T., Jr. 1983. *The Politics of Public Utility Regulation.* Pittsburgh: University of Pittsburgh Press.

Gormley, William T., Jr. 1979. "A Test of the Revolving Door Hypothesis at the FCC." *American Journal of Political Science* 23 (November): 665–83.

Graham, James M., and Kramer, Victor H. 1976. *Appointments to the Regulatory Agencies.* Washington, D.C.: Committee Print. U.S. Senate, Committee on Commerce, 94th Congress, 2d Session.

Gramlich, Edward M. 1981. *Benefit/Cost Analysis of Government Programs.* Englewood Cliffs, N.J.: Prentice-Hall.

Gray, C. Boyden. 1983. "Regulation and Federalism." *Yale Journal on Regulation* 1: 93–110.

Graymer, LeRoy, and Thompson, Frederick, eds. 1982. *Reforming Social Regulation: Alternative Public Policy Strategies.* Beverly Hills, Calif.: Sage Publications.

Greenwood, Ted. 1984. *Knowledge and Discretion in Government Regulation.* New York: Praeger.

Grodzins, Morton. 1960. "The Federal System," in President's Commission on National Goals, *Goals for Americans.* Englewood Cliffs, N.J.: Prentice-Hall, pp. 265–282.

Hadden, Susan G., ed. 1984. *Risk Analysis, Institutions, and Public Policy.* Port Washington, N.Y.: Associated Faculty Press.

Hambright, James K. 1984. "Comments," in George C. Eads, and Michael Fix, eds., *The Reagan Regulatory Strategy.* Washington, D.C.: Urban Institute Press, pp. 180–83.

Harris, Richard A., and Milkis, Sidney M. 1983. "Deregulating the Public Lobby Regime: A Tale of Two Agencies." Paper presented at the meeting of the American Political Science Association, Chicago.

Hawkins, Keith, and Thomas, John M. 1984. *Enforcing Regulation.* Boston: Kluwer-Nijhoff Publishing.

Heclo, Hugh, and Salamon, Lester M., eds. 1981. *The Illusion of Presidential Government.* Boulder, Colo.: Westview Press.

Hedge, David M., and Menzel, Donald C. 1985. "Loosening the Regulatory Ratchet: A Grassroots View of Environmental Deregulation." *Policy Studies Journal* 13 (March): 599–606.

Heffron, Florence. 1983. *The Administrative Regulatory Process.* New York: Longman.

Hibbing, John R. 1985. "The Independent Regulatory Commissions Fifty Years After *Humphrey's Executor v. U.S.,*" *Congress & the Presidency* 12 (Spring): 57–68.

Hofstadter, Richard. 1955. *The Age of Reform: From Bryan to F.D.R.* New York: Knopf.

Holden, Matthew, Jr. 1970. "Political Bargaining and Pollution Control," in James E. Anderson, ed., *Politics and Economic Policy-Making.* Reading, Mass.: Addison-Wesley, pp. 435–452.

Institute of Medicine. 1986. *Improving the Quality of Care in Nursing Homes.* Washington, D.C.: National Academy Press.

Jones, Charles O. 1975. *Clean Air: The Policies and Politics of Pollution Control.* Pittsburgh: University of Pittsburgh Press.

Joskow, Paul L., and Schmalensee, Richard. 1983. *Markets for Power: An Analysis of Electric Utility Deregulation*. Cambridge, Mass.: MIT Press.

Kahn, Alfred. 1970. *The Economics of Regulation*, Vol. I. New York: John Wiley.

Kaplan, Daniel P. 1986. "The Changing Airline Industry," in L. W. Weiss, and M. W. Klass, eds., *Regulatory Reform: What Actually Happened*. Boston: Little, Brown, pp. 40–77.

Katzmann, Robert A., 1984. "The Attenuation of Antitrust." *Brookings Review*, (Summer), pp. 23–27.

Kaufman, Herbert. 1960. *The Forest Ranger*. Baltimore: Johns Hopkins University Press.

Keiser, K. Robert. 1980. "The Regulation of Health and Safety." *Political Science Quarterly* 95 (Fall): 479–91.

Kelman, Steven. 1982. "The Ethics of Regulatory Competition." *Regulation* 6 (May/June): 39–47.

Kelman, Steven. 1983. "Economic Incentives and Environmental Policy: Politics, Ideology, and Philosophy," in Thomas Schelling, ed., *Incentives for Environmental Protection*. Cambridge, Mass.: MIT Press, pp. 291–331.

Kelman, Steven. 1981a. "Regulation and Paternalism." *Public Policy* 29 (Spring): 219–54.

Kelman, Steven. 1981b. "Cost-Benefit Analysis: An Ethical Critique." *Regulation* (January-February): pp. 33–40.

Kelman, Steven. 1981c. *Regulating America, Regulating Sweden: A Comparative Study of Occupational Safety and Health Regulations*. Cambridge, Mass.: MIT Press.

Kelman, Steven. 1981d. *What Price Incentives? Economists and the Environment*. Boston: Auburn House.

Kelman, Steven. 1980. "Occupational Safety and Health Administration," in James Q. Wilson, ed., *The Politics of Regulation*. New York: Basic Books, pp. 236–66.

Kemp, Kathleen A. 1983. "The Regulators: Partisanship and Public Policy." *Policy Studies Journal* 11 (March): 386–95.

King, Jonathan F. 1985. "In on the Act." *Sierra* (May/June), pp. 32–34.

Kirp, David L., and Soffer, Eileen M. 1985. "Taking Californians to the Cleaners." *Regulation* (September/October): pp. 24–26.

Kneese, Allen V. 1984. *Measuring the Benefits of Clean Air and Water*. Washington, D.C.: Resources for the Future.

Kneese, Allen V., and Schultze, Charles L. 1975. *Pollution, Prices, and Public Policy*. Washington, D.C.: The Brookings Institution.

Kohlmeier, Louis M., Jr. 1969. *The Regulators*. New York: Harper and Row.

Kolko, Gabriel. 1965. *Railroads and Regulation, 1877–1916*. Princeton: Princeton University Press.

Kraft, Michael E. 1982. "The Use of Risk Analysis in Federal Regulatory Agencies: An Exploration." *Policy Studies Review* 1 (May): 666–75.

Krasnow, Erwin G., Longley, Lawrence D., and Terry, Herbert A. 1982. *The Politics of Broadcast Regulation*, 3rd ed. New York: St. Martin's Press.

Krier, James. 1982. "Marketlike Approaches: Their Past, Present, and Probable Future," in LeRoy Graymer and Frederick Thompson, eds., Beverly Hills, Calif.: Sage Publications, *Reforming Social Regulation*, pp. 151–58.

Kurland, Philip B., et al. 1984. *Supreme Court Review, 1983*. Chicago: University of Chicago Press.

Lash, Jonathan, Gillman, Katherine, and Sheridan, David. 1984. *A Season of Spoils: The Reagan Administration's Attack on the Environment*. New York: Pantheon.

Lasswell, Harold. 1936. *Politics: Who Gets What, When, How*. New York: McGraw-Hill.

Latham, Earl G. 1952. "The Group Basis of Politics." *American Political Science Review* 46 (June): 376–97.

Lave, Lester B. 1981. *The Strategy of Social Regulation: Decision Frameworks for Policy.* Washington, D.C.: The Brookings Institution.

Lave, Lester B., and Omenn, Gilbert. 1981. *Clearing the Air: Reforming the Clean Air Act.* Washington, D.C.: The Brookings Institution.

Levin, Michael H. 1985. "Building a Better Bubble at EPA." *Regulation* (March/April): pp. 33–42.

Levine, Michael E. 1981. "Revisionism Revised? Airline Deregulation and the Public Interest." *Law and Contemporary Problems* 44 (Winter): 179–95.

Lewin, Marion Ein, ed. 1985. *The Health Policy Agenda.* Washington, D.C.: American Enterprise Institute.

Lindberg, Leon N., and Maier, Charles S., eds. 1985. *The Politics of Inflation and Economic Stagnation.* Washington, D.C.: Brookings Institution.

Lindblom, Charles E. 1977. *Politics and Markets: The World's Political-Economic System.* New York: Basic Books.

Lindblom, Charles E. 1965. *The Intelligence of Democracy.* New York: Free Press.

Lindblom, Charles E., and Cohen, David K. 1979. *Usable Knowledge: Social Science and Social Problem Solving.* New Haven, Conn.: Yale University Press.

Litan, Robert E., and Nordhaus, William D. 1983. *Reforming Federal Regulation.* New Haven: Yale University Press.

Litan, Robert E. 1985. "Regulatory Policy in the Second Reagan Term." *Brookings Review* (Spring), 21–27.

Lowi, Theodore J. 1969 and 1979. *The End of Liberalism.* New York: W. W. Norton.

Lowrance, William W. 1976. *Of Acceptable Risk: Science and the Determination of Safety.* Los Altos, Calif.: William Kaufman.

MacIntyre, Angus. 1985. "Administrative Initiative and Theories of Implementation: Federal Pesticide Policy, 1970–1976." in R. Kenneth Godwin, and Helen M. Ingram, eds., *Public Policy and the Natural Environment.* Greenwich, Conn.: JAI Press, pp. 205–38.

MacRae, Duncan, Jr., and Wilde, James A. 1979. *Policy Analysis for Public Decisions.* North Scituate, Mass.: Duxbury Press.

Marcus, Alfred. 1980. "Environmental Protection Agency," in James Q. Wilson, ed., *The Politics of Regulation.* New York: Basic Books, pp. 267–303.

Mazmanian, Daniel A., and Sabatier, Paul A. 1983. *Implementation and Public Policy.* Glenview, Ill.: Scott, Foresman.

McCaffrey, David P. 1982. "Corporate Resources and Regulatory Pressures: Toward Explaining a Discrepancy." *Administrative Science Quarterly* 27 (September): 398–419.

McCraw, Thomas K. 1984. *Prophets of Regulation.* Cambridge, Mass.: Harvard University Press.

McCraw, Thomas K., ed. 1981. *Regulation in Perspective.* Cambridge Mass.: Harvard University Press.

McCraw, Thomas K., 1980. "Regulatory Change, 1960–79, in Historical Perspective," in U.S. Congress Joint Economic Committee, Special Study on Economic Change, Vol. 5, *Government Regulation: Achieving Social and Economic Balance.* Washington, D.C.: Committee Print, 96th Cong., 2d Sess., December 8.

McFarland, Andrew S. 1984a. "An Experiment in Regulatory Negotiation: The National Coal Policy Project." Paper presented at the meeting of the Western Political Science Association, Sacramento, Calif., September.

McFarland, Andrew S. 1984b. *Common Cause: Lobbying in the Public Interest.* Chatham, N.J.: Chatham House.

Meier, Kenneth J. 1985. *Regulation: Politics, Bureaucracy, and Economics.* New York: St. Martin's Press.

Melnick, R. Shep. 1983. *Regulation and the Courts: The Case of the Clean Air Act.* Washington, D.C.: The Brookings Institution.

Mendeloff, John. 1983. "Measuring Elusive Benefits: On the Value of Health." *Journal of Health Politics, Policy and Law* 8 (Fall): 554–80.

Meyer, Richard E., and Vartabedian, Ralph. 1986. "Aircraft Safety: Cracks Begin to Show in the System." *Los Angeles Times* (March 30).

Mishan, Edward J. 1976. *Cost-Benefit Analysis*. New York: Praeger.

Mitnick, Barry M. 1980. *The Political Economy of Regulation*. New York: Columbia University Press.

Moe, Terry. 1985. "Control and Feedback in Economic Regulation: The Case of the NLRB." *American Political Science Review* 79 (December): 1094–1116.

Moe, Terry. 1980. *The Organization of Interests*. Chicago: University of Chicago Press.

Moe, Terry M. 1982. "Regulatory Performance and Presidential Administration." *American Journal of Political Science* 26 (May): 197–224.

Moore, Thomas Gale. 1986. "Rail and Trucking Deregulation," in L. W. Weiss, and M. W. Klass, eds., *Regulatory Reform: What Actually Happened*. Boston: Little, Brown, pp. 14–39.

Morone, James A., and Dunham, Andrew B. 1985. "Slouching Towards National Health Insurance: The New Health Care Politics." *Yale Journal on Regulation* 2 (2): 263–91.

Mosher, Frederick C. 1984. *A Tale of Two Agencies: A Comparative Analysis of the General Accounting Office and the Office of Management and Budget*. Baton Rouge, Louisiana: Louisiana State University Press.

Lawrence Mosher. 1981. "Will EPA's Budget Cuts Make It More Efficient or Less Effective?" *National Journal*, August 15, p. 1468.

Murray, Francis X., ed. 1978. *Where We Agree: Report of the National Coal Policy Project*. 2 vols. Boulder, Colo.: Westview Press.

Nadel, Mark V. 1971. *The Politics of Consumer Protection*. Indianapolis: Bobbs-Merrill.

Nader, Laura, and Nader, Claire. 1985. "A Wide Angle on Regulation: An Anthropological Perspective," in Roger G. Noll, ed., *Regulatory Policy and the Social Sciences*, Berkeley, Calif.: University of California Press, pp. 141–60.

Nader, Ralph. 1965. *Unsafe at Any Speed: the Designed-in Dangers of the American Automobile*. New York: Grossman.

Nager, Glen D. 1982. "Bureaucrats and the Cost-Benefit Chameleon," *Regulation* (September/October): pp. 37–42.

Nance, John J. 1986. *Blind Trust: How Deregulation Has Jeopardized Airline Safety and What You Can Do About It*. New York: Wm. Morrow Co.

Nash, Roderick, 1967 and 1983. *Wilderness and the American Mind*. New Haven, Conn.: Yale University Press.

Nathan, Richard. 1983. *The Administrative Presidency*. New York: John Wiley.

Needham, Douglas. 1983. *The Economics and Politics of Regulation: A Behavioral Approach*. Boston: Little, Brown.

Neustadt, Richard E. 1980. *Presidential Power: The Politics of Leadership from FDR to Carter*. New York: John Wiley.

Noll, Roger G. 1985. *Regulatory Policy and the Social Sciences*. Berkeley, Calif.: University of California Press.

Noll, Roger G., and Owen, Bruce M. 1983. "What Makes Reform Happen?" *Regulation* (March/April) pp. 19–24.

Oates, Wallace E. 1985. "The Environment and the Economy: Environmental Policy at the Crossroads," in John M. Quigley, and Daniel L. Rubinfeld, eds., *American Domestic Priorities*. Berkeley, Calif.: University of California Press, pp. 311–44.

Okun, Arthur. 1970. *The Political Economy of Prosperity*. Washington, D.C.: The Brookings Institution.

Olson, Mancur. 1965. *The Logic of Collective Action*. Cambridge, Mass.: Harvard University Press.

Owen, Bruce M., and Gottlieb, Paul D. 1986. "The Rise and Fall and Rise of Cable Television Regulation," in L. W. Weiss, and M. W. Klass, eds., *Regulatory Reform: What Actually Happened.* Berkeley, Calif.: University of California Press, pp. 78–104.

Page, Talbot. 1978. "A Generic View of Toxic Chemicals and Similar Risks." *Ecology Law Quarterly* 7: 207–44.

Peirce, Neal R. 1985. "Environmental Activists Taking a New Tack." *National Journal*, August 3, p. 1808.

Peltzman, Sam. 1976. "Toward a More General Theory of Regulation." *Journal of Law and Economics* 19: 211–48.

Perrow, Charles. 1984. *Normal Accidents: Living with High-Risk Technologies.* New York: Basic Books.

Pertschuk, Michael. 1982. *Revolt Against Regulation. The Rise and Pause of the Consumer Movement.* Berkeley: University of California Press.

Peterson, Cass. 1985. "How Much Risk Is Too Much?" *Sierra* (May/June), pp. 62–4.

Piper, Dennis, and Ladd, Fred. 1985. "Toxics on Tap." *Sierra* (July/August), pp. 56–60.

Pope, Carl. 1985. "An Immodest Proposal." *Sierra* (September/October), pp. 43–48.

Portney, Paul R. 1984. "The Benefits and Costs of Regulatory Analysis," in V. Kerry Smith, ed., *Environmental Policy under Reagan's Executive Order.* Chapel Hill, N.C.: University of North Carolina Press, pp. 226–40.

Pressman, Jeffrey L., and Wildavsky, Aaron. 1973. *Implementation.* Berkeley: University of California Press.

Price, Don K. 1983, 1985. *America's Unwritten Constitution: Science, Religion, and Political Responsibility.* Baton Rouge, La.: Louisiana State University Press, and Cambridge, Mass.: Harvard University Press.

Price, Don K. 1982. "The Institutional Presidency and the Unwritten Constitution," in James Sterling Young, ed., *Problems and Prospects of Presidential Leadership.* Washington, D.C.: University Press of America, pp. 57–84.

Purcell, Edward A., Jr. 1967. "Ideas and Interests: Businessmen and the Interstate Commerce Act." *Journal of American History* 54 (December): 561–78.

Quarles, John. 1976. *Cleaning Up America: An Insider's View of the Environmental Protection Agency.* Boston: Houghton Mifflin.

Quigley, John M., and Rubinfeld, Daniel L., eds. 1985. *American Domestic Priorities: An Economic Appraisal.* Berkeley: University of California Press.

Quirk, Paul J. 1981. *Industry Influence in Federal Regulatory Agencies.* Princeton: Princeton University Press.

Rabkin, Jeremy. 1984. "Captive of the Court: A Federal Agency in Receivership." *Regulation* (May–June), pp. 27–35.

Reagan, Michael D. 1985. "The Reagan 'Mandate', Public Law, and the Ethics of Policy Change." *Congress & the Presidency* 12 (Autumn): 153–64.

Reagan, Michael D. 1972. *The New Federalism.* New York: Oxford University Press.

Reagan, Michael D. 1963. *The Managed Economy.* New York: Oxford University Press.

Reagan, Michael D. 1961. "The Political Structure of the Federal Reserve System." *American Political Science Review* 55 (March): 64–76.

Reagan, Michael D., and Sanzone, John G. 1981. *The New Federalism*, 2nd edition. New York: Oxford University Press.

Redford, Emmette S. 1965. *American Government and the Economy.* New York: Macmillan.

Redford, Emmette S. 1952. *Administration of National Economic Control.* New York: Macmillan.

Reeves, Mavis M. 1985. *The Question of State Government Capability: A Commission Report.* Washington, D.C.: Advisory Commission on Intergovernmental Relations, January.

Regens, James L. 1982. "Risk Assessment in the Policy-making Process: Environmental Health and Safety Protection." Paper presented at the meeting of the American Political Science Association, Denver, Colorado.

Reynolds, Larry. 1981. "Foundations of an Institutional Theory of Regulation." *Journal of Economic Issues* xv (September): 641–56.

Rhoads, Steven E. 1980. *Valuing Life: Public Policy Dilemmas.* Boulder, Colo.: Westview.

Rhoads, Steven E. 1985. *The Economist's View of the World: Government, Markets, and Public Policy.* New York: Cambridge University Press.

Roe, David. 1984. *Dynamos and Virgins.* New York: Random House.

Rosenbaum, Walter A. 1985. *Environmental Politics and Policy.* Washington, D.C.: CQ Press.

Rosenberg, Morton. 1981a. *Presidential Control of Agency Rulemaking.* Committee Print. Washington, D.C.: Committee on Energy and Commerce, U.S. House of Representatives, 97th Cong., 1st Sess., June 15.

Rosenberg, Morton. 1981b. "Beyond the Limits of Executive Power: Presidential Control of Agency Rule-making Under Executive Order 12291." *Michigan Law Review* 80 (December): 193–247.

Rottenberg, Simon, ed. 1980. *Occupational Licensing and Regulation.* Washington, D.C.: American Enterprise Institute.

Rourke, Francis E. 1984. *Bureaucracy, Politics, and Public Policy,* 3rd ed. Boston: Little, Brown.

Rowland, C. K., and Marz, Roger. 1982. "Gresham's Law: The Regulatory Analogy." *Policy Studies Review* 1 (February): 572–80.

Salamon, Lester M. 1981. "Federal Regulation: A New Arena for Presidential Power?" in Hugh Heclo, and Lester M. Salamon, eds., *The Illusion of Presidential Government.* Boulder, Colo.: Westview Press, pp. 147–73.

Schelling, Thomas C., ed. 1983. *Incentives for Environmental Protection.* Cambridge, Mass.: MIT Press.

Scholzman, Kay Lehman. 1984. "What Accent the Heavenly Chorus? Political Equality and the American Pressure System." *Journal of Politics* 46 (November): 1006–32.

Schmandt, Jurgen. 1984. "Regulation and Science." *Science, Technology, and Human Values* 9 (Winter): 23–38.

Schultze, Charles L. 1977. *The Public Use of Private Interest.* Washington, D.C.: The Brookings Institution.

Schultze, Charles L. 1968. *The Politics and Economics of Public Spending.* Washington, D.C.: The Brookings Institution.

Seligman, Daniel. 1986. "How Much Money Is Your Life Worth?" *Fortune* (March 3), pp. 25–27.

Shapiro, Martin. 1982. "On Predicting the Future of Administrative Law." *Regulation* (May/June): pp. 18–25.

Shepherd, William G. 1985. *Public Politics Toward Business,* 7th ed. Homewood, Ill.: Richard D. Irwin.

Shover, Neal, et al. 1984. "Regional Variation in Regulatory Law Enforcement," in Keith Hawkins, and John M. Thomas, eds., *Enforcing Regulation.* Barton: Kluwer-Nijhoff Publishing, 1984, pp. 121–144.

Simons, Henry C. 1948. *Economic Policy for a Free Society.* Chicago: University of Chicago Press.

Slovic, Paul, et al. 1985. "Regulation of Risk: A Psychological Perspective," in Roger G. Noll, ed., *Regulatory Policy and the Social Sciences.* Berkeley: University of California Press, pp. 241–78.

Smith, V. Kerry, ed. 1984. *Environmental Policy under Reagan's Executive Order: The Role of Benefit-Cost Analysis.* Chapel Hill, N.C.: University of North Carolina Press.

Sohn, Michael, and Litan, Robert. 1981. "Regulatory Oversight Wins in Court." *Regulation* (July/August): pp. 17–24.

Stanfield, Rochelle L. 1985. "Air Toxics Debate Clouded by Mistrust, Philosophical Dispute Over Remedies." *National Journal,* June 29, 1516–20.

Stanfield, Rochelle L. 1984a. "Ruckelshaus Casts EPA as 'Gorilla' in States' Enforcement Closet." *National Journal,* May 26, pp. 1034–38.

Stanfield, Rochelle L. 1984b. "Few Are Satisfied with Statutes Aimed at Controlling the Chemical Revolution." *National Journal,* November 11, pp. 200–205.

Stanfield, Rochelle L. 1986. "The Elusive Bubble," *National Journal* (April 5), pp. 820–22.

Stenberg, Carl W. 1985. "States Under the Spotlight: An Intergovernmental View." *Public Administration Review* 45 (March/April): 319–26.

Stewart, Richard B. 1975. "The Reformation of American Administrative Law." *Harvard Law Review* 88: 1667–1813.

Stigler, George J. 1975. *The Citizen and the State.* Chicago: University of Chicago Press.

Stigler, George J. 1971. "The Theory of Economic Regulation." *Bell Journal of Economics and Management Science* 2 (Spring): 3–21.

Stone, Alan. 1982. *Regulation and Its Alternatives.* Washington, D.C.: CQ Press.

Sullivan, Timothy J. 1984. *Resolving Development Disputes Through Negotiations.* New York: Plenum Press.

Sunstein, Cass R. 1984. "Deregulation and the Hard-Look Doctrine," in Philip B. Kurland, et al., eds., *Supreme Court Review, 1983.* Chicago: University of Chicago Press, pp. 177–213.

Sunstein, Cass R. 1981. "Cost-Benefit Analysis and the Separation of Powers." *Arizona Law Review* 23: 1267–82.

Taylor, Serge. 1977. "The Politics of Charges," in Frederick Anderson, et al., eds., *Environmental Improvement Through Economic Incentives. Environmental Improvement Through Economic Incentives.* Baltimore, Md.: Johns Hopkins University Press, pp. 145–91.

Thayer, Frederick C. 1984. *Rebuilding America: The Case for Economic Regulation.* New York: Praeger.

Thompson, Frank J., and Scicchitano, Michael J. 1985. "State Enforcement of Federal Regulatory Policy: The Lessons of OSHA." *Policy Studies Journal* 13 (March): 591–98.

Tietenberg, T. H. 1985. *Emissions Trading: An Exercise in Reforming Pollution Policy.* Baltimore, Md.: Resources for the Future.

Tolchin, Susan J. 1984. "Cost-Benefit Analysis and the Rush to Deregulate." *Policy Studies Review* 4 (November): 212–18.

Tolchin, Susan J., and Tolchin, Martin. 1983 and 1985. *Dismantling America: The Rush to Deregulate.* Boston: Houghton Mifflin; and New York: Oxford University Press.

Tombari, Henry A. 1984. *Business and Society.* Chicago: Dryden Press.

Truman, David B. 1951. *The Governmental Process.* New York: Knopf.

U.S. Federal Trade Commission. 1984. *Consumer Guide to the FTC Funeral Rule.* Washington, D.C.: FTC.

U.S. President's Commission on National Goals. 1960. *Goals for Americans.* Englewood Cliffs, N.J.: Prentice-Hall.

U.S. President's Committee on Administrative Management. 1937. *Administrative Management in the Government of the United States.* Washington, D.C.: President's Committee on Administrative Management.

U.S. Senate. 1977a. Study on Federal Regulation, vol. V, *Regulatory Organization,* Committee Print. Washington, D.C.: Committee on Government Operations, 95th Congress, 1st Session, December.

U.S. Senate. 1977b. Study on Federal Regulation, vol. II, *Congressional Oversight of Regulatory Agencies,* Committee Print. Washington, D.C.: Committee on Government Operations, 95th Congress, 1st Session, February.

Vig, Norman J., and Kraft, Michael E. 1984. *Environmental Policy in the 1980s: Reagan's New Agenda.* Washington, D.C.: CQ Press.

Viscusi, W. Kip. 1984a. *Regulating Consumer Product Safety.* Washington, D.C.: American Enterprise Institute.

Viscusi, W. Kip. 1984b. "The Influence of Legislative Mandates on the Oversight of Risk Regulation Agencies," in Susan G. Hadden, ed., *Risk Analysis, Institutions, and Public Policy.* Port Washington, N.Y.: Associated University Press, pp. 117–32.

Vogel, David. 1986. *National Styles of Regulation.* Ithaca, N.Y.: Cornell University Press.

Vogel, David. 1981. "The 'New' Social Regulation in Historical and Comparative Perspective," in Thomas K. McCraw, ed., *Regulation in Perspective.* Cambridge, Mass.: Harvard University Press, pp. 155–85.

Walker, Jack L. 1983. "The Origins and Maintenance of Interest Groups in America." *American Political Science Review* 77 (June): 390–406.

Weaver, Paul H. 1978. "Regulation, Social Policy, and Class Conflict," in Chris Argyris, ed., *Regulating Business.* San Francisco: Institute of Contemporary Studies, pp. 193–216.

Weidenbaum, Murray L. 1979. *The Future of Business Regulation.* New York: AMA CON.

Weingast, Barry R., and Moran, Mark J. 1982. "The Myth of Runaway Bureaucracy: The Case of the FTC." *Regulation* (May-June): pp. 33–38.

Weiss, Leonard W., and Klass, Michael W., eds. 1986. *Regulatory Reform: What Actually Happened.* Boston: Little, Brown.

Weiss, Leonard W., and Klass, Michael W., eds. 1981. *Case Studies in Regulation: Revolution and Reform.* Boston: Little, Brown.

Welborn, David M. 1977. *Governance of Federal Regulatory Agencies.* Knoxville, Tenn.: University of Tennessee Press.

Wenner, Lettie McSpadden. 1978. "Pollution Control: Implementation Alternatives." *Policy Analysis* 4 (Winter): 47–65.

Wessel, Milton, R. 1976. *The Rule of Reason: A New Approach to Corporate Litigation.* Reading, Mass.: Addison-Wesley.

West, William F. 1985. *Administrative Rulemaking: Politics and Processes.* Westport, Conn.: Greenwood Press.

West, William F., and Cooper, Joseph. 1985. "The Rise of Administrative Clearance," in George C. Edwards, et al., eds., *The Presidency and Public Policy Making.* Pittsburgh: University of Pittsburgh Press, pp. 192–214.

Whelan, Elizabeth M. 1985. "Cancer Paranoia vs. Common Sense." *Los Angeles Times,* October 14, Section II, p. 5.

White, Lawrence J. 1986. "The Partial Deregulation of Banks and Other Depository Institutions," in L. W. Weiss, and M. W. Klass, eds., *Regulatory Reforms: What Actually Happened.* Boston: Little, Brown, pp. 169–209.

Wilcox, Clair. 1955. *Public Policies Toward Business,* 2nd ed. Homewood, Ill.: Richard D. Irwin.

Wilcox, Clair, and Shepherd, William G. 1975. *Public Policies Toward Business,* 5th ed. Homewood, Ill.: Richard D. Irwin.

Wildavsky, Aaron, 1984. *The Politics of the Budgetary Process*, 4th ed. Boston: Little, Brown.

Willey, W. R. Z. 1982. "Some Caveats on Tradable Emissions Permits," in Roy N. Graymer, and Frederick Thompson, eds., *Reforming Social Regulation*, Beverly Hills, Calif.: Sage Publications, pp. 165–70.

Wilson, James Q., ed. 1980. *The Politics of Regulation*. New York: Basic Books.

Wilson, James Q. 1967. "The Bureaucracy Problem." *Public Interest* No. 6 (Winter): 3–9.

Wilson, Woodrow. 1887. "The Study of Administration." *Political Science Quarterly* 2 (June): 197–222.

Wolf, Charles Jr. 1979. "A Theory of Nonmarket Failure." *Journal of Law and Economics* xxii (April): 107–39.

Woolley, John T. 1984. *Monetary Politics: The Federal Reserve and the Politics of Monetary Policy*. New York: Cambridge University Press.

Wright, Deil S. 1982. *Understanding Intergovernmental Relations: Public Policy and Participants' Perspectives in Local, State, and National Governments*, 2nd ed. Monterey, Calif.: Brooks/Cole.

Wright, Deil S. 1985. "A Quarter-Century Window on the U. S. Federal System, 1935–1960," in Lawrence E. Gelfand and Robert J. Neymeyer, eds., *Changing Patterns in American Federal-State Relations*. Iowa City: Center for the Study of the Recent History of the United States.

Yaffee, Steven Lewis. 1982. *Prohibitive Policy: Implementing the Federal Endangered Species Act*. Cambridge, Mass.: MIT Press.

Young, James Sterling. 1982. *Problems and Prospects of Presidential Leadership in the Nineteen-Eighties*. Vol. I. Washington, D.C.: University Press of America.

Zeckhauser, Richard J., and Leebaert, Derek, eds. 1983. *What Role for Government? Lessons from Policy Research*. Durham, N.C.: Duke University Press.

ACRONYMS

ABA	American Bar Association
AEC	Atomic Energy Commission
AIDS	Acquired Immune Deficiency Syndrome
AMA	American Medical Association
APA	Administrative Procedure Act
CAB	Civil Aeronautics Board
CBA	Cost-Benefit Analysis
CBO	Congressional Budget Office
CEQ	Council on Environmental Quality
COWPS	Council on Wage and Price Stability
CPSC	Consumer Product Safety Commission
CERCLA	Comprehensive Environmental Response, Compensation and Liability Act
CRS	Congressional Research Service
DIDC	Depository Institutions Deregulation Committee
DIDMCA	Depository Institutions and Monetary Control Act
DRG	Diagnostic Related Group
EEOC	Equal Employment Opportunity Commission
EDF	Environmental Defense Fund
EPA	Environmental Protection Agency
FAA	Federal Aviation Administration
FCC	Federal Communications Commission
FDA	Food and Drug Administration
FDIC	Federal Deposit Insurance Corporation
FERC	Federal Energy Regulatory Commission
FIFRA	Federal Insecticide, Fungicide, and Rodenticide Act
FMC	Federal Maritime Commission
FPC	Federal Power Commission
FRB	Federal Reserve Board
FTC	Federal Trade Commission
GAO	General Accounting Office
ICC	Interstate Commerce Commission
IGR	Intergovernmental Relations
IRCs	Independent Regulatory Commissions

NCPP	National Coal Policy Project
NEPA	National Environmental Policy Act
NHTSA	National Highway Traffic Safety Administration
NLRB	National Labor Relations Board
NRC	Nuclear Regulatory Commission
NRDC	Natural Resources Defense Council
OCR	Office of Civil Rights
OIRA	Office of Information and Regulatory Affairs
OMB	Office of Management and Budget
OSHA	Occupational Safety and Health Administration
OSHRC	Occupational Safety and Health Review Commission
OSM	Office of Surface Mining
OTA	Office of Technology Assessment
PIG	Public Interest Group
RCRA	Resource Conservation and Recovery Act
SEC	Securities and Exchange Commission
SIP	State Implementation Plan
TSCA	Toxic Substances Control Act

INDEX

Note: Authors mentioned only in parenthetical citations are listed (with titles and publications) in the References.